W9-CON-986

NOVA SCOTIA
COLOURGUIDE
SEVENTH EDITION

Colleen Abdullah
Photographs by Keith Vaughan

FORMAC PUBLISHING COMPANY LIMITED
HALIFAX

CONTENTS

Formac Publishing Company Limited recognizes the support of the Province of Nova Scotia through the Department of Tourism, Culture and Heritage. We acknowledge the financial support of the Government of Canada through the Book Publishing Industry Development Program (BPIDP) for our publishing activities.
For photo credits please see page 216.

Library and Archives Canada Cataloguing in Publication

Abdullah, Colleen
    Nova Scotia colourguide / Colleen Abdullah ; photographs by Keith Vaughan. — 7th ed.

(Colourguide series)
Includes index.
ISBN-13: 978-0-88780-722-0
ISBN-10: 0-88780-722-4

    1. Nova Scotia—Guidebooks. I. Vaughan, Keith, 1943- II. Title. III. Series.
FC2307.P66 2007   917.1604'5   C2006-906912-3

CONTENTS

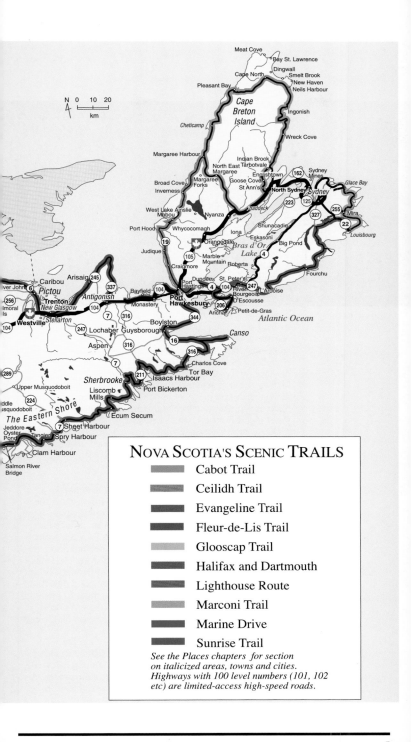

NOVA SCOTIA'S SCENIC TRAILS

- Cabot Trail
- Ceilidh Trail
- Evangeline Trail
- Fleur-de-Lis Trail
- Glooscap Trail
- Halifax and Dartmouth
- Lighthouse Route
- Marconi Trail
- Marine Drive
- Sunrise Trail

See the Places chapters for section on italicized areas, towns and cities. Highways with 100 level numbers (101, 102 etc) are limited-access high-speed roads.

GETTING AROUND

CABOT TRAIL

Though Nova Scotia is Canada's second-smallest province, its land mass is equal to the combined area of Massachusetts, New Hampshire and Vermont. Shaped somewhat like the lobster found off its coast, Nova Scotia stretches 730 kilometres from Yarmouth to Sydney. This distance can be driven in under eight hours along new highways, but plan to take the older, more scenic routes for a relaxing trip with plenty of opportunities for sightseeing, and for visiting interesting local museums and shops. The 100-series highway routes, which extend to all areas of the province, are an excellent way to reach particular destinations in a hurry. While they bypass the picturesque villages, many of them offer panoramic vistas not seen on older routes.

AMHERST ENTRY POINT

Most motoring visitors enter the province at Amherst, at the border point with New Brunswick. A trip through the Wentworth Valley via the Cobequid Pass toll highway is the fastest route to the central point of Truro, or take the slower route, winding around Folly Lake. To reach scenic Cape Breton meander along the Northumberland Shore on the Sunrise Trail (Route 6) to Pictou. Following the Trans-Canada Highway to Cape Breton and on to Baddeck brings you to the Alexander Greham Bell Museum, and then on to the Cabot Trail and the counter-clockwise route from Ingonish to Cheticamp. Try to include a visit to Fortress Louisbourg and the Glace Bay Miners' Museum on the east side of the island.

If you are heading for Halifax and want a more interesting drive, take the Glooscap Trail (Route 2) along the Minas Basin to Truro where you can join Highway 102 which will take you in to the Halifax metropolitan area. A couple of days can be enjoyed taking in the sights of the city and its museums, but be sure to include a drive to spectacular Peggys Cove. Day trips can be planned to the South Shore or Annapolis Valley, but it's better to plan two or three days to make the loop along one route to Yarmouth, following the shoreline one way, and driving through the province's agricultural heartland on the other. Or shorten the loop by cutting across on Route 8 from Liverpool on the Lighthouse Route to Annapolis Royal on the Evangeline Trail, passing Kejimkujik National Park enroute.

YARMOUTH ENTRY POINT

Arriving at Yarmouth by ferry from Maine, you have the choice of following the Lighthouse Route (see p. 94) along the province's scenic South Shore, or taking the Evangeline Trail (see p. 114) along the French Shore and through the pastoral Annapolis Valley. Both routes lead to Halifax. Enjoy the best of both worlds by taking either route one way and the other on the return journey. Depending on your schedule, you might plan one to three days to enjoy charming villages and historic sites each way. Both routes have a wealth of history to exhibit, opportunities for recreation, and spectacular scenery to enjoy.

HALIFAX ENTRY POINT

If you fly into Halifax International Airport your first stop will probably be Halifax. The Halifax metro area (see p. 75) requires at least a day for sightseeing, but two or three days would be better, especially if you include a side trip to Peggys Cove. A visit to Halifax Citadel National Historic Site, stroll on the waterfront and shopping at Historic Properties are some of the many activities available. Evening entertainment might include taking in a play at Neptune Theatre, or experiencing Shakespeare by the Sea in Point Pleasant Park. A water excursion on Halifax Harbour and the Northwest Arm adds a different perspective to your visit.

Visitors beginning their Nova Scotia tour at Halifax have the opportunity to plan two to three days exploring the Annapolis Valley and South Shore. A day could be enjoyed along Marine Drive, and if more time is available, a visit to Cape Breton should be planned.

Plan a day or two for the drive to Cape Breton, taking in some sights along the way, such as historic Sherbrooke Village on Marine Drive (see p. 143). After crossing the Canso Causeway, follow Route 4 through St. Peter's and along the Bras d'Or Lakes. Perhaps you will have time for tea at Rita's Tea Room in Big Pond.

A couple of days in Cape Breton will leave you wanting to stay longer. From Sydney you can visit the Fortress of Louisbourg, which deserves a full day, but don't miss it even if you can only manage a half day (see p. 163), and take in the Miners' Museum in Glace Bay (see p. 168). The Cabot Trail (see p. 146) can be done in a day, but you will want to make a list of things to do and places to stop on your next trip. An overnight stay at Baddeck, or perhaps Cheticamp or Margaree, will let you enjoy a taste of the Celtic and Acadian cultures of those areas.

If you have to head for home, take another day to enjoy some of the Sunrise Trail (see p. 135) or the Glooscap Trail (see p. 130) on your way back to Halifax.

LAND AND SEA

BY ROBERT J. MCCALLA AND AL KINGSBURY

CANOE ON MUSQUODOBOIT RIVER

Spectacular scenery, a rich blend of history and culture in seaside villages and vibrant metropolitan areas, and a full calendar of festivals and events combine to offer the visitor to Nova Scotia an unforgettable experience.

Located on Canada's East Coast, within a day's drive of the United States border, and just hours from the major airports in Boston and New York, Nova Scotia prides itself on being "Canada's Ocean Playground," with its 7,450-kilometre coastline of beaches, coves, salt marshes, headlands and cliffs. Its geology, climate, plants and animals — as well as its peoples — have all been shaped by the sea.

Nova Scotia is part of the Appalachian Region, which extends from the southeastern United States to Newfoundland in the northeast. Along the Atlantic coast, rugged beauty, such as the mass of granite rising from the

ROCKHOUNDING AT JOGGINS

sea at Peggys Cove, draws thousands of visitors each year. By contrast, Cape Breton Island and the northern mainland along the Northumberland Strait boast some fine beaches. The world's highest tides have carved spectacular sea cliffs along the shores of the Bay of Fundy. The effects of the Fundy tides are most dramatic at Advocate Bay along Cape Chignecto (see p. 132) and in the area of Cape Split, which divides the Minas Channel from the Minas Basin.

Millions of years ago, this area was swampland; deposits of organic matter later became coal, which has been mined at Joggins, Springhill, and in communities in Pictou, Inverness and Cape Breton counties. Underground coal seams at the Springhill Miners' Museum (see p. 131) and the Miners' Museum at Glace Bay (see p. 168) are open to visitors for tours. Embedded within the sedimentary rocks is an excellent record of past plant and animal life. The areas around Joggins and near Parrsboro are famous for fossils (see pp. 132–33).

The province's land surface has been scarred by glaciers at least four times during the last 100,000 years, leaving behind deposits of drumlins (egg-shaped hills) and erratics (large boulders).

The melting of the glaciers caused a rise in sea level which flooded the shoreline, creating deep bays and sheltered harbours along the Atlantic coast. Halifax Harbour, one of the world's finest, owes its existence to both glacial erosion and a rise in sea level.

TIDES

Coastal Nova Scotia is influenced by the twice-daily ebb and flow of the tides. These effects are most spectacular in the upper reaches of the Bay of Fundy where the tidal range has exceeded 16 metres and at low tide huge mud flats are exposed. Several companies take advantage of the upriver surge, known as the tidal bore, by providing white-water rafting excursions on the Shubenacadie River. The tidal phenomenon can be seen along many of the rivers that flow into Cobequid Bay and the Cumberland Basin.

CLIMATE

Nova Scotia has a modified continental climate. Once again, the sea exerts its influence, making winters warmer and summers cooler than in the Canadian interior. The same effect takes place within the province; temperatures become more continental as you move away from the coast. And while you can

THESE TWO IDENTICAL VIEWS SHOW THE CONTRAST BETWEEN LOW TIDE, TOP, AND HIGH TIDE, ON THE BAY OF FUNDY

TIDAL RIPS AT CAPE SPLIT

FALL COLOURS (TOP)

blame the ocean for Nova Scotia's cold, damp springs (the sea is slow to warm), it is also responsible for our fine autumns (it takes just as long to cool).

Precipitation is plentiful and evenly distributed throughout the year. On average, Halifax records precipitation on 171 days of the year. The Cape Breton Highlands and southwestern mainland receive more moisture than the northern mainland and the Annapolis Valley, mainly because of onshore winds.

FLORA

The forests of Nova Scotia are mixed, typical of the Acadian Forest found throughout the Maritime provinces. Softwood — mostly balsam fir, red, white and black spruce, and white pine — are generally found in poorly drained areas, while the hardwoods — mainly red maple, yellow birch, sugar maple, and white birch — prefer drier ground. During autumn, many Nova Scotian hillsides blaze with colour as hardwood leaves turn from soft greens to vivid yellows, oranges and reds. The most dramatic display of fall colour is along Cape Breton's Cabot Trail.

The natural open spaces in Nova Scotia — the salt marshes, bogs, coastal dunes, shallow lakes and ponds, stream banks and barrens — have their own distinctive plant communities. In the salt marshes, for example, angiosperms, algae and grasses trap sediment and help in the transition of the marsh from a saltwater environment to a freshwater one. Many of these marshes are found in the Minas Basin and Chignecto Bay, although large areas, like Grand Pré, have been converted to dykeland.

BIRDS AND MAMMALS

With its diverse landscape and strategic position along the Atlantic flyway, Nova Scotia hosts a wide variety of birds. Some, like jays, grouses and sparrows, are typical of boreal forest regions. Others create more of a stir. Bald eagles and osprey can be found close to marine and freshwater feeding areas, particularly in the more remote areas of the northern mainland and on Cape Breton Island. Eagle tours are provided in Cape Breton's Bras d'Or Lakes region (see p. 158).

In August, huge flocks of shorebirds (sandpipers, plovers and phalaropes) gather in the upper reaches of the Bay of Fundy to feed on the nutrient-rich mudflats before resuming their southward migration (Evangeline Beach, near Grand Pré, is a crowded stopover). They can also be found at Brier Island, where they take advantage of nutrient upwelling, and along the Atlantic coast in sheltered harbours with exposed mudflats and salt marshes.

The best place to observe seabirds — razorbills, guillemots, kittiwakes, cormorants, and puffins — is at Hertford and Ciboux, tiny islands off the coast of Cape

Dauphin in Cape Breton. The "Bird Islands" are protected sanctuaries and can only be reached by boat tours that leave from Big Bras d'Or and Englishtown.

Nova Scotia's land mammals range in size from the mole to the moose. Moose and deer are found throughout the province. Other species (skunks, for example) that are found on mainland Nova Scotia are not present on Cape Breton Island. The coyote, a relatively recent arrival, is the most vilified of Nova Scotia's mammals, given its penchant for killing sheep.

Marine mammals, including seals, whales, porpoises and dolphins, are among the province's most popular attractions. Numerous species of whales visit Nova Scotia's coastal waters. The Bay of Fundy near Brier Island is a good place to see fin and humpback whales; pilot and minke whales are often sighted in the Gulf of St. Lawrence, especially along the west coast of Cape Breton Island.

NOVA SCOTIA IS HOME TO A WIDE VARIETY OF BIRDS AND ANIMALS

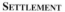SETTLEMENT

The prehistoric evidence of native settlement is sparse. At the time of European contact an estimated 3,000–3,500 Mi'kmaq were living in the area that is now Nova Scotia, New Brunswick and Prince Edward Island. In Nova Scotia the largest concentration was probably on Cape Breton Island.

A recent theory places the Chinese in Cape Breton long before John Cabot. European exploration of Nova Scotia may have included the Norse, but there is no hard evidence to show this. Prince Henry Sinclair of Orkney is believed by some to have sailed to Nova Scotia in 1398. Certainly the English and Portuguese had explored the coast by the beginning of the 16th century.

The story of European settlement starts with the French at Port Royal in 1604 and includes the Acadian population which numbered 13,000 at the time of their deportation in 1755. The story of subsequent immigration (and the return of the Acadians) is told in the following chapters.

Today, more than 900,000 people live in Nova Scotia. Although upwards of 350,000 live in Halifax Regional Municipality, Nova Scotia is mainly a rural and small-town area. Even the urban communities are small. Truro has fewer than 12,000 people; Yarmouth, in southwest Nova Scotia, has a population of only 7,500; Amherst, at the border with New Brunswick, has fewer than 10,000; Lunenburg's population is under 3,000; and 115,000 reside in the Cape Breton Regional Municipality.

There are more than 70 ethnic groups in the province (identified by mother tongue), but the majority of people trace their roots to the British Isles. Nova Scotia's telephone books are full of Scottish surnames, especially on Cape Breton Island and along the Northumberland Shore. Still, other peoples — the Mi'kmaq and Acadians are most visible — have retained strong cultural identities that will certainly enrich any visit to Nova Scotia.

GENEALOGY

TERRY PUNCH

Nova Scotia was home to Canada's first French settlement four centuries ago, and several waves of people — English, Blacks, Scots, Germans, Irish and Dutch — have followed, so it's not surprising that many descendants of those immigrants visit the province each year in search of their family roots. Residents, too, have developed a keen interest in genealogy, and have put extensive efforts into compiling, preserving and cataloguing data. As a result, there are many sources of research available that can be used both before and during a visit to the province by people trying to trace their roots.

Details critical to finding family links are name, place and date (within two to three years) of births, deaths and marriages. If a place within Nova Scotia is not known, religion or ethnicity might help to localize a family. My book *In Which County? Nova Scotia Surnames from Birth Registers: 1864 to 1877*, gives the distribution of 5,000 surnames. And before you do too much work, you should check Allan E. Marble's *A Catalogue of Published Genealogies of Nova Scotia Families.* Perhaps your family has been done before, and you will need only to connect or update your branch of the family tree.

In Nova Scotia, no government records of births and deaths were kept prior to 1864. Township books help in a few areas, and an incomplete set of marriage licenses exists, going back to 1763. Otherwise, church registers, newspaper notices or headstone data must be used. Government records prior to 1908 can be viewed at the Nova Scotia Archives & Records Management (NSARM). Records after that date are available through the provincial Deputy Registrar-General. A register of deaths in Halifax from 1890 to 1908 was recently put online at the NSARM website.

The major repository in the province, NSARM on University Avenue in Halifax, is closed to the public on Sundays and public holidays, and Saturdays on holiday weekends. Americans should note that three Canadian holidays differ from their own: Victoria Day (the Monday before May 25), Canada Day (July 1), and Thanksgiving (the second Monday in October).

Church records are an invaluable resource for genealogical research, and many of these are available in Nova Scotia. Typically, registers open in the 1800s, although some start decades earlier. Catholic records of the French era (pre-1755) are best explored through the Centre d'Etudes Acadiennes at New Brunswick's Université de Moncton. Members of the Church of Jesus Christ of Latter Day Saints (Mormons) microfilmed many church records, and these are accessible through their worldwide library system. NSARM has many pre-1908 church registers, especially Anglican, Methodist and Presbyterian. Other records are in church repositories or in local custody.

Many headstone inscriptions have been transcribed, and the results are often available at NSARM or with local historical or genealogical societies. Most surviving inscriptions date from after 1840, and these are particularly useful for deaths in the 1875–1950 period.

Newspaper announcements of marriages and deaths were predominantly those of Anglophones, the prominent and the Protestant until about 1850, after which coverage grew increasingly general. NSARM has microfilm of most of the old newspapers, and vital records from the Halifax press (1769–1856) have been published by the Genealogical Association of Nova Scotia. Other information available at the archives includes census data, poll tax records, land grants and deeds, and probate records.

Township books were kept in areas settled by New Englanders in western Nova Scotia. These generally covered births, marriages and deaths from the 1760s to the 1820s. They often recorded only those families having shares in the township, neglecting minorities, transient families and immigrants.

EARLY SETTLER RE-ENACTORS, SHERBROOKE VILLAGE

The provincial organization for family history is the Genealogical Association of Nova Scotia. GANS publishes *The Nova Scotia Genealogist*, an annual list of members' interests, readers' queries, book reviews, interesting short articles and other useful information. They offer a series of publications containing the 1838 census data.

Other active organizations that can be of help to anyone researching their family roots can be found in the Listings section at the end of this book. Further particulars of existing records and where to find them can be obtained by consulting two standard works I've written about the subject: *Genealogist's Handbook for Atlantic Canada Research* and *Genealogical Research in Nova Scotia*. They are available at NSARM and at many local libraries, or may be purchased from GANS.

MUSEUMS

78TH HIGHLANDERS, HALIFAX CITADEL

Nova Scotia is an interesting old place. Its modern history is diverse, abundant and, by New World standards, long. The area has witnessed some cataclysmic events in the evolution of the earth. Fascinating stories of the ages before human settlement are visible in its rocks and land formations. The history of its first people, the Mi'kmaq, stretches back 16,000 years to the end of the last Ice Age. Europeans visited Nova Scotia as early as the 11th century, and came to stay in 1604. Thankfully, the riches of the past have been collected, treasured and preserved and are now artfully and creatively presented at more than 100 museums in Nova Scotia.

Credit for this good stewardship belongs to the provincial and federal governments and to local community groups, as well as philanthropists and enthusiasts who have helped preserve fragments of social and natural history. A Nova Scotia Museum Pass (available at www.museum.gov.ns.ca, by calling 1-800-632-1114, or at any Nova Scotia Museum site) is a great bargain, especially for families ($38 per adult; $75 per family), and will admit you to all 25 Nova Scotia Museum sites. Parks Canada administers several important National Historic Sites in the province, including the Halifax Citadel and the Fortress of Louisbourg. There are also many excellent community museums. Check before you go out of your way to visit a museum, as many are only open during the summer season.

If you are coming to Nova Scotia by ferry, you can get your first history hit as soon as you disembark in the old seaport of Yarmouth. Kids love fire trucks. Get their vacation off to a roaring start at the Firefighters' Museum of Nova Scotia. It houses a rare collection of firefighting memorabilia from the 19th and early 20th centuries, including leather water buckets and antique toy fire engines. While you're in town, the award-winning Yarmouth County Museum is worth a walkabout.

The stories of Nova Scotia's earliest settlers unfold along the Evangeline Trail. Along the Acadian Shore you will witness evidence of the faith, industry and tenacity of Nova Scotia's 17th-century French settlers. Beautiful St. Mary's Church in Church Point/Pointe de l'Eglise is the largest wooden church in North America (56 metres from floor to steeple). The church houses le Musée Ste-Marie, comprising church artifacts such as vestments, furnishings, documents and photographs. Further along is St. Bernard Church, an impressive Gothic structure of granite, with a small museum.

When you arrive at the graceful old town of Annapolis Royal, you can stretch your legs on the earthworks of Fort Anne National Historic Site, which affords great views of the Annapolis Basin. The gunpowder building is the only surviving structure of the first 1708 French fort. The museum in the officers' quarters (circa 1797) presents a chapter in the struggle between France and Britain for supremacy in the New World. An amazing tapestry represents 400 years of the area's history.

Nearby, Port Royal National Historic Site is a reconstruction, based on a detailed drawing by Samuel de Champlain, of Canada's first European colony — a fur-trading post established here in 1605. High wooden walls around the habitation bring to mind the dangers of fierce weather, the intrusion of wildlife and fear of the wilderness. Inside the habitation, costumed interpreters perform the daily chores that made it possible for the French to maintain a European lifestyle.

Also on the Evangeline Trail is the Prescott House Museum, in Starrs Point, former home of the Honourable Charles R. Prescott, a Halifax merchant who became a horticulturalist. He introduced new varieties of apples to the Annapolis Valley and helped establish the Fruit Growers Association. The house (circa 1814) is now part of the Nova Scotia Museum. The heritage perennial gardens are delightful.

Past Wolfville is the Grand-Pré National Historic Site, which commemorates the deportation of the Acadians in 1755. The site paints a vivid picture of the lives of the first French settlers around Minas Basin. Henry Wadsworth Longfellow's epic poem *Evangline* and the novel *The Sea is So Wide* by Evelyn Eaton are fictional accounts

FORT ANNE NATIONAL HISTORIC SITE

based on the tragic events of 1755. Acadian families can find their ancestors' names on the lists in the church at Grand Pré.

The town of Windsor claims bragging rights to being the birthplace of Canada's great game on ice. At the Hockey Heritage Centre fans can see wooden pucks, handmade one-piece hockey sticks and early memorabilia of the game. Also in Windsor are two Nova Scotia Museum sites — the mid-Victorian Haliburton House, former home of Thomas Chandler Haliburton, writer of the famous Sam Slick stories, and the late-Victorian Shand House.

The Glooscap Trail leads you along the Fundy shoreline. Here is history of another, much older sort — the history of ancient rocks and life forms. The Joggins Fossil Centre has an excellent collection of 300-million-year-old fossils and gives some explanation of the geological phenomena in this area. There are also guided tours of the nearby fossil cliffs.

The Fundy Geological Museum at Parrsboro is a great place to take young dinosaur enthusiasts. There are some Jurassic tales here to tell the kids back home.

Nova Scotia has an extensive shipbuilding heritage. Huge wooden vessels were built on the beaches of this shore. The Age of Sail Heritage Centre at Port Greville highlights the history of lumbering and shipbuilding with artifacts and hands-on exhibits. On the other side of Minas Basin is the Lawrence House Museum in Maitland where the *William D Lawrence*, the largest wooden ship ever built in Canada, was launched in 1874.

AGE OF SAIL HERITAGE CENTRE, PORT GREVILLE

Visitors can go deep into a dark coal mine at the Miners' Museum in Springhill, a coal-mining town that has seen more than its share of tragedy, and learn about the stories of heroism and survival around the chilling disaster of 1891, the 1916 subterranean fire, the 1956 explosion and the major "bump" in 1958.

There aren't many places where you can still see a huge Scottish granite millstone in action, but at the Balmoral Grist Mill Museum you can watch how it's done and sample toasted oats that have been ground the same way as they were in 1784. Freshly ground flour and baked goods are sold at the museum shop.

The idyllic brook-side setting is a great location for a picnic.

At Pictou's Hector Heritage Quay, costumed guides and exhibits let you feel the hardships of the 1773 voyage that brought early Scottish settlers to "New Scotland." Step aboard the full-size replica of the ship *Hector* and imagine yourself crossing the Atlantic in the crowded space below decks.

In nearby Stellarton, the Nova Scotia Museum of

ANIMATORS AT THE
FORTRESS OF
LOUISBOURG

Industry celebrates 200 years of progress with more than 18,000 artifacts and many interactive exhibits. It is built over the famous Albion mine. The museum helps explain technology and the province's industries, past, present and future.

Across the Canso Causeway in Cape Breton there are some very fine museums, beginning in Baddeck with the Alexander Graham Bell National Historic Site. The well-designed museum deserves a half-day visit. It shows the diverse interests and accomplishments of the man behind the telephone, Alexander Graham Bell. Most of Bell's later years were spent in Baddeck, and the museum demonstrates the impressive breadth of his inventiveness, including his method for teaching speech to the deaf, his giant kites, airplanes and hydrofoils. The view of the Bras d'Or Lakes from the museum is breathtakingly beautiful.

At Fortress of Louisbourg National Historic Site, Nova Scotia's pre-eminent historical attraction, you will be transported back to 1744. Dozens of costumed actors portraying townsfolk and soldiers carry on as if the 21st century weren't just beyond the site's walls. There's a lively tavern, period homes to explore, and women at work in the authentic kitchen gardens. A hefty loaf of bread from the baker is the same as the soldiers ate, except for the absence of floor sweepings formerly added to augment the flour. Atop the ramparts at the back of the fortress there's a bird's-eye view of the harbour and town, with the children at play and the soldiers doing their drills. The fortress is best experienced over a full day.

On the other side of the island, the Ceilidh Trail promotes, preserves and presents its music-making heritage at the Celtic Music Interpretive Centre in Judique, with live music, vintage recorded music and collections of musical family histories. The biggest fiddle in the world makes for a fun photo opportunity.

Returning to the mainland, the ruggedly beautiful Marine Drive makes for a very different view of Nova Scotia. Along the way, at the Lighthouse Interpretive Centre at Port Bickerton, the lore of the lighthouse and the lightkeeper is kept alive. The lighthouse gives a great view of the sea and community.

Sherbrooke Village is a must-see. Like Louisbourg, it is a living history museum, depicting rural life in Nova Scotia between 1860 and the First World War. A weaver's cottage, a blacksmith's shop, a doctor's office and the home of an affluent master mariner are as they looked 100 years ago.

The Fisherman's Life Museum in Jeddore Oyster Pond is a little gem. An early 1900s inshore fisherman, his wife and his family of 13 daughters lived here. Women of the Eastern Shore tell stories of the family and how they lived, while they bake, tend the garden and preserve its wonderful produce, just as it was done several generations ago. The pump organ in the parlour, the hooked mats and the embroidered samplers all bring the close-knit family into focus.

In Halifax, be sure to visit the Maritime Museum of the Atlantic. Many are unaware of Halifax's close connection to the *Titanic* disaster. It was from Halifax that search and recovery operations were conducted. The museum has the world's largest collection of wooden artifacts from the *Titanic* (sit in a replica deck chair from the *Titanic* for a great souvenir photo).

The powerful exhibit "A Moment in Time" captures the devastation wrought by the Halifax Explosion of 1917. Exhibits on the Age of Sail, shipwrecks and the navy are part of the big picture of a great port city in a maritime province.

Halifax is crowned by the star-shaped Halifax Citadel National Historic Site. The Citadel is surrounded by a dry defensive ditch. The earthen ramparts provide great views of the city and harbour. Constructed between 1828 and 1856, the Citadel is a fine example of a bastioned fort of the "smooth bore" era. The site's exhibit, *"Fortress Halifax — Warden of the North"*, describes Halifax and its defences. In summer, students portray soldiers of the Royal Artillery and the 78th Highlanders of 1869 and fire the noonday gun.

At the Museum of Natural History there is something to fascinate all ages and tastes — a house full of live exotic butterflies, life in a busy beehive (located safely behind glass), and models of a life-sized whale, soaring eagles, a moose, a puffin colony and Canada's oldest dinosaurs.

HALIFAX CITADEL NATIONAL HISTORIC SITE

Many Canadians have a neighbour who came to Canada as a war bride, or had a great-uncle who went off to war, or know a family who came to Canada as

refugees. A gateway to North America for more than a million people, Pier 21 National Historic Site recollects the experiences of many individuals who arrived between 1928 and 1971. The facility houses interactive displays and artifacts, touching first-hand accounts, and exhibits celebrating the ethnic diversity and cultural heritage of Canada.

If you are touring the South Shore, there are a couple of museums you really shouldn't miss. Even if the Lighthouse Route isn't on your agenda, it's an easy day trip from Halifax to New Ross and the town of Lunenburg, a World Heritage Site. In 1816, William Ross, an army captain, and his wife Mary arrived in Nova Scotia with 172 disbanded soldiers to take up lands granted to them by the Crown. Today, the Ross Farm Living Museum of Agriculture is alive with costumed heritage interpreters who take you back to the early 1800s at a vintage store, the Ross farmhouse, barns and workshops, a village school, a blacksmith's shop and a cooper's shop. The farm is populated with heritage animals — horses, cows, oxen, sheep, pigs and poultry. The baby farm animals are always popular with children. Kids who have never seen a cow up close can try to milk one. Slightly older children (and their grandparents) might enjoy demonstrations of spinning, flax processing, bread making, yarn dying and woodworking.

In Lunenburg, the Fisheries Museum of the Atlantic is one of the Nova Scotia Museum's largest and most popular sites. *Bluenose* buffs will enjoy the exhibit of memorabilia and photos of the famous schooner built here. Old salts will tell you all you want to know about lobster fishing and demonstrate fishing skills. There's an exhibit on Lunenburg's rum-running days and a wonderful aquarium with peep holes at just the right level for pint-sized observers. You can board the schooner *Theresa E. Connor* and see what the life of a Grand Banks fisherman was like.

In Liverpool is the Sherman Hines Museum of Photography and Galleries, the only museum of photography east of Montreal; it contains artifacts dating from the beginnings of photography in the Maritimes, as well as vintage photographs by Karsh, Notman, MacAskill, Hines and others. The Queens County Museum and Perkins House give important insights into colonial life and times.

For nearly 80 years, the Barrington Woolen Mill Museum supplied yarn for fishermen's warm woolies. Its carding machines, spinning mule, loom twister and skeiner remain in their original places. There are also exhibits on raising sheep on the islands offshore and on wool processing and demonstrations of hand spinning.

Acadians returning to Nova Scotia after the expulsion settled the Pubnico area, which remains a strong Acadian community to this day. The Historical Acadian Village of Nova Scotia (Village Historique Acadien) at West Pubnico depicts the lifestyle of the Acadians from the mid-1600s to mid-1800s.

Nova Scotians have a right to be proud of the museums in their communities — and there are many more. Large and small, these sites provide entertainment and education to people of all ages. Many of them are run by volunteers and all of them try to give an authentic glimpse into their region's social and natural heritage.

ART AND CRAFTS

ADRIANE ABBOTT

CANDICE PRIOR AT THE SHOW OF HANDS ART FAIR, HALIFAX

GRUNT GLASS

Nova Scotia is more than seafood, fishing villages and lively fiddle music. It's fertile ground for some of the country's best visual arts and home to numerous talented artists, designers and craftspeople. It's all a matter of locating their various studios, workshops and sheds to get a glimpse of their creativity and the 'collecting' opportunity. The Studio Rally map, created by Adriane Abbott and Beverly McClare 15 years ago, is one way to find some of the finest artists. The map leads you to 100

studios that feature diverse creations — traditional landscape paintings, contemporary fashion, fine pottery vessels, mailboxes adorned with whimsical barnyard creatures and much more. The free guide illustrates and describes the work of each

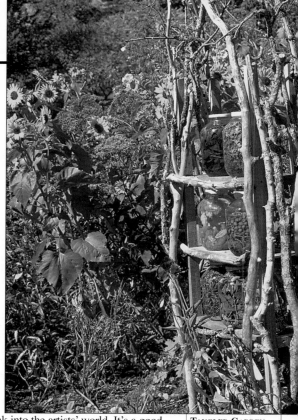

participating artisan. Choose a region to visit and you'll be sure to find welcoming people who will gladly show you their latest works.

Every year on the last weekend of May, all studios on the map throw open their doors to welcome visitors and demonstrate their talents and show off the best of their winter's work. This is a collector's dream. This event marks the opening of the season, but most of the studios are open year-round for self-directed travellers. So take a fun Sunday drive off the beaten path to sneak into the artists' world. It's a good idea to call before you stop in, though. All the artists welcome your visit, but as their studios often double as their homes, it's best to catch them when they're not taking the kids to soccer or sorting their laundry.

TANGLED GARDEN

On the Evangeline Trail entering the Annapolis Valley region, Grand Pré's Tangled Garden is a studio, garden and gallery showing Beverly McClare's sculptures of natural materials and George Walford's paintings. While you're there, sample some of the Tangled Garden jams and jellies and then pop out to the garden to appreciate the source of the ingredients! The neighbouring town of Wolfville is home to Frank Hill, a "bodger" — a crafter of Windsor chairs and tables who uses hand tools and traditional techniques. In Annapolis Royal, as well as the many great artists listed on the map, there is the Annapolis Region Community Arts Council which operates an artist-run centre and gallery, and it's right across the street from the Annapolis Royal Historical Gardens. In Yarmouth, there is a new branch of the Art Gallery of Nova Scotia.

Along the Glooscap Trail is Raspberry Bay Stone, a perfect summer stop in the community of Bass River. In Heather Lawson's gardens, hand-carved stone pieces dot the grounds. Also located near Bass River is Joy Laking, a watercolour painter and printmaker whose works of villagescapes, interiors,

21

salt marshes and lyrical flower portraits have been exhibited in major public collections. West of Parrsboro is ArtWare, Krista Wells's collection of colourful polymer clay and mixed media masks, décor, clocks and jewellery, and her line of block prints.

Lunenburg County has as many artists and craftspeople, studios and galleries as would make a sizeable city proud. Mahone Bay is a veritable beehive of artistic activity: potters, painters, printmakers, pewterers. Amos Pewter's interpretive workshop shows how their renowned jewellery, ornaments and vessels are crafted. Another notable local artist is realist painter Tom Ward. Mahonne Arts offers workshops in a wide range of media conducted by local professional artists. Details at www.mahonnearts.com. In the town of Lunenburg, Nova Terra Cotta Pottery features Joan Bruneau's thrown and altered earthenware of rich, painterly surfaces and distinct shapes. Lunenburg's Houston North Gallery celebrates Inuit people and their art, and shows Nova Scotian artists whose work harmonizes with the featured Arctic prints and sculptures. The Art Gallery Association of Lunenburg publishes a catalogue and a gallery map that provides a self-guided walking tour of approximately 20 galleries showing diverse media and styles. The maps are available at the Visitor Information Centre and at the galleries. For more about the Lunenburg galleries visit lunenburgart.com.

The truly adventurous should press on and head

LEATHER WORKER JOHN ROBERTS, INDIAN BROOK

further along the South Shore to Tudor Tile in Little Harbour, near Sable River, for Rebecca Tudor's handmade, custom-designed ceramic tiles, which are inspired by the land and seascape surroundings, then have lunch at Charlotte Lane Café & Crafts located in the historic waterfront properties of Shelburne.

POTTERY FROM CAPE BRETON CLAY

On the other side of the province, the Sunrise Trail leads to the town of Antigonish. The Lyghtesome Gallery is a good place to see the region's talent. The gallery has a long-standing reputation for promoting local artists through its monthly exhibition schedule. Nearby studios boast the painting talents of Alice Reed and the exquisite wood works of the McLean Brothers.

Along Cape Breton's Cabot Trail, there are numerous studios dotting this celebrated route. Sunset Art Gallery in Cheticamp is the studio of William Roach, a local folk artist — and a real character! He welcomes visitors anytime in the summer, and by appointment in the off-season, to view his spirited painted wood carvings. John C. Roberts' leather goods range from bags, buckets, belts and bowls to wallets, aprons and dog leashes. The town of Baddeck is another artisan hot spot, with Carol and Gordon Kennedy's Iron Art & Photographs: Working Forge & Gallery and Bell Fraser's Cape Breton Clay which help celebrate Maritime cuisine. If making a visit to Louisbourg, take a side trip to Grey Seal Weaving Studio in Point Michaud to see a large loom in a small cabin with a great view of the Atlantic, to say nothing of the breathtaking silk weavings.

JOY LAKING WATERCOLOUR

ART GALLERY OF NOVA SCOTIA

The Studio Rally map is best suited to those with wheels, since solitude-seeking artists often live on the roads less taken. But for those who are visiting Halifax, all that's needed is time, a sense of adventure and the wherewithal to walk the hilly city. If you take a stroll along the city's picturesque harbourfront docks, continue walking south to the Pier 21 Arts Annex building. Jeffery Cowling Architectural Interior Accessories welcomes visitors to the Arts Annex. His wooden architectural boxes are also containers for documents, jewellery and CD collections. Though not all of the studios are open to the public, a cluster of Studio Rally artists can be found there, from jewellers to extraordinary wood turners.

ELIZABETH GOLUCH'S LIZZY BUGS

On the other side of the Citadel, closer to Halifax Harbour's Northwest Arm, Elizabeth Goluch's Lizzy Bugs will make friends out of entomophobes. Her studio is filled with metal insects — from sculptures of giant articulated praying mantis to larger-than-life bees and roaches. Her work is truly unique and despite the description, it's utterly stunning.

Halifax has several galleries and museums that provide a solid cross-section of local art and crafts. A visit to the Art Gallery of Nova Scotia will give you a feel for the diversity of talent and the work of local folk and contemporary artists. The AGNS Gallery Shop offers work by local artists. Studio 21 features the work of local and nationally recognized artists in three galleries within its warehouse space close to the redeveloped Pier 21 area. Zwicker's Gallery,

Eastern Canada's oldest commercial art gallery, carries original oil and watercolour paintings, drawings, sculpture and prints by over 80 Maritime and other Canadian artists. The Secord Gallery offers traditional and modern works — paintings, drawings, original prints and photographs. Argyle Fine Art represents regional, national, international, historic and contemporary artists. Page and Strange Gallery on Granville Mall, next to the Nova Scotia College of Art and Design (NSCAD), gives the scoop on emerging artists.

Just a short drive from Halifax, you'll come upon a cluster of studios along Purcells Cove Road. Joy Pennick's jewellery and metalworks, Kathy Brown's seacoast-inspired watercolours and Sally Ravindra's stoneware and porcelain vessels are all minutes away from one another.

When you visit an artist's studio you get to know the creator, which enhances your appreciation of the work, and you may acquire a really meaningful souvenir of your visit to Nova Scotia.

For a free copy of a Studio Rally map stop by any tourist information desk in Nova Scotia, or download a copy of the map at www.studiorally.ca. Call 1-800-565-0000 for further information, or visit www.novascotia.com for information on more artists and craftspeople in Nova Scotia. See the Listings section of this book for the addresses and phone numbers of the artists and resources mentioned above.

SHOW OF HANDS CRAFT FAIR, HALIFAX

THEATRE

LINETTE CHIASSON

GRAFTON STREET DINNER THEATRE

With more than thirty working venues and a list of companies that grows longer every year, actors, directors and playwrights are flocking to Nova Scotia, producing works that are commanding international attention.

The first theatrical production in Nova Scotia (and arguably in the New World) was a masque devised by Marc Lescarbot, a settler at Port Royal, in 1606. The theatrical tradition of the area is continued to this day at King's Theatre, site of the Annapolis Royal Summer Theatre Festival, held each year in July and August.

The numerous theatre festivals in Nova Scotia constitute a good reason for a trip just in themselves. Festival Antigonish is a popular event, with attendees from around the globe — a treat for any theatre lover and set in a jewel of a town. The Liverpool International Theatre Festival, held at the Astor Theatre every other May; the Atlantic Theatre Festival in Wolfville, which runs from June to September; and the Chester Theatre Festival at the Chester Playhouse in July and August are all worth checking out. The Internet is a valuable tool when planning a festival expedition, with listings and information about plays and show times.

The Atlantic Fringe Festival is an excellent opportunity to see some new and innovative pieces. Because the festival draws from local, national and international companies, it provides a diverse range of styles. It also gives a rare opportunity for up-and-coming artists from the area (and smaller established companies) to showcase their work. Fringe prices are so reasonable it's well worth seeing half a dozen performances.

In the metro area, there are a host of other companies and venues to see — most notably Shakespeare by the Sea, set against the natural beauty and fantastic forts and ruins around Point Pleasant Park each summer. Check out Dartmouth-based Eastern Front Theatre located at Alderney Landing, a fun few minutes by ferry from downtown Halifax. This is the area's only professional company whose mandate places emphasis on producing plays of regional provenance and social relevance.

The recently-renovated Neptune Theatre started life in 1915 as the Strand Theatre vaudeville house, but since 1963 the company has been producing shows almost year-round. The Fountain Hall main stage is a grand space with beautiful acoustics, while the smaller Studio Theatre provides a more intimate setting. With the addition of the studio series, the Neptune season offers a fine mix of old and new works. Ticket prices are available on the theatre's website, but if you're not able to book ahead, a limited number of rush tickets are sold a half hour before most performances for about half price. Both of the Neptune venues also serve as host theatres for touring productions and smaller companies, so it's worth calling the box office ahead of time to find out what's happening when you're going to be in town.

Keep your eyes peeled and peruse the *Coast* (a free Halifax weekly) for complete area entertainment listings, as there are many smaller companies in the metro area that produce shows on a less regular schedule. Names to watch for

NEPTUNE THEATRE

SHAKESPEARE BY THE SEA

STEVEN McCARTHY IN 2B THEATRE COMPANY'S *REVISITED*

MERMAID THEATRE'S *MIXED-UP CHAMELEON*

include the Irondale Ensemble, Zuppa Circus, 2b, Exodus Theatre and Two Planks and a Passion (a touring company dedicated to bringing theatre to the masses). Watch also for performances at some of the smaller venues, such as The Space on Agricola Street and Bus Stop Theatre, also in the city's North end. DalTheatre, the Dalhousie University theatre department, runs an interesting season from the Sir James Dunn Theatre in the Dalhousie Arts Centre — also the home of the Rebecca Cohn auditorium. Year-round fun can be found at Halifax's two dinner theatres — Halifax Feast Dinner Theatre and Grafton Street Dinner Theatre, both within the downtown core.

For a true taste of Nova Scotia culture and history, don't miss the summer performances of *Évangéline* at Université Ste-Anne. This musical is based on Longfellow's famous poem, with shows in Acadian French and English. The story is so familiar and the staging so evocative that this piece is really best experienced in its original tongue. If you don't have much French but can't make an English show,

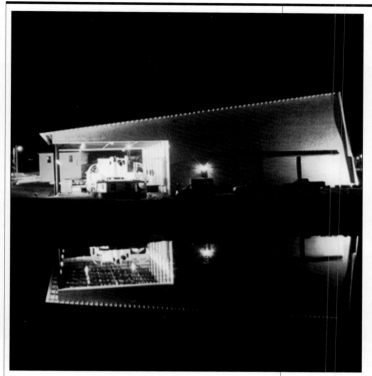

SHIP'S COMPANY
THEATRE,
PARRSBORO

simultaneous translation headsets are available for a small additional fee.

Mermaid Theatre, an internationally acclaimed touring puppet theatre based in Windsor, is focussed on children, but is equally magical for adults. It's well worth the trip from anywhere in the province.

If your taste runs to unusual venues, you shouldn't miss the Ship's Company Theatre in Parrsboro. The theatre is housed in a converted car ferry, the MV *Kipawo*, and the performances are just as innovative. Ship's Company often performs interesting and appealing Canadian works, often with a local connection. For more historic savour, there's the Savoy Theatre in Glace Bay, built in the 1920s in the manner of a Victorian show house. Although extensively renovated in the 70s, the theatre retains all of its original period charm. In addition to its regular season, it hosts a wide range of touring and cultural activities, including the original Cape Breton Summertime Revue, with comedy and music blended in perfect proportion.

With so much to choose from, theatre aficionados will have no difficulty finding exciting productions across the province. The key is to keep abreast of the many new companies, productions and venues popping up all the time. Check websites, ask at your place of accommodation, and pay attention to signs and posters.

Music

PEGGY WALT

HOCHIWITCHI, ATLANTIC JAZZ FESTIVAL

Nova Scotia is alive with the sound of music. From pop music to Celtic, down-home bluegrass to hard-core jazz — touring Nova Scotia can be an eclectic symphony of sounds.

One of the headliners in this soundscape is Symphony Nova Scotia (www.symphonynovascotia.ca). SNS's season runs from September to May at Halifax's Rebecca Cohn Auditorium, with programming extending beyond the core symphonic repertoire to include diverse local artists such as El Viento Flamenco, singer/songwriter Lennie Gallant and local rocker Matt Mays. Much of the credit for the creative partnerships with Maritime musicians goes to Nova Scotian conductor/arranger Scott Macmillan, whose highly acclaimed *Celtic Mass for the Sea* and MacKinnon's *Brook Suite* have been featured nationally on CBC and sold throughout the world. Symphony musicians perform in several smaller ensembles at festivals throughout the province. Rhapsody Quintet performs a Light Music/Palm Court repertoire, and the Blue Engine String Quartet features women composers and innovative arrangements, including songs of Leonard Cohen with actor/singer Cliff Le Jeune. SuddenlyLISTEN produces improvisational music concerts led by SNS principal cellist, Norman Adams, also a member of the Upstream New Music Ensemble.

Complementing the orchestra's season, in late May and early June the Scotia Festival of Music produces a world-class chamber music series in Halifax with artists of exceptionally high calibre. Scotia Festival features an artist-in-residence program that has brought in such prestigious talent as the Prazak Quartet, Pierre Boulez and Philip Glass.

For 10 months of the year the St. Cecilia Concert Series (www.stcecilia.ca) brings a wide range of performers to Nova Scotia audiences at venues in the Halifax region and on the South Shore. During the summer months visitors will be delighted to find Music at the Three Churches in Mahone Bay, Musique Saint Bernard on the Acadian Shore and Musique Royale at various historic venues around the province. These classical concert series engage musicians from across Canada.

For traditional musical tastes, each area of Nova Scotia offers its own musical pedigree: in Cape Breton, the fiddle shares the stage with Celtic singers; in southwest Nova Scotia, Acadian musicians blend Louisiana cajun, modern folk and fiddle tunes for a distinctive and lively sound. Each community has its own stellar entertainers: for example, fiddler Buddy MacMaster is king of the Ceilidh Trail, and from the French-speaking communities in the district of Clare come celebrated groups such as Grand Dérangement and Blou, heard at festivals such as the Festival Acadien de Clare. Acadian kitchen parties are held at various local restaurants on the French Shore throughout the summer as part of Musique de la Baie (www.baiesaintemarie.com).

The Mabou Ceilidh, a tradition for more than 20 years, is a weekly event all year round. The musicians range from stars such as Natalie MacMaster to gifted youngsters who are itching to get in the spotlight. People at all levels of dancing ability are welcome to participate. You can learn the steps from seasoned regulars.

Seaside Folk, a non-profit organization of music fans, hosts monthly concerts at the Italy Cross fire hall, featuring performers as diverse as Scotland's Battlefield Band to local favourites such as Ian Janes. And then there's Pictou's Hector Festival, celebrating celtic music and heritage each August at the deCoste Centre.

RHAPSODY QUINTET

DRUM! HALIFAX

LUNENBURG FOLK HARBOUR FESTIVAL

In late May, the Apple Blossom Festival in the Annapolis Valley, an annual event since 1933, mixes pageantry with music. Well-known Canadian music performers, including the Barenaked Ladies and Atlantic Canada's Great Big Sea, have appeared on stage at the festival.

All the pomp and circumstance of the province's rich military history comes alive at Halifax's Metro Centre the first week in July with the Royal Nova Scotia International Tattoo (www.nstattoo.ca). Nova Scotia's spine-tingling massed pipes and drums share the floor with the best international military bands at one of the world's most prestigious musical events. Pipe and drum bands abound throughout the province, and one of the newest groups to spring from this tradition is Squid, four young precision drummers who are taking audiences by storm (www.tastysquid.com).

On Cape Breton Island, the tempo picks up in June, especially in Port Hawkesbury, with a weekly ceilidh at the Creamery (Tuesdays; www.ceilidh.ca) and free Granville Green concerts (Sundays, July and August, www.granvillegreen.com). There are ceilidh dances each Wednesday all summer long at The Barn in the Margaree Valley (www.normaway.com).

Communities like Bridgewater, Avon Valley and Stewiacke have built amazing concerts and camping festivals spotlighting the unique down-home sounds of Bluegrass.

In summer, concerts are advertised in the local newspapers, tourist bureaus and on community cable channels. You can also check Music Nova Scotia's website at www.musicnovascotia.com.

The *Coast*, a weekly newspaper found all over Halifax, gives details on the what and where of live music, be it pop, jazz, fusion, hard-core rock or anything in between. Halifax also hosts the best pub scene in Canada. Mainstays such as the The Old Triangle, Lower Deck and Peddler's Pub feature live entertainment. In the fall, Pier 20 at the Halifax waterfront is home to the hit show DRUM! (www.drumshow.ca), a musical celebration of four founding cultures of Nova Scotia (Black, Mi'kmaq, Acadian and Scottish), utilizing rhythm, dance and video montages in a powerful celebration of Nova Scotia's culture and history.

The Atlantic Jazz Festival (www.jazzeast.com) in early July is the place to see solo artists and ensembles from Canada and the international scene. In addition to free jazz during the day on Halifax's Spring Garden Road, the festival hosts events in many different venues throughout the city.

More great music from around the world abounds at the annual Multicultural Festival, held on the Dartmouth waterfront each June (www.multifest.ca). Flamenco, African drumming, Korean dance and great food await you.

GUERILLA VACATION, ATLANTIC JAZZ FESTIVAL, HALIFAX

The Stan Rogers Festival, named for one of the country's best-loved folk musicians, can lay claim to being one of Canada's best folk festivals, held each July in Canso (www.stanfest.com).

In August the Lunenburg Folk Harbour Festival (www.folkharbour.com) hosts folk musicians such as Susan Crowe, Ron Hynes, Lennie Gallant and many others from various parts of the world in a fishing town steeped in history. The New Glasgow Riverfront Jubilee (www.jubilee.ns.ca) set against the backdrop of the beautiful New Glasgow riverfront, offers the best in East Coast and Canadian talent ranging from pop to Celtic.

New on the scene is Wolfville's Deep Roots Festival in mid-September in the beautiful Annapolis Valley, showcasing local, national and international folk artists (www.deeprootsmusic.ca).

CELTIC COLOURS FESTIVAL DANCERS

The festival season draws to a close in October with the internationally acclaimed Celtic Colours International Festival (www.celtic-colours.com) in Cape Breton, drawing enthusiastic crowds to listen to the best of Celtic music from the new and old worlds — Slainte Mhath, Mary Jane Lamond, Bela Fleck and Capercaillie.

For details about music festivals and events call 1-800-565-0000, check out www.novascotia.com or ask at a local visitor information centre.

DINING

BY ELAINE ELLIOT

ZUPPA DI PESCE AL MODENESE, LA PERLA RESTAURANT, DARTMOUTH

FLEUR DE SEL, LUNENBURG

With an abundant supply of local fresh fruit, produce and seafood, Nova Scotia's chefs will treat you to memorable dining experiences.

Seafood is our forte. Seventy percent of visitors order seafood, and menus around the province offer a generous selection. Atlantic lobster, the king of the crustacean family, is very popular. Dining on lobster should be a casual affair; it is, after all, a hands-on experience. Choose a table overlooking the sparkling

Atlantic waters at the Quarterdeck Grill at Summerville Beach, join the folks at the Shore Club's lobster suppers in Hubbards or visit the Halls Harbour Lobster Pound and Restaurant at Halls Harbour on the Bay of Fundy. At the pound, meals are served outdoors, picnic-style, overlooking the ever-changing tides of this picturesque village. Throughout the province locals celebrate the beginning of lobster season

POTATO-CRUSTED
SNOW CRAB CAKES,
CHIVES CANADIAN
BISTRO, HALIFAX

with church or community suppers. A visit to any
tourist information centre should provide details of
times and places. For the faint of heart who cannot
bear to tackle a whole lobster, lobster rolls (soft buns
stuffed with lobster meat) are featured on menus
throughout the province.

In addition to lobster, world-renowned Digby
scallops, North Atlantic crab, farm-raised salmon and
blue mussels, haddock, halibut, tuna and swordfish
are but a few of our seafood dining options.
Succulent scallops are featured on most menus and
while some may be content with the simple sautéed
version, look for innovative adaptations of this
delicious bivalve. Chef Martin Ruiz-Salvador of
Lunenburg's Fleur de Sel restaurant serves scallops
with morel mushrooms, while Dartmouth's La Perla
Restaurant chef James MacDougall serves his
scallops with Italian flair. Large and tender cultivated
mussels served steamed in the shell with an
accompanying sauce are a popular choice as an
appetizer, especially with crusty bread for dipping!

Try "planked" Atlantic salmon, a specialty at
Liscombe Lodge on the Province's eastern shore.
There, diners are invited to watch each evening as
the chef arranges the hot embers, bastes his fish with
butter and turns the planks to ensure an even
cooking. Cedar-planked salmon is not to be confused
with "cold smoked" salmon, a delicacy known
around the world as Nova Scotia smoked salmon,
used mainly in appetizers or perhaps in a pasta sauce.
Smokehouses are scattered along the province's
shores and some, such as Willy Krauch's Danish
Smokehouse at Tangier and St. Mary's River

SALAD OF ORGANIC
FIELD GREENS WITH
ORANGE SHALLOT
VINAIGRETTE,
CHIVES CANADIAN
BISTRO, HALIFAX
(RIGHT)
OUTDOOR CAFÉ,
ARGYLE STREET,
HALIFAX (BELOW)
CURRIED BUTTERNUT
SQUASH AND
CAULIFLOWER SOUP,
SAEGE BISTRO,
HALIFAX (MIDDLE)
LOBSTER
CROQUETTES, OPA!,
HALIFAX (BOTTOM)

Smokehouse at Sherbrooke, welcome visitors and ship worldwide.

Halifax and Dartmouth offer the most diversified food experiences in the province. Intimate restaurants tucked in 19th-century buildings compete with upscale dining rooms, and most are a short walk from downtown hotels. Canadian cuisine is featured at Chives Canadian Bistro where the menu changes with the seasons. Halliburton House Inn and Bish World Cuisine on the waterfront both offer fine dining experiences. Authentic Italian fare may be enjoyed at elegant Da Maurizio or more casual Il Mercato, companion establishments to Bish. Il Mercato has two locations, one in the busy Spring Garden Road shopping district, the other a short drive from the city's downtown in a smart Bedford mall. Tucked in a little courtyard off Dresden Row you will find Fid, offering a creative fusion menu highlighting local ingredients. Various ethnic restaurants serve Greek, Thai, Indian, Korean or Japanese fare. Opa! is your place for traditional Greek favourites, while Cheelin in the trendy Brewery Market or Baan Thai are excellent choices for Chinese or Thai fare. Several restaurants such as Jane's on the Commons, Deco Restaurant or Saege Bistro offer fashionable lighter dishes, including vegetarian, pasta and stir-fry combinations.

As well as spectacular scenery, the South Shore offers excellent regional cuisine — succulent lamb at Rhubarb Grill at Oceanstone Inn and Cottages in Indian Harbour, chunky chowders from Mahone Bay's Innlet Café, seasonal fruit desserts at Charlotte Lane Café in Shelburne. And for a truly Acadian experience, visit Restaurant Chez Christophe at Grosses Coques on the French Shore, where chef Paul Comeau will introduce you to fricot, fish cakes and rappie pie.

ROAST BREAST OF PHESANT IN DRIED-CRANBERRY JUS, STORIES RESTAURANT AT HALLIBURTON HOUSE INN (INSET) CAST IRON SEARED DEEP OCEAN SCALLOPS WITH BEETROOT BEURRE BLANC AND MANGO SALSA AT TEMPEST RESTAURANT (BOTTOM)

In the Annapolis Valley, vine ripened strawberries become delightful desserts at Wolfville's Tempest Restaurant while blueberries are incorporated into dressings, sauces and desserts at Between the Bushes, a casual but fine-dining restaurant located, aptly, between the bushes at a commercial blueberry farm.

No holiday in Nova Scotia is complete without spending at least three or four days enjoying the magnificent scenery and sampling the local fare of the Northumberland Shore, Pictou, Antigonish and Cape Breton Island. Piper's Landing at Lyons Brook and Gabrieau's Bistro of Antigonish present varied menus reflecting local ingredients. In Cape Breton look for porridge or bannock breads, surprisingly tasteful presentations of root vegetables

PORK TENDERLOIN STUFFED WITH RED ONION CRANBERRY CONFIT, GABRIEAU'S BISTRO, ANTIGONISH

and local lamb. Gowrie House Country Inn in Sydney Mines and Chanterelle Country Inn at North River Bridge both offer exquisite fine dining. The Red Shoe Pub in Mabou, run by the Rankin sisters of singing fame and under the guidance of chef Craig Flinn, offers excellent casual dining.

Fine dining is never complete without a glass of wine or ale. Ask the restaurateurs to suggest a local wine, perhaps from Jost Vineyards in Malagash, Grand Pré Winery near Wolfville or Sainte Famille Wines in the Windsor area. Grand Pré Winery also offers Stultz Cider. Lunenburg County Winery, Newburne, makes enjoyable fruity dessert wines. At brewpubs scattered across the province, beers or ales are crafted for on-premise consumption: Rudder's Seafood Restaurant and Brew Pub, Yarmouth; Paddy's Brew Pub, Kentville; Chedabucto Bay Brewing Company in the Rare Bird Pub and Eatery, Guysborough.

Advance planning is the key to a good vacation. If travelling with children, look for establishments offering services and menus adapted to little ones. White Point Beach Resort at Hunts Point and Inverary Resort in Baddeck are ideal family destinations. Call before you begin a foray into the countryside as many rural inns and restaurants are seasonal, operating from early May through October; a few offer limited public dining, while others have just one seating. Consider your expectations, check menus on websites or ask your innkeeper to recommend regional dining specialties. Reservations are strongly suggested at peak travel times, such as July and the height of fall foliage viewing.

ORGANIC FINGERLING POTATO SKINS WITH LEMON AND RED PEPPER AIOLIS, TEMPEST RESTAURANT, WOLFVILLE

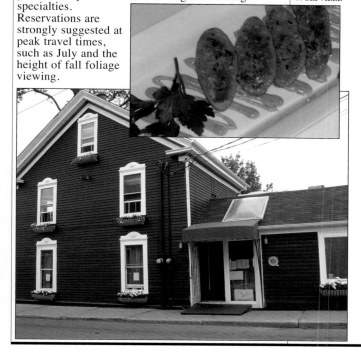

FAIRS, FESTIVALS AND EVENTS

ALAN LYNCH

ROYAL NOVA SCOTIA INTERNATIONAL TATTOO	Samuel de Champlain launched a dining club, the Order of Good Cheer, as a way to break up the winter boredom of 1605. Champlain's idea set the tone for Nova Scotia's passion for fairs, festivals and food. Nova Scotians use any excuse to eat, drink and be merry.

As if to prove the gregarious nature of Nova Scotians, the province's calendar is crammed with over 700 fairs, festivals and special days. Many festivals are inspired by the bountiful fruits of Nova Scotia's fertile land and generous sea. There's the Apple Blossom Festival held in the Annapolis Valley in late May; maple syrup festivals in Dean and Maplewood in early spring, and wine festivals in Falmouth, Lunenburg and Malagash in early fall. There are a staggering number of strawberry socials, lobster suppers, chowder festivals, and bean and sausage or ham and scalloped potato dinners. These events are fantastic bargains for residents and visitors alike, with plates stacked high by cooks used to feeding farm hands and fishermen.

Agricultural exhibitions take place throughout the summer. Three of the largest are the South Shore Exhibition (late July to early August), the Nova Scotia Provincial Exhibition at Bible Hill (late August) and Nova Scotia's oldest, the Hants County Exhibition in Windsor (held over two weekends in mid-September). These exhibitions have all the traditional elements:

fruit, vegetable and flower competitions, quilt shows and livestock displays. The ox-pulls are the main attraction at the South Shore Exhibition (the "Big Ex") in Bridgewater. Teams of these impressive beasts pull three times their own weight. The Maritime Fall Fair, held in October just outside Halifax, lets city kids get up close to animals, and it is a must for those who enjoy equestrian events.

The fishery is the focus for many other community events across the province. There's the Pictou Lobster Carnival in mid-July, Digby Scallop Days and the Louisbourg Crab Festival in August. In mid-August, Lunenburg hosts the Nova Scotia Fisheries Exhibition and Fishermen's Reunion. A number of fishermen's competitions take place at these festivals, including net mending, fish filleting, scallop shucking and the hotly contested dory races.

When Nova Scotians do move away from the table, they celebrate with some blockbuster events. In 2006, Queen Elizabeth, to mark her 80th birthday, granted Royal status to the Nova Scotia International

NOVA SCOTIA TATTOO PARADE

Tattoo, making it the Royal Nova Scotia International Tattoo. With over 2,000 performers from Canada and around the world, this musical extravaganza held at Halifax's Metro Centre in late June to early July is the largest military tattoo in North America. Following on the Tattoo's heels is the Atlantic Jazz Festival, which fills downtown Halifax with cool vibes. Then for 10 days in early August, Halifax hosts the International Buskers' Festival, which feels like the circus has come to town as 50 street performers from around the world take over wharves and pedestrian walks with their fun, eccentric and offbeat talents.

The Mahone Bay Classic Boat Festival (end of July) has a parade, music, seafood and boat-building demonstrations on the water's edge. The highlight of the three-day event is the "Fast and Furious" competition in which teams build and then race unique wooden boats, often with hilarious results. The Lunenburg Folk Harbour Festival (early August) is

MAHONE BAY CLASSIC BOAT FESTIVAL

four days of international folk music in the historic surroundings of this world heritage town. Also in the folk vein, the Stan Rogers Folk Festival in Canso on the first weekend in July celebrates the life of the late singer/songwriter with a variety of genres from Celtic to country. Two other not-to-be-missed festivals are the Riverfront Music Jubilee on the

New Glasgow riverfront and the new Deep Roots Music Festival (mid-September) in Wolfville. If your schedule doesn't allow you to take in the festivals mentioned, don't worry, Nova Scotia hosts 136 music festivals every year!

And then there are the waterside festivals. Around the Canada Day Weekend, the folks in Pictou are looking up with their new Maritime Kite and Kayak Festival. A windy holiday brightens the hearts of young and old as this ancient joy is revived. In early August — but just for one day, so come early — 40 of the province's celebrated folk artists participate in the Nova Scotia Folk Art Festival in Lunenburg. Their brightly painted, primitive and fantastical creations are quickly finding homes in some of the world's best art collections. Even if you're not a collector, these creations provide a great touch of humour.

Another type of artistry, married to invention and engineering, is celebrated in Shelburne's Whirligig Festival (late July). Look for a field of fun, magical creations spinning wildly on the harbourfront. Equally amazing are the temporary creations crafted at the Clam Harbour Beach Sandcastle Contest, where wild imaginations and hidden talents are unleashed.

For those making a fall visit to Nova Scotia, the Windsor–West Hants Pumpkin Regatta on the waterfront in Windsor takes place the second Sunday of October. Competitors actually race huge — and we mean really big (up to 800 pounds) — pumpkins across Lake Pesaquid. Some are paddled, some are motorized. It's truly unique!

Some of Cape Breton Island's stunning celebrations include the Fête de Saint Louis — a baroque-styled celebration at the Fortress of Louisbourg that ends with an antique fireworks display that recreates the great siege of the fortress, and the Celtic Colours International Festival, a week-long celebration of Celtic music, with over 300 concerts held across the Island. During the summer months, there are smaller musical surprises like the ceilidhs held Tuesdays in Mabou and Wednesdays in Judique. Ceilidhs are impromptu musical evenings of toe-tappin' wild fiddles, throbbing bodhrans (flat Irish hand drums) and plaintive bagpipes, mixed with step dancing and singers.

Nova Scotians also celebrate the diverse cultures that make up the population of the province. Mi'kmaq traditions are demonstrated at the

WINDSOR-WEST HANTS PUMPKIN REGATTA

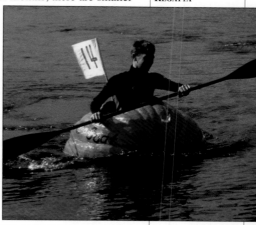

Millbrook First Nations Powwow in August. Black Loyalists are remembered in Amherst in January. Haligonians eagerly anticipate the Greek Festival in early June, which kicks off a summer season of feasting and festivity. The Multicultural Festival on the Dartmouth waterfront in mid-July is an opportunity to hear world music while munching your way through a global food court. There's a Polish festival in Sydney. There are a dozen special events celebrating our Acadian heritage and population, such as Musique de la Baie, a summer-long music festival throughout the District of Clare, Journées Acadienne de Grand Pré (a music and cultural fair), and Festival de l'Escaouette in Cheticamp. One of the biggest, the Festival Acadien de Clare, includes games, traditional dances, an ox-haul, fishing tournament and many other community-based activities that last a whole week in early July.

The culture of one of the largest groups of settlers, the Scots, takes over a number of open spaces in summer to hold highland games, where you'll see traditional heavy events such as the caber toss, when a telephone-pole-sized log is tossed end-over-end. These games also include traditional dancing and pipers. So, if you can't live without a touch of the tartan, look for the Gathering of the Clans in Pugwash (Canada Day), Festival of the Tartans in New Glasgow (July), the Inverness Gathering (July), and the Halifax Highland Games and Scottish Festival (July). The Antigonish Highland Games, the oldest (since 1861) and largest highland games held outside Scotland, are the best bet. Each August, the Gaelic College of Celtic Arts and Crafts at South Gut St. Anns, in Cape Breton, holds the Gaelic Mod, a weekend of Gaelic language and song.

CABER TOSS, ANTIGONISH HIGHLAND GAMES

Watch for numerous other celebrations and fairs based on Nova Scotia's traditional music, culture, crafts and culinary specialties, as well as its natural history, and anniversaries of major events, such as the first flight in the British Empire or the sinking of the *Titanic*. There's also a wealth of music, theatre, dance and visual arts festivals, and many others that are just an excuse to have fun. It's been over 400 years since explorer Samuel de Champlain founded the Order of Good Cheer and Nova Scotians are still partying, proving that having fun never goes out of fashion.

For specific times and information about these fairs and festivals, and for a full list of all 700 events held annually, visit www.novascotia.com and click on What to Do, or call 1-800-565-0000. You can also pick up a copy of the *Nova Scotia Festival and Events Guide* at a visitor information centre.

GOLF

ELEANOR ANDERSON

With just the right mix of classic and contemporary designs, breathtaking scenery, warm hospitality and affordable green fees, Nova Scotia is the perfect choice for a golf vacation.

Rolling landscapes and seaside vistas are highlights of the more than 60 golf courses found throughout Nova Scotia. Most courses offer the challenging game that golf enthusiasts are seeking yet provide layouts that can appeal to the novice golfer. The golf season typically runs from May through to October. The *Nova Scotia Golf Travel Guide*, available at visitor information centres and travel information kiosks throughout the province, identifies the golf courses that welcome green-fee play. Approximate fees range between $13 and $35 for 9 holes and from $29 to $125 for 18 holes.

Golf courses throughout the province are easily found by following the blue highway signs bearing a golfer symbol. Peak season times (July and August) should be booked well in advance to avoid disappointment. Optimal tee times are before 10 am, with weekends busier than the weekdays. On Monday to Thursday afternoons most courses have tee times available on shorter notice.

Services offered at most clubs range from club rentals and tee times to golf clinics and lessons. Well-

HIGHLAND LINKS, INGONISH

appointed pro shops are the norm across the province; they can meet your immediate requirements and provide you with great souvenirs.

Many accommodation operators, both large and small, across Nova Scotia offer golf as part of their accommodation packages. They will often arrange tee times and include some meals. Each package has varying characteristics and should be clarified upon booking. Keltic Lodge is located next door to Highlands Links and offers Tee Off Packages with one night's accommodation and one round of golf, as well as a range of customized Golf Getaway vacation packages to choose from. Rates are subject to change and are higher in peak season.

Additional golf packages are offered through experienced accommodation operators such as White Point, the Digby Pines Resort and Cape Breton Resorts, whose "Ultimate Golf Package" includes three nights accommodation in properties across Cape Breton Island and a round at each of the Fabulous Foursome golf courses. The annually produced golf travel guide provides an extensive list of golf/accommodation packages.

Golf in Nova Scotia can be challenging, with courses cut from unforgettable landscapes; most are built with a view of one of the world's greatest water hazards, the Atlantic ocean. Golfers of all skill levels will enjoy a diversity of courses from the classic Stanley Thompson–designed Highlands Links to the gem of southern Nova Scotia, the Digby Pines Resort Golf Course. Highlands Links, dramatically cut from the highlands of Cape Breton, is ranked the 71st best golf course in the world by *GOLF Magazine*, and ranked the number one public course in Canada by *SCOREGolf* magazine. It's well worth driving the meandering but modern highway up Smokey Mountain, each kilometre adding to your anticipation as you get closer to this true links course. Framed by the rugged Atlantic coastline and the mountainous

contours of the Cape Breton Highlands, the brilliance of Stanley Thompson's design invites all to experience and enjoy his legacy. At the other end of the province is The Pines, carved out of a superb setting through an evergreen forest. Many professional golfers consider

BELL BAY

this to be one of the most challenging and picturesque golf courses in the country.

Golf in this vibrant seaside province has advanced in recent years with the opening of other championship layouts, such as the impeccable Glen Arbour Golf Club just outside Halifax, and Baddeck's Bell Bay Golf Club, which *SCOREGolf* ranked the most underrated golf course in Canada in 2002.

The Pines, Highlands Links, Bell Bay and Glen Arbour are the more familiar names to visiting golfers. However, there are many other must-play experiences. These include the Graham Cook–designed Osprey Ridge 18-hole golf club, which offers a blend of links and parkland golf as well as outstanding panoramic vistas from many of the tees, and Granite Springs, which features granite outcroppings that make for an interesting and sometimes challenging round. This memorable course is just 25 minutes from Halifax on Route 333 on the way to Peggys Cove, perhaps the most photographed harbour in the world and a must on any visitor's itinerary.

Travelling between the golf courses in the southern portion of Nova Scotia allows visiting golfers to experience the world's highest tides and one of North America's greatest concentrations of marine life. These courses are designed along shorelines cooled by summer breezes and framed by rugged coastlines and splendid white-sand beaches. The salty fresh scent of the sea greets and relaxes you.

OSPREY RIDGE

GLEN ARBOUR

NORTHUMBERLAND LINKS, NEAR PUGWASH

Nestled in the Acadian community of Clare, the Clare Golf & Country Club welcomes visitors with its charming rustic clubhouse and a truly challenging layout for golfers of all abilities. For a completely different golf experience, the delightful nine-hole facility at White Point is a golf club and cozy resort complete with sandy beaches, gourmet dining room, tennis courts and high-quality accommodations. Other South Shore golf courses to include on your itinerary are the historic Chester Golf Club and River Hills in Shelburne.

The entertainment capital of the province, Halifax offers gourmet dining, endless shopping and nightlife galore. Nova Scotia's capital city has wonderful golf as well. New and enhanced courses around which to plan your golf vacation include Glen Arbour (ranked number 19 in Canada by *SCOREGolf*), which is challenging yet rewarding regardless of your skill level, and Granite Springs. Closer to Dartmouth, the Links at Montague offers an executive nine-hole

experience that should not be missed. This course is the designated national training centre for Atlantic Canada by the Royal Canadian Golf Association and has an "old world" flavour and ambience with its restored rock fences and classically designed clubhouse.

A burgeoning golf cluster is being nurtured in the centre of the province. Less than an hour's drive from Halifax, Truro is a bustling urban centre with shopping, restaurants, festivals and, of course, lots of great golf to choose from. Whether you book your tee time with the oldest course in the province, the Truro Golf Club, located most appropriately on Golf Street close to downtown, or venture to the surrounding areas and visit Mountain Golf Club or the delightful nine-hole offerings at Greenfield or Riverrun, you will not be disappointed.

Touring the scenic shores of Northumberland Strait, you will come upon the oceanside Northumberland Links. This Scottish links–style course offers spectacular seascapes and a view of all three Maritime provinces. As you travel further north in Nova Scotia, the landscape becomes more rugged and a mystical island awaits. On Cape Breton Island there are three things you will always remember: the majesty of the land, the friendliness of its people and the great golf. Nova Scotia's masterpiece is home to a

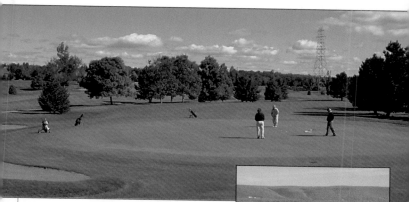

masterpiece in golf — Cape Breton Island's Fabulous Foursome. The fall is a great time to experience some of the finest golf and scenery Atlantic Canada has to offer. Panoramic landscapes painted in spectacular autumn colours surround the Bell Bay Golf Club, Dundee Resort & Golf Club, Le Portage Golf Club and Highlands Links. Ranked the 29th best golf destination in the world by *Golf Digest*, there are opportunities for a memorable round for both novice and championship players alike. Most accommodation providers offer room and green-fee packages and make these arrangements on behalf of their visitors. Individually, these courses offer challenging and unique golfing experiences and, collectively, they make up a fine golfing destination.

DUNDEE RESORT AND GOLF CLUB

In Nova Scotia, you are never more than a one-and-a-half- to two-hour driving distance between golf courses. The pristine natural beauty found across the province is simply not to be missed. From the Bay of Fundy to the majesty of the Cape Breton Highlands, the viewscapes are unspoiled and unmatched. Nature is treasured in Nova Scotia, as evidenced by Highlands Links being the first course in Atlantic Canada to hold the designation of "Certified Audubon Cooperative Sanctuary."

Golf in Nova Scotia includes excellent nine-hole facilities that attract golfers and families to value-priced, well-groomed fairways. Putting greens and driving ranges are common and easy to locate. The selection of nine-hole courses offer affordable, accessible and enjoyable play.

The *Nova Scotia Golf Travel Guide* contains course profiles and information such as yardage/slope, hours of operation, practice greens, teaching pros, pull or electric carts, food and beverage services, rates and contact information. For a free copy of the guide or more information on golf in Nova Scotia, visit www.golfnovascotia.com or www.golfcapebreton.com. For golf and accommodation packages in Nova Scotia, contact 1-800-565-0000 or visit www.novascotia.com

CYCLING

DALE DUNLOP

Nova Scotia has been a popular destination for cyclists and cycling tours for many years. Although most of the touring is on roads rather than specially constructed bicycle paths, there is no problem finding paved byways in scenic areas that see a minimum of auto traffic. Nova Scotian motorists are generally polite and mindful of cyclists. Nova Scotia's temperate climate makes for pleasant cycling six months of the year. When it does get particularly hot, choosing a route that skirts the ocean usually ensures that you'll get a cooling onshore breeze.

FRENCH MOUNTAIN, CABOT TRAIL

When considering where to cycle, any one of the

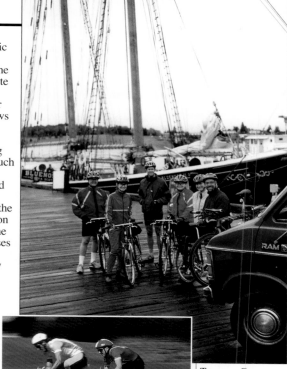

province's designated scenic routes is a good place to start. The Lighthouse Route along the South Shore is popular because it follows the coast very closely and has many interesting historic towns such as Chester, Mahone Bay and Lunenburg at which to spend the night. The portion of the Evangeline Trail that traverses the Annapolis Valley is equally popular for its gentle pastoral landscape, fine inns and fine dining. Those looking for a challenge should consider the Cabot Trail, which is strenuous, but rewards strong legs and lungs with

TOURING GROUP WITH *BLUENOSE II*, LUNENBURG

spectacular seascapes and highland valleys. The loop around the small island of Isle Madame, linked to Cape Breton Island by a bridge, provides a complete contrast of gentle cycling and captivating scenery. For a real off-the-beaten-path cycling experience, Marine Drive follows a twisting and rolling route along the coast from Halifax to Cape Breton Island, passing through some of the most remote and well-preserved fishing villages in all Canada. Stop at any harbour along the way — Ship Harbour, Spry Harbour, Sheet Harbour, Isaacs Harbour — for a glimpse into the past and a good night's rest.

Those who prefer to do their cycling in day trips from a central base have two outstanding choices in Nova Scotia. Lunenburg, a UNESCO World Heritage Site, offers not only a great base to come home to each night, but an amazing number of interesting coastal peninsulas to explore on day trips. For over a hundred years, the Blue Rocks peninsula has been a favourite with artists and photographers who delight in its tiny colourful fishing shacks that perch upon the unusual blue polished slate shoreline. In contrast, First Peninsula and Second Peninsula are more pastoral, with tranquil coves in a time-forgotten setting. The Lunenburg Bike Barn (www.bikelunenburg.com) on Blue Rocks Road offers a variety of rentals and plenty of suggestions for day trips in the area.

Many paved roads radiate out through the countryside from the college town of Wolfville, making it an equally popular choice as a base. In late spring, the apple blossoms are in full bloom and a trip through the rolling hills of the Gaspereau Valley, just outside of town, will provide a memorable day's outing. Those up for a more strenuous day should consider biking up North Mountain to the look-off for amazing views of the Minas Basin and the patchwork quilt of fields and orchards far below. Further along is Scots Bay, with its agate-strewn beach and the entrance to the hiking trail at Cape Split. After descending the mountain, a series of roads follow the red sandstone shoreline back to Wolfville.

For more information on Nova Scotia cycling, a copy of *Bicycle Tours in Nova Scotia* can be ordered from Bicycle Nova Scotia (www.bicycle.ns.ca). Those interested in taking a cycling tour of Nova Scotia with a Nova Scotian-based company should consider Freewheeling Adventures (www.freewheeling.ca), which has been building a solid reputation for many years. Should it be necessary to have your bike serviced, there are repair shops in almost all localities. An up-to-date listing can be found under the Atlantic Canada Cycling directory at www.atl-canadacycling.com, which offers organized large group tours along various routes on an annual basis. The Equipment Rentals section of the *Nova Scotia Doers' and Dreamers' Guide* lists places to rent bikes throughout the province.

BOTTOM: TOURING CYCLISTS NEAR CHETICAMP

HIKING

DALE DUNLOP

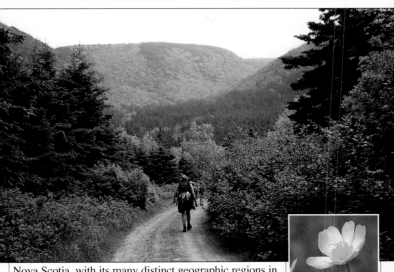

Nova Scotia, with its many distinct geographic regions in a compact area, offers a wide variety of hiking trails that should appeal to hikers of all skill levels and experience. Over the past decade, the number of kilometres of trails has increased dramatically, particularly with the opening of large portions of the Trans Canada Trail.

Hiking as a recreational pastime is exceeded perhaps only by sea kayaking as a sector of rapid growth in Nova Scotia's tourist industry.

With over 7,000 kilometres of coastline, hiking, whether over the rugged granite outcrops on the Atlantic, atop the heights of highland Cape Breton or at the base of the fantastic seascapes of the Fundy coast, is an extremely popular way to enjoy Nova Scotia. Although a volume this size can't begin to describe all of the trails, what follows are some of the best.

On the Eastern Shore's Marine Drive at Taylor Head Provincial Park, a series of trails lead out to rugged, windswept headlands overlooking the clear, cold waters of the Atlantic. On the South Shore, the trail to St. Catherine's River Beach at Kejimkujik National Park Seaside Adjunct, recently lengthened, crosses a coastal barren to arrive at a spectacular white-sand beach where seals and seabirds frolic just offshore. Inland, Kejimkujik National Park offers a great number of trails, including a few that traverse some of the last remaining old-

CAPE BRETON HIGHLANDS

HIKING, CABOT TRAIL

CAPE BRETON HIGHLANDS

growth forests in Nova Scotia. On the Fundy Shore, there are a number of great hiking sites, including Cape Chignecto Provincial Park, which is located in one of the most remote areas of the province. This park features strenuous wilderness trails that make their way up and over coastal hills to secluded valleys, deserted settlements and tiny coves not accessible along the shore. Serious hikers can make a triangular loop of the park that can take up to a week. Those less daring might prefer to hike along the beach to Red Rocks and other very unusual and rare rock formations. At Five Islands Provincial Park, trails follow the top of the Fundy Cliffs to a series of look-offs over such well-known landmarks as the Old Wife and Red Head. In the Annapolis Valley the very popular Cape Split trail follows the spine of a peninsula that juts out into the Bay of Fundy to its very tip; from there the tremendous force of the tides can be viewed first-hand.

Cape Breton Island offers a myriad of coastal hiking opportunities, in particular Cape Breton Highlands National Park, one of the oldest in Canada's park systems, which offers over 25 trails of varying length and difficulty. It is hard to recommend just a few, but Middle Head Trail, which starts right behind Keltic Lodge and winds its way to the tip of Middle Head, provides great views of the sea and highlands in all directions. Also of

KEMPTOWN INTERVALE

note are the Skyline Trail, which, as its name suggests, climbs high above the waters of the Gulf of St. Lawrence; the Coastal Trail, which explores hidden coves and a waterfall along a gentle portion of the park; and Franey Mountain Trail, which climbs very steeply to one of the best viewpoints in the province. Here,

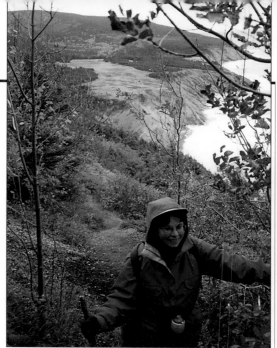

eagles and hawks often soar hundreds of metres below you as they rise up in the thermals from the valley below. Not to be overlooked are the Mabou Highlands and Cape Smokey Provincial Park, which provide trails and vistas equal to the national park but with fewer people.

Aside from the coastal hikes, Nova Scotia has some great hiking to waterfalls, including Economy Falls and Ward Falls in the Bay of Fundy area and Uisge Bahn, Beulach Bahn and Mary Ann Falls, all in Cape Breton.

AUTUMN ALONG THE COAST

People who prefer their hiking on the less strenuous scale have a number of venues from which to choose, many on reclaimed railbeds that now form part of the Trans Canada Trail system. These trails are uniformly flat and well maintained to the point that some of them are suitable even for strollers. Some of the best sections of these railbed trails are the Mabou Harbour Trail in Cape Breton; the Musquodoboit Railway Trail on the Eastern Shore; the Salt Marsh Trail, which starts just outside the Halifax metropolitan area; and the St. Margaret's Bay Trail, which skirts the bay of that name between Halifax and Hubbards. All in all, there is definitely something for everyone on the hiking trails of Nova Scotia.

Those with a serious interest in hiking have a number of guidebooks from which to chose, including two by Michael Haynes, whom most consider the dean of Nova Scotia hiking. His *Hiking Trails of Nova Scotia* and *Hiking Trails of Cape Breton* are revised regularly and provide detailed descriptions of over 70 trails. On the internet there are a number of sites, the best of which is Trails Nova Scotia (www.trails.gov.ns.ca) which has up-to-date information on the Trans Canada Trail as well as descriptions of dozens of trails in all parts of the province. There are also a number of local and international companies that feature hiking tours of Nova Scotia. One reputable Nova Scotia company that has been in business for many years is Scott Walking Tours (www.scottwalking.com).

ECONOMY FALLS

BEACHES

Nova Scotia is a seaside adventure. Visitors come to be invigorated by the fresh salt breeze, to be soothed by the murmur of the waves and to savour that sand-between-the-toes feeling. You will want to spend your time here in close communion with the sea — in it, on it, by it. You can't get a much closer salt water experience than at one (or several) of the 400-odd accessible beaches that scallop the 7,400-kilometre-long coastline of this almost-island province.

You don't have to be a beach bum or a bathing beauty to enjoy the sand, the surf and the sea. Nova Scotia's beaches are as varied as its geography. Young or young-at-heart, sociable or solitary, athletic or aesthetic — whatever your age or inclination, Nova Scotia has a beach experience for you.

Junior geologists and paleontologists will have a heyday at beaches along the shores of the Minas Basin, where gemstones, minerals and fossils are constantly liberated from the cliffs by the Fundy tides. Rockhounding on the shores at Blomidon

Provincial Park and Scots Bay on the Evangeline Trail may yield agates and amethysts. In the Parrsboro area of the Glooscap Trail, where Jurassic Age dinosaur bones have been discovered, you might see a real dig in progress on the beach at Wasson Bluff.

At Five Islands, you can dig up some lunch. Clam-digging is great fun for the whole family — see a squirt and dig like fury. If you brought a camp stove along, you can steam or grill the clams on the spot. On the same shore at Economy, when the Fundy tide is out — and it goes waaay out — you can walk for (what seems like) miles on the ocean floor. The cool red sand flats are great therapy for the foot-weary.

Those who are seeking peace and solitude can snuggle into the lee of a warm sand dune with a good book. Sand Hills Beach Provincial Park near Barrington, or Carters Beach at South West Port Mouton are perfect.

Beaches also set the scene for romance. Honeymooners and lovers stroll along a water's edge bathed in moonlight, lost in dreams and each other. You'll feel like the only people in the world at Ingonish Beach near Keltic Lodge.

Little kids can amuse themselves for hours observing starfish, jellyfish, sea urchins and periwinkles in sun-warmed tide pools at Hirtle and Crescent beaches on the South Shore, Bayswater on the Aspotogan Peninsula and Rushton Beach near Tatamagouche. Big kids, too, like to pick up shells, pretty pebbles and interesting bits of driftwood. Mavillette Beach on the Acadian Shore is a good place to beachcomb for lovely shells deposited on the shore by the tide.

Bird watching is a bona fide beach activity. Nova Scotia is almost completely surrounded by water — ergo lots of sea and shore birds. At Taylors Head on Marine Drive a variety of sea ducks and shore birds can be seen. The beach at Gulf Shore Provincial Park on Wallace Bay is a good starting point to observe the more than 160 bird species recorded in the area. Many beaches have signs marking nesting grounds of the endangered piping plover. During nesting season, stick to boardwalks or marked paths and you may be rewarded with a glimpse of this rare little shorebird.

The ocean is capricious and can go from calm to choppy in pretty short order. Some revel in the

MELMERBY BEACH

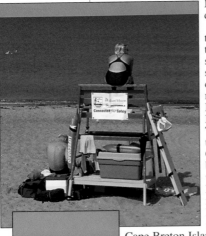

SURFERS AT LAWRENCETOWN

excitement of wild seas and white caps. When the surf's up, local and itinerant surfers head for Lawrencetown Beach, just outside Dartmouth (which, incidentally, has several supervised beaches on lakes within its boundaries). Scuba diving is popular at Terence Bay. Children delight in the age-old games of jumping waves and racing them up the shore at Queensland on St. Margarets Bay, a convenient drive from Halifax.

If you insist on being a traditionalist and *must* swim in the ocean, there are actually some very fine beaches ideally suited to that purpose, with change houses, lifeguards and, most importantly, warm water. Melmerby Beach, not far from New Glasgow on the Sunrise Trail, is a great place to break the journey enroute to or from Cape Breton. This one is apt to be relatively crowded on weekends, but the Northumberland Shore sports many other warm-water (and less peopled) beaches, including supervised Heather Beach. On Cape Breton Island, the beaches along the Ceilidh Trail also benefit from the warming effects of the waters from the Gulf of St. Lawrence. There is a nice supervised beach at Inverness.

Braver souls may relish a dip in the ocean on the Eastern Shore where the waters are bracing but the beaches are spectacular. Martinique has almost 5 kilometres of fine white sand and you might be the only soul in sight. In mid-August, you could participate in the annual Clam Harbour Beach Sandcastle and Sculpture Contest or simply stroll the beach and judge for yourself. This lovely fine-sand beach is supervised and has full amenities. There is a whole string of gorgeous beaches with fine white sand along the Lighthouse Route — Summerville, Rissers, and five beaches at Lockeport, including the famous Crescent Beach, featured for years on the $50 bill.

A few cautionary words — never underestimate the power of the ocean. Do not swim where yellow signs warn of dangerous currents. Strangers to the seaside may not be aware that on foggy or hazy days at the beach, the sun can still scorch the skin so sunscreen and wide-brimmed hats are a good idea, as well as shirts for the children. For a complete list of supervised beaches, contact the Nova Scotia Lifeguard Service at (902) 477-6155.

You can drive right up to the edge of some beaches, jump out of the car and into the water. Others are the reward at the end of a pleasant hike like St. Catherines River Beach at Kejimkujik Seaside Adjunct, a naturalist's dream. Some beaches are on islands and make a nice sailing or sea-kayaking destination. While touring Nova Scotia by car, there is no better place to stretch the legs and clear the head than a beach (and there is sure to be one handy). Stop for a picnic. Spread out your car rug, or if you're squeamish about sand in your sandwiches, many beaches offer picnic tables. There are dozens of little provincial and community parks with picnic tables and a beach. These are well indicated with signs on the highways. In northern Cape Breton, you might encounter a fishing boat arriving at Neils Harbour with a catch of queen crab. If you can prevail upon the fisherman to part with a few, take yourselves along to Black Brook on the Cabot Trail and cook them up at picnic facilities overlooking a fine beach. Now there's a picnic! Kids getting fractious? Hit the beach near you with buckets and spades — or reasonable facsimiles. Cool travel-weary bodies and tempers with a refreshing dip and a race up and down the edge of the wave-packed water's edge.

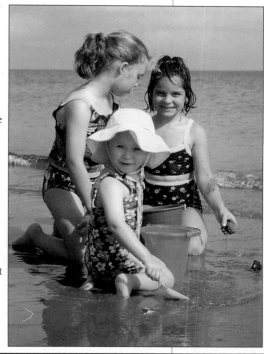

Many accommodations offer front-row beaching. The Quarterdeck at Summmerville Beach and Salty Rose at Rose Bay come to mind as good examples. MacLeod Cottages at Petite Rivière and White Point Beach Resort have been favourites with families for generations. By the

CRYSTAL CRESCENT BEACH

Dock of the Bay Cottages at Margaretsville are mere steps from the water. An early walk along the shingle will set you up for a busy day's sightseeing.

If you fancy camping at the beach, there are many provincial beach parks with camping facilities. Thomas Raddall Park at East Side Port L'Hèbert, with secluded campsites and white sand beaches, and Caribou and Munroes Island Park near Pictou, with its red sand and warm water, are good choices. For RVers, there is a great spot right across the road from Louis Head Beach near Sable River on the Lighthouse Route. To find and book beachside accommodations, check the *Nova Scotia Doers' and Dreamers' Guide* or call 1-800-565-0000.

There are beautiful beaches within a short drive of metro Halifax. Conrads Beach and Rainbow Haven outside Dartmouth and Crystal Crescent just beyond the fishing village of Sambro are popular beaches within easy access of the city.

Take a dip, take a hike, take a break at one of Nova Scotia's beautiful beaches — or two, or three. And take home a healthy glow, a relaxed body, a head full of precious memories (and a little salt water in your veins) from Canada's ocean playground.

CRYSTAL CRESCENT BOARDWALK

SAILING

MICHAEL ERNST

As a sailing destination, Nova Scotia offers thousands of kilometres of beautiful, natural, accessible coastline, dotted with innumerable small harbours, sheltered coves and uninhabited islands with sandy beaches. "The sailing here is better than Chesapeake Bay," commented one of our sailing companions. It was a sunny day, winds steady at 12 knots, beautiful scenery, clear waters and very few boats on the horizon. A typical Nova Scotia summer day. Yes, the sailing is good!

Nova Scotia is renowned for its many and varied sea birds, and sailing is a great way to observe them, along with seals, porpoises and, in some areas, whales. Our summers are usually dry and warm with steady southwesterly winds, and we can sail comfortably from June to October. And when the day's sailing is done? There are fine onshore amenities including quality accommodations, restaurants and unique cultural experiences.

Nova Scotia's history has been written by the sea. It is a rich mixture of sea battles, shipwrecks, privateers, buried treasure and ghosts. Nova Scotians have been going down to the sea in ships since the province was first settled. The Mi'kmaq arrived over 10,000 years ago. They lived on the coast during the summers and travelled the waters by birch-bark canoe. The first European visitors may have been Vikings, a Scottish prince named Henry Sinclair in 1398 or John Cabot in 1497. Permanent European

SAILBOATS IN CHESTER HARBOUR

HMS *ROSE* IN HALIFAX HARBOUR

settlements were established in the early 17th century, and over the next hundred years the province changed ownership between the French and English four times. During the American Revolutionary War and the War of 1812 many battles were fought along the coast. Nova Scotia's coast was also a haven for privateers and the cause of thousands of shipwrecks.

Sailing is part of the Nova Scotian culture; it's in our bones and blood. Recreational sailors started flocking to Nova Scotia in the 1920s and 30s. Yacht clubs scattered throughout the province provide locals and summer

MAHONE BAY

residents with high-quality competitions and onshore amenities. The number of visiting yachts increases annually and marina facilities are being developed to keep pace with the demand. The majority of visitors on cruises are from the U.S. and Canada, but Nova Scotia is also being recognized internationally as a sailing destination. These visitors are attracted by the quality of our sailing areas, the warm summers, fair winds and our rich and diverse culture.

Any visitor who wants to sail can enjoy our wonderful province in a variety of environments and sailing craft. Sailing operators offer a wide range of activities that will meet practically all tastes.

Visitors who have never sailed before but yearn to try can cruise with an experienced skipper, letting someone else do the work while they savour the salt air and the scenery, or they may want to take the helm and help sail the boat.

Some providers will offer sailing lessons to individuals and families who are only going to be in Nova Scotia for a short vacation. Visitors who plan to spend the summer or several weeks at one location could check out the availability of lessons for adults or kids at the nearest yacht club.

Whatever option you choose, being properly equipped

OAK ISLAND INN AND MARINA

is important. Hat, sunblock, sunglasses, summer clothing, sweater, rain jacket and non-slip shoes are essential items. Being properly prepared can make for a more pleasurable sailing experience.

If you are a seasoned sailor and plan to sail your own boat, or charter one, Mahone Bay and the Bras d'Or Lakes may have what you are looking for.

Nova Scotia is approximately 34,000 square kilometres in area — about the same size as Belgium. With approximately 7,400 kilometres of coastline, the sailing is quite spread out. This is a brief summary of what visitors can expect. However, it must be stressed that tourism businesses can be transitory. What exists one year may not be there the next.

Halifax, with the second-largest natural harbour in the world, has very strong links to the province's maritime history. Learn about this history and such famous events as the sinking of the *Titanic*, the Halifax Explosion and sea battles of both world wars at the Maritime Museum of the Atlantic, located on the city's waterfront. Close by are sailing tours that provide a unique way to explore the harbour. The tall ship *Silva* (Canadian Sailing Expeditions) and the *Mar II* (Murphy's on the Water) both offer short cruises. The *Bluenose II*, a replica of Canada's most famous sailing vessel, spends part of the summer in Halifax and offers sailing cruises to the public. The schedule changes every summer, but up-to-date information can be found at www.bluenose2.ns.ca.

Just an hour southwest of Halifax is Mahone Bay, which shares its name with the scenic village located at its head waters. Beautiful scenery, sheltered waters, fair winds and warm summer weather make the bay a sailor's paradise. This area was a haven for privateers during the many wars between France and England in the 17th and 18th centuries. Local legends tell of raids, buried treasure and ghost ships. There are over 100 islands in Mahone Bay. Many are uninhabited and have small beaches — great stopping places for picnics and exploration. The most famous is Oak Island, where the longest on-going treasure hunt in the world has been taking place since 1795.

Three sailing schools that are affiliated with the Canadian Yachting Association operate in Mahone Bay and provide cruises and lessons. Sou'west Adventures and Discovery Charters, based at the Oak Island Resort, offer CYA cruising qualification courses. If you are looking for a live-aboard cruise, then Discovery Charters will provide this experience on its 11-metre yacht. Sail Mahone Bay offers single-day Introductory and Improver sessions as well as the multi-day CYA courses.

Two boating events of importance in Mahone Bay are Chester Race Week, the largest keel-boat regatta in Eastern

MAR II

AVON SPIRIT

Canada, and the Mahone Bay Classic Boat Festival. The festival is a celebration of Nova Scotia's shipbuilding industry through music, water and shore-based activities — great fun for sailors and landlubbers alike.

In nearby Lunenburg, there are sailing cruises of this historic harbour on the *Eastern Star*, a 14-metre ketch. These tours leave from the wharf near the Fisheries Museum of the Atlantic — a must for anyone interested in boats and the sea. You may be lucky enough to sail on the *Bluenose II*, which was built here and is now based in Lunenburg, but booking ahead is recommended.

On Cape Breton Island, a three-hour drive from Halifax, the Bras d'Or Lakes claim to offer the finest sailing in the world. This warm, inland saltwater sea is approximately 600 square kilometres in size with breath-taking scenery, sheltered waters and islands (and no fog). Visiting yachts can access the lakes through the historic St. Peter's Canal. There are opportunities to explore the Lakes by sail; two of these are the *Elsie*, built in 1917 for Alexander Graham Bell, and the schooner *Amoeba*. Both sail from Baddeck. Further north you can 'See the Whales by Sail' on the schooners *Avon Spirit* and *Tom Saylor*, which both sail in the Ingonish area. This is a great way to experience these sea creatures and view the wonderful bird life of this coast.

The freedom of the sea, the excitement of a lively boat responding to a brisk wind, the challenge of navigation and learning every time you sail — these are a few of the rewards of this great sport. Whether you are an old salt or a novice, Nova Scotia can offer great sailing opportunities. The serenity of our waters, the beauty of the environment, the encounters with wildlife, the sense of exploration and the knowledgeable professional guides will provide memories that will make you want to set sail for Nova Scotia again and again.

SEA KAYAKING

SCOTT CUNNINGHAM

Sea kayaking has become increasingly popular in recent years and Nova Scotia, with its countless harbours and headlands, inlets and islands offers a world-class destination. Our meandering shoreline is extensive (over 7,000 km), access is easy (nowhere are you more than 55 km away) and the contrasts are exceptional. Within a short time you can travel between paddling venues as diverse as the rugged Atlantic coast and the sandy beaches of the Northumberland Strait; or between the highlands of Cape Breton and the tides of the Bay of Fundy. There is something for paddlers of every taste and skill level. You will find protected day trips for the beginner as well as challenging multi-day routes, and everything in between. And you can explore all this in relative solitude, because with several thousand kilometres of waterfront there is plenty of space to find a spot for yourself.

My favourite realm, and my home, is along the rugged Eastern Shore, where an isolated band of islands stretches from Clam Harbour to Canso. This forgotten wilderness forms a compelling mix of natural and human history. Some of these outposts are just tiny specks, scarcely breathing air at high water, while others are huge forest-covered expanses that dominate the horizon, and beckon to the inquisitive traveller. There are abandoned lighthouses and shipwrecks to explore, vanishing signs of our own transient history to uncover, or deserted isles to camp on where your only

OAK ISLAND

BOTTOM:
MAHONE BAY

companions are the seals and the sea birds. There are no bridges or ferries to this archipelago, and few fishing or pleasure craft — only a dramatic and pristine isolation far from the summer bustle. Tangier is an ideal place from which to start. This is where Coastal Adventures, the pioneer in sea kayaking in the province, is located and offers day trips, extended tours and courses.

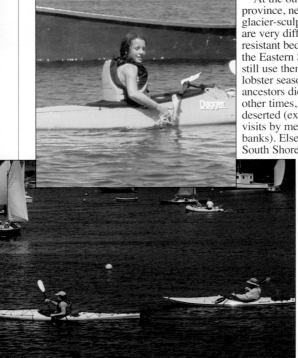

At the other end of the province, near Yarmouth, the glacier-sculpted Tusket Islands are very different from the resistant bedrock outposts of the Eastern Shore. Fishermen still use them as a base during lobster season, much as their ancestors did for centuries. At other times, they are also deserted (except for frequent visits by meandering fog banks). Elsewhere along the South Shore, there are dozens of idyllic places to put in and explore, including the Kejimkujik Seaside Adjunct, the La Have Islands, Blue Rocks, Mahone Bay and Prospect, and a number of operators to help you out (Rossignol Surf and Kayak, Mahone Bay Adventures, Hubbards Cove Outfitters, East

Coast Outfitters, Sea Sun). Even Halifax with its eclectic waterfront and harbour islands merits a visit by kayak.

On Cape Breton Island, the paddling possibilities are also numerous, both along its rugged east coast and on the more protected Bras d'Or Lake. However, the gem is certainly the Highlands. This majestic plateau occupies the

INGONISH HARBOUR

northwestern tip of the island, where it rises abruptly from the Gulf of St. Lawrence, and it is particularly imposing when viewed from the perspective of a sea kayak. Sea spires, caves and a colourful geology decorate the perimeter, while the Cabot Trail winds out of sight and sound far above. Rich deciduous valleys alternate with barren vertical cliffs, washed by waterfalls. Here you will certainly spot bald eagles and seals. If lucky you will also paddle with the whales, as I have done many a time. By mid-summer the water can warm up considerably (to 20°C), but this is an open coast and experience is advised. Outfitters offering trips here include Cape Breton Sea Coast Adventures, Coastal Adventures and North River Kayak Tours.

The Bay of Fundy is perhaps our most distinctive region. The highest tides recorded on earth wash these shores, sculpting cliffs and inundating massive salt marshes and mud banks with surprising speed. Experience is essential, but novices can take advantage of a knowledgeable outfitter (Coastal Adventures and Hinterland Adventures both run tours here). Cape

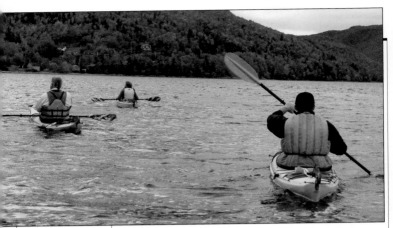

INGONISH HARBOUR

Chignecto, which juts into the bay separating the Minas Basin from Chignecto Bay, is the jewel of the Fundy. This is the boundary where an early Africa was thrust up against North America eons ago, and where the details of a cataclysmic upheaval can be read in rock strata of the exposed escarpment.

Even for those with little knowledge of geology, the striking melange of colours, textures and forms is fascinating. The abrupt cliffs, numerous pinnacles and sea caves combine with tides exceeding 13 metres (40 feet) to create a spectacular land/seascape. In the remote river valleys, remnants of a lost era play hide-and-seek among the shifting gravel. This is where some of our largest wooden vessels were constructed during the "Age of Sail". Elsewhere in the bay, along the Minas shore, the layered sandstones and dark basalt of the Five Islands and Economy Mountain offer another intriguing destination.

If you arrive early in the season when the Atlantic coast may be draped in fog, or if the Highlands and the Fundy shore are too exposed for your taste, you should try the province's north shore. Along the Northumberland Strait you will be treated to the warmest saltwater north of the Carolinas (or so the tourist propaganda runs) and, after numbing your toes in the Atlantic, this can be a real pleasure. Fog has been banned, and the miles of sandy shores and salt marsh estuaries offer protected paddling for the entire family. Kayakers are not the only ones who enjoy soaking up a few summer rays, and this shore has become a mecca for the vacation crowd. However, secluded corners can still be found. Outfitters along this coast include Shoreline Adventures and Coastal Spirit Expeditions.

There are many other exciting areas of our coastline to entice you and your sea kayak. A comprehensive guide (*Sea Kayaking in Nova Scotia*, available at most bookstores), with detailed descriptions of over 40 routes, will help. Bring your own kayak and paddle on your own, or accompany a local outfitter (other than those mentioned, provincial tourism literature lists over 25) who can introduce you to the biology, geology, and human history of this fascinating environment where the land meets the sea.

BIRDING

JOAN WALDRON

Nova Scotia has endless beaches, tucked-away fishing villages, hundreds of years of culture and a special natural beauty. With its rich marshlands, forests and lakes at every turn, it has perfect habitats for all kinds of birds. Whether the birds visit your backyard feeder, scurry around you on the beach or add to the sounds of nature on a stroll through the woods, you may wonder what kind they are, and whether they are local or just visiting. Some 305 birds have been listed in the province, with about 50 of these noted as regular strays or seldom seen. The avid birder may seek these rarities. For example, the rare Bicknell's thrush spends its summers in the Cape Breton Highlands; Canada's only breeding American oystercatchers have spent the past few years with their families on Cape Light, just off the fabulous birding area on Cape Sable Island. Visiting birders may want to see birds that Nova Scotians take for granted, such as the magnificent osprey, the provincial bird, which is commonly seen around beaches and harbours. Seabirds abound off Nova Scotia's endless shoreline. Puffins breed off Cape Breton Island; on sea-bound trips one can spot shearwaters, phalaropes and storm petrels and, with luck, a jaeger or skua as well. It's a treat to see these feeding alongside huge whales.

As in most places, Nova Scotia's birds have a time and a place. A winter birding trip can produce visiting seabirds such as the tiny dovekie, murres and Glaucous and Iceland gulls. And if you want to spend a quick weekend in winter ogling eagles, scores of bald eagles can be seen during the Sheffield Mills Eagle Watch in the Annapolis Valley at the end of January.

Spring and early summer birding offers the sounds of warblers. Their sounds are so varied you often wonder what bird you are hearing. The ovenbird, for example, yells "teacher-teacher." Twenty-two species of warblers breed in Nova Scotia, which is filled with woodland roads and parks (both national and provincial). The national parks have birding lists and may offer field trips. The *Atlas of Breeding Birds of the Maritimes* by Anthony J. Erskine will help pinpoint where particular birds can be found. Also, in late springtime, a careful walk on a quiet beach might give you a glimpse of the breeding endangered piping plover that Nova Scotians are trying so hard to protect. Late July features more than 20 species of shore birds, which stop in Nova Scotia to fatten up on the way south from their northern breeding grounds. Fall is delightful, when scores of bird species are coming and going, and there's always the chance that one of Nova Scotia's edge-of-the-continent weather surprises can bring a rarity or two or three.

In addition to the actual excitement and anticipation of birdwatching, most birders enjoy the homework they must do before a trip. Information about birding in all parts of Nova Scotia is on-line, but if a computer is not yet part of your life, write a letter requesting information to the Nova Scotia Bird Society, c/o Nova Scotia Museum, 1747 Summer Street, Halifax, Nova Scotia, B3H 3A6. The Nova Scotia Bird Society's website

BIRDERS AT HARTLEN POINT

EAGLES AT SHEFFIELD MILLS

(www.chebucto.ns.ca/Recreation/NS-BirdSoc/) offers a range of information, including contacts throughout the province and recommended reading. If you are in Nova Scotia for a Bird Society meeting, join some local birders. Nova Scotians are very friendly, particularly the binocular-wearing species. The dates and meeting topics are included on-line, as are upcoming field trips to which visitors are most welcome. Try to let the leader know you are joining the group.

An important part of the society's website is its links to other birding websites. Birders can browse various sites and plan their birding locations. The Cape Sable Island Important Bird Area website includes wonderful photos of the shorebirds you can expect to see at this location (users.auracom.com/csiba/index.htm). Ted D'Eon's homepage has great photos and shows his achievements in helping to preserve the endangered roseate tern. The classic *Birds of Nova Scotia* by Robie W. Tufts is also linked to the site.

A visit through cyberspace will offer thousands of websites linked to birding in Nova Scotia. The Birding the Americas website (www.birdingtheamericas.com), maintained by Blake Maybank, includes trip reports from Nova Scotia that will give visiting birders a sense of what they can expect to see. Blake also maintains the Nova Scotia rare bird alert site at www.group.yahoo.com/group/NS-RBA.

There are many bird reference books and field guides available. A handy reference guide to keep in your pocket or on the kitchen counter is the *New Formac Pocketguide to Nova Scotia Birds*.

BIRDERS ON THE TRAIL

LIGHTHOUSES

PEGGYS COVE

ANNAPOLIS ROYAL

Lighthouses are part of the history, the lore and the mystique of a province whose life, growth and prosperity have been shaped by the sea. Without these "signposts of the sea," many mariners would have been lost in fog, darkness and stormy seas. The first lighthouse in Canada was a circular stone tower built by the French between 1731 and 1734 at Louisbourg. Twice replaced, the present octagonal tower is now part of the Fortress of Louisbourg National Historic Site.

Originally lit by oil, then kerosene, and finally electricity, several hundred lighthouses have guided ships past the dangers off Nova Scotia's complex and perilous seacoast. Many lights were isolated, and the keepers and their families were often the only inhabitants on desolate islands. Totally automated today, many of the remaining 150 lighthouses and range lights (a pair of towers used to direct vessels into port) are being replaced with modern towers of fibreglass or metal. Others have been replaced by buoys, self-guiding harbour sector lights, or skeleton masts, as modern vessels rely increasingly on satellite navigational systems. The Sambro Light is the oldest operational lighthouse in North America.

About 80 lights are accessible (with varying degrees of difficulty) on the Nova Scotia mainland, 12 of which are open to visitors. More than a dozen others invite you to picnic in their shade. Many other lighthouses can be viewed as you tour the coast.

A few lights have been incorporated into public or historic parks by local community groups and are open seasonally. One of the most photographed lighthouses in North America is the tall tapering tower at Peggys Cove. First erected in 1868 at the entrance to St. Margarets Bay, the original light was replaced with the present octagonal tower in 1915.

At Burntcoat Head on the Bay of Fundy, a lovely little park incorporates a replica of the keeper's house surmounted by a lantern. The Nova Scotia Lighthouse Interpretive Centre houses photographs and memorabilia in a restored 1930s keeper's home with roof-mounted light at Port Bickerton on Marine Drive along the rugged Eastern Shore. Open seasonally and situated beside a modern operational light tower, the lighthouse allows visitors to appreciate the dedicated work of the light keeper. Another roof-mounted light at Gilbert Cove near Digby has also been restored by a local group.

One of the most common designs for lighthouses along our shores is the wooden tapered square or pyramid style commonly referred to as a "pepper shaker." The non-operational restored light at Walton Harbour, situated in a quiet little park with commanding views of the Bay of Fundy, is open to the public. A similar light graces the waterfront in Annapolis Royal. The small Five Islands lighthouse, moved several times due to constant shoreline erosion, can be seen in a local campground. Another tapered-design light has been relocated to the Historical Acadian Village in West Pubnico. The little light tower overlooking the Bay of Fundy at Spencers Island is now a heritage property. Famous as the home port of the ghost ship *Mary Celeste*, this tiny village is nestled along a gravel beach. At Margaretsville, a viewing platform surrounds the base of its lighthouse. The beauty of Neils Harbour, with its colourful fishing boats and the wharf below its lighthouse, is the subject of many a photograph.

The unique "apple core" tower at Cape Forchu, near Yarmouth, is perhaps out-photographed only by the rock-mounted light at Peggys Cove. Although the Forchu light isn't open to the public, the keeper's house displays artifacts of a bygone era. A replica of the Seal Island light is open seasonally in Barrington, while the lovely setting of the uniquely designed lighthouse at Fort Point in Liverpool makes it a popular attraction. The Cape d'Or light near Advocate Harbour isn't unusual, but its location is dramatic, hugging the edge of a steep cliff. The tower at Cape George, north of Antigonish, is similar in design to the one at Peggys Cove and offers a sweeping view of the Canso Strait.

The romance and reality of the lighthouse have been the inspiration for many high-profile books. *We Keep a Light* by Evelyn Richardson chronicles a lighthouse family's life. A lighthouse keeper features in Frank Parker Day's *Rockbound,* a bestseller set on an island along Nova Scotia's Lighthouse Route.

Detailed information about lighthouses in Nova Scotia is available on the website of the Nova Scotia Lighthouse Preservation Society (www.nslps.com).

PLACES

HALIFAX

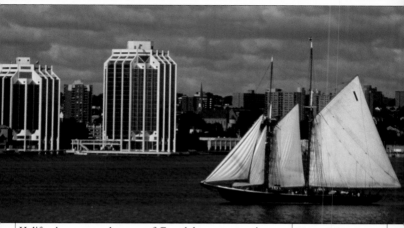

Halifax has emerged as one of Canada's most attractive cities to visit. It's a relatively small city in an appealing setting, offering a variety of attractions. Halifax is at its best in summer and fall — and fall lasts longer here than in the rest of Canada, with many beautiful days in October and even into November. Spring, on the other hand, often comes late, and there are even years when it doesn't seem to come at all.

The waterfront area has become the most popular place to spend time in the summer. It's a long, vibrant boardwalk along the harbour, with many attractive cafés, bars and restaurants, street entertainment, the Maritime Museum of the Atlantic and the Historic Properties. The city's best bargain, and one kids love, is the ferry trip across the harbour. All this, together with the added thrill of the occasional container ship, navy vessel or cruise ship passing by, appeals to residents and visitors alike. Almost every visitor makes the trip up to the Citadel, a historical attraction with wonderful views of the harbour. The Spring Garden Road area rivals the waterfront for friendly, low-key street life and its variety of shops, bars and restaurants.

Within 40 minutes' drive of downtown there are beautiful ocean beaches at Crystal Crescent and Lawrencetown, fine for warm summer afternoons when small children (and hardy adults) don't mind the relatively cool temperatures of the Atlantic shore. In the evenings, Halifax offers a surprisingly wide range of entertainment options, and that is one of the reasons why most visitors to Nova Scotia make a point of including the city on their itinerary. One caution: in recent years, summer and fall tourism has been on the increase, but accommodation hasn't expanded as quickly as demand. Don't count on being able to find a downtown hotel in summer or fall unless you've booked well in advance. If you don't have

HALIFAX HARBOUR

Major Routes to Halifax

102 Provincial arterial
1 Exit
Main roads
- - - Ferry

Middle Sackville

HALIFAX REGIONAL MUNICIPALITY

3 km
2 miles

Lower Sackville

Bedford

Burnside

Bedford Basin

Dartmouth

Bayers Lake

Halifax

Northwest Arm

Halifax Harbour

McNabs Island

time to book much in advance, don't be surprised if you're offered a room in one of the old-fashioned motels along the Bedford Highway, some distance from the downtown. Depending on your preferences, that may not be as appealing as being downtown, but the motels have their own 1950s charm. Halifax also has some excellent inns and B&Bs.

Halifax sits atop a great slab of slate that rises from the harbour. There is precious little topsoil. It was the harbour that attracted the Mi'kmaq for centuries and the British in 1749. The harbour extends inland about 16 kilometres from its seaward approaches, through the Narrows, spanned by two bridges connecting Halifax and Dartmouth, and into Bedford Basin. Except for an occasional freakish episode, it remains ice-free — a point long stressed by those interested in steering winter traffic the way of Halifax. Recreational sailors happily coexist with shipping in the harbour. During the summer months, Bedford Basin is flecked

MACDONALD BRIDGE

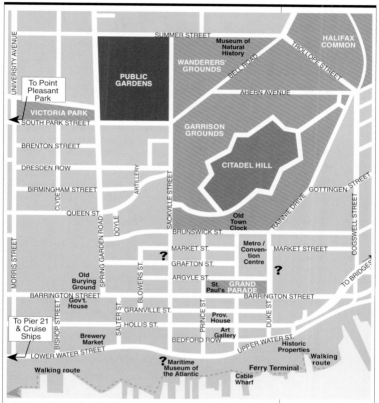

UNIVERSITY AVENUE

SUMMER STREET

Museum of
Natural
History

HALIFAX
COMMON

TROLLOPE STREET

PUBLIC
GARDENS

WANDERERS'
GROUNDS

BELL ROAD

To Point
Pleasant
Park

AHERN AVENUE

VICTORIA PARK

SOUTH PARK STREET

GARRISON
GROUNDS

BRENTON STREET

DRESDEN ROW

CITADEL HILL

BIRMINGHAM STREET

ARTILLERY

CLYDE

QUEEN ST.

SACKVILLE STREET

GOTTINGEN STREET

RANNIE DRIVE

COGSWELL STREET

SPRING GARDEN ROAD

DOYLE

Old
Town
Clock

BRUNSWICK ST.

MORRIS STREET

?

MARKET ST.

Metro /
Convention
Centre

MARKET STREET

TO BRIDGES

GRAFTON ST.

BLOWERS ST.

?

Old
Burying
Ground

ARGYLE ST.

St.
Paul's

GRAND
PARADE

BARRINGTON STREET

Gov't.
House

SALTER ST.

GRANVILLE STREET

PRINCE ST.

BARRINGTON STREET

DUKE ST.

To Pier 21
& Cruise
Ships

BISHOP STREET

HOLLIS ST.

Prov.
House

Historic
Properties

Walking
route

Brewery
Market

BEDFORD ROW

Art
Gallery

UPPER WATER ST.

LOWER WATER STREET

?

Maritime
Museum of
the Atlantic

Ferry Terminal

Walking route

Cable
Wharf

with hundreds of colourful sailboats. The Northwest Arm,
on the southwest side of the Halifax peninsula, is also a
yachting haven.

Summers in Halifax tend to be mild, with sunny days
made fresh by sea breezes. Winters are cool and snowy.
Although there are days in January that are cold enough to

**EARLY MORNING FOG
IN HALIFAX
HARBOUR**

draw wisps of sea smoke off the harbour, Haligonians are accustomed to spending much of their winters around the freezing point. Nice spring days are cherished because they are few. But autumn — Nova Scotia's finest season — flatters Halifax. Then, the days are crisp and bright, and the city's tree-lined streets blush with colour.

Halifax was established in 1749 to counter the military threat posed by the French Fortress of Louisbourg.

TOP: INTERNATIONAL VISITOR CENTRE, BARRINGTON STREET
MIDDLE: MARTELLO TOWER, POINT PLEASANT PARK

During the last century, the city's magnificent harbour served as a marshalling area for North Atlantic convoys during two world wars. Halifax's economic fortunes have flowed during conflict and ebbed with peace.

Today, the Citadel in the heart of the city and the historic fortifications at Point Pleasant Park and York Redoubt are celebrated aspects of Halifax's military landscape, but there is also a contemporary military presence to go along with those reminders of the past. Warships regularly ply the harbour and helicopters fly overhead. A substantial number of military personnel are stationed here and sailors from the NATO fleet are regular visitors.

Despite the steady thrum of naval activity, Halifax is no longer primarily a military town. In post-war Halifax, rapid growth in the research, transportation and public service

YORK REDOUBT

sectors has turned the old garrison town into a vital

commercial and government centre. This is Atlantic Canada's largest city. The provincial legislature is here, and a substantial federal bureaucracy works out of the city. There is a thriving alternative scene, and the city's four universities, including Nova Scotia College of Art and Design University (NSCAD) provide much of the impetus for it.

Halifax serves up some startling contrasts. The same city that annually hosts the popular Royal Nova Scotia International Tattoo, with its regimental bands and drill teams, also stages the Atlantic Fringe Festival — alternative theatre that scandalizes the city's conservative element. The military is here, but so is Vajradhatu, the headquarters for an international network of Buddhist meditation centres. Burgers and draught beer or bean sprouts and herbal tea — the downtown pubs and bistros cater to a city with multiple personalities.

A walk along Hollis Street, one of the city's oldest, tells some of the story. Government departments and law offices operate cheek by jowl in high-rises that stand along the street's northern end.

You can explore the downtown area by foot, as the heart of the city extends for just a few — but very hilly — blocks.

The Grand Parade, framed by Argyle and Barrington Streets, sits between Citadel Hill and the waterfront. Special activities, like the Remembrance

PROVINCE HOUSE, HOLLIS STREET

HOLLIS STREET (BELOW) 1ST BATTALION MIDDLESEX REGIMENT AT HALIFAX CITADEL (BOTTOM)

Day service and the New Year's Eve party, take place here, and Halifax City Hall is situated on the north side. On mild nights, people collect at the Grand Parade as they go from bar to bar, and summer days see business people patronizing hot dog vendors in the square.

Completed in 1750, St. Paul's Anglican Church still occupies the south side of the Parade. It was patterned on James Gibbs' design for St. Peter's on Vere Street in London. Gibbs apprenticed with Christopher Wren, and his work includes the beautiful St. Martin-in-the-Fields on Trafalgar Square. St. Paul's is the oldest Protestant church in Canada. Local legend has it that the profile of the vicar who died in the Explosion of 1917 can still be seen in one of the upper windows on the Argyle Street side of the church. Church tours are available in summer. St. Paul's Cemetery (the Old Burying Ground) on Barrington Street was the town's original cemetery. Information on the headstones is available at the church.

Nearby, on Hollis Street, is Province House, the seat of provincial government. Opened in 1819, it is a fine example of the Palladian style. During a visit to Halifax in 1842, Charles Dickens described it as "a gem of Georgian architecture." The building really is beautiful — remarkably so, given that as far as anyone can tell the plans were drawn up by John Merrick, a local contractor. Tour guides are on hand to take you through the building's splendid interior. Highlights include the Red Chamber, with its tall windows and ornate plasterwork, where you can see the oak table from the *Beaufort*, the ship that brought Queen Victoria's father, Prince Edward to Halifax in June of 1749. The Legislative Library, complete with hanging staircases and a three-sided balcony, is also magnificent.

The city's turn-of-the-century commercial success is reflected in the Barrington and Granville streetscapes. Many of these buildings were of steel beam construction, a new technology that emerged in the wake of the Chicago fire of 1871. The walls of these structures were not load-bearing, so they were often built high with lots of windows and decorative arches. Contemporaries questioned their extravagance, but millionaires like George Wright could afford the best. The Wright Building still stands at 1672-4 Barrington Street. (Wright was one of 33 millionaires to go down with

ST. PAUL'S ANGLICAN CHURCH

PROVINCE HOUSE (BELOW)

the *Titanic* in 1912.)

This area is also the old stomping ground of Anna Leonowens, immortalized in the Rodgers and Hammerstein musical *The King and I*, and several movies, including the film *Anna and the King* starring Jodie Foster. In 1876 Leonowens moved here with her daughter and son-in-law. Soon after, Leonowens was actively involved in establishing libraries, reading clubs and a Shakespeare Club. Today, NSCAD University represents the culmination of Leonowens's interest in the local artistic community. Halifax jewellers and graphic designers — and

there are many — share in her legacy.

The Art Gallery of Nova Scotia, a modern facility located in a heritage building on Hollis Street, houses a collection of historic and contemporary art, and an acclaimed folk art collection. Paintings by Nova Scotian artists can be purchased at the Art Sales and Rental Gallery. The work of many of the province's best craftspeople and designers is displayed at the Nova Scotia Centre for Craft and Design on Marginal Road.

ST. MARY'S CATHEDRAL BASILICA, SPRING GARDEN ROAD (ABOVE)
ART GALLERY OF NOVA SCOTIA (BELOW)

Unique Nova Scotian wares can also be found in Barrington Place and the shops at Granville Mall, adjacent to the Delta Barrington Hotel.

Continue south on Hollis to the Brewery — Alexander Keith's Nova Scotia Brewery, that is, the oldest working brewery in North America. (Keith's beer, now brewed by Labatt, is sold far beyond Nova Scotia). Year-round brewery tours feature stories and songs and, of course, beer sampling. The Brewery is frequently held up as an example of what can be achieved by preservation-minded developers. Its arches and gothic windows provide a comfortable setting for one of Halifax's

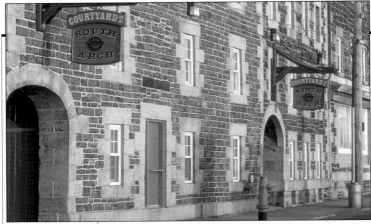

THE BREWERY MARKET, LOWER WATER STREET

best restaurants, Da Maurizios. On Saturday mornings, the Brewery bustles with a farmers' market where local crafts, baked goods and produce are available.

Further south, walk up Bishop Street to Barrington. Here is Government House, another example of a beautiful Georgian building in the Palladian style. When John Wentworth became Lieutenant-Governor of Nova Scotia in 1792, he sought to upgrade his accommodation. A member of a well-connected family who knew royalty on the most intimate terms, he was probably justified in doing so. The cornerstone of Government House, the Wentworths' new residence, was laid in 1800. It has served as the Lieutenant-Governor's residence ever since. Although it is normally not open to the public, the Lieutenant-Governor continues a long-standing tradition of hosting a New Year's Day levee, when everyone is invited inside for a look (and a glass of sherry).

GOVERNMENT HOUSE, BARRINGTON STREET

Backtracking on Barrington, you come to Spring Garden Road. There are a number of fine boutiques and craft shops in the Spring Garden Road area. The Halifax Folklore Centre provides the city's best introduction to the

ST. MARY'S CATHEDRAL BASILICA

traditional music of Nova Scotia. Jennifer's of Nova Scotia sells everything from small souvenirs to the prized works of some of Nova Scotia's best artisans. Fine foods and wines are available at the Spring Garden Place Market, and at Port of Wines and the Italian Market on Doyle Street. There are also a number of good bookstores and coffee shops along the city's most fashionable street. Nearby, on the other side of the Public Gardens, the Museum of Natural History features the natural wonders of Nova Scotia's land and sea — whales, fossils, dinosaurs and birds, along with a number of other permanent and temporary exhibits.

The Halifax Citadel, a national historic site operated by Parks Canada, is Nova Scotia's most visited attraction. Built between 1828 and 1856, the fortification is the fourth to occupy the hilltop site, with its commanding view of Halifax Harbour.

The present Citadel was built through the semi-divine intervention of the "Iron Duke," Arthur Wellesley. The Duke of Wellington, a strong proponent of colonial defenses at a time when opinion was sharply divided, used his prime ministerial authority to push approval for the project through the British Parliament. In his view, a strong fortification was needed to defend against the American threat, which remained palpable in the wake of the War of 1812. The fort was designed to prevent a land-based attack on the naval dockyard. It was left to the harbour defenses to repel an attack from the sea. Whether the Citadel was a necessary discouragement is open to debate — no attack ever came. The Citadel's smooth-bore cannons were never fired in anger.

During the summer months,

ENTRY TO THE CITADEL (TOP)
RE-ENACTORS AT THE HALIFAX CITADEL (BELOW)
AERIAL VIEW OF CITADEL HILL (BOTTOM)

Citadel staff re-enact the fort's military routines as they were carried out during the years 1869–71. At that time, the Citadel was manned by soldiers from the 78th Highlanders and the Royal Artillery, along with sailors of the Naval Brigade. Today, students take on these roles, drilling according to instructions laid out in the 1860s manuals, hoisting the signal flags and standing watch at the sentry posts. The firing of the noon gun is heard throughout downtown Halifax year-round. The signal flags flying above the ramparts once told civilians what ships were in the harbour and where they were docked. They were also used to send messages to the other harbour fortifications. At one time, a series of signalling stations could be used to reach as far as Quebec!

Tour guides help explain the Citadel's rituals and exhibits in French or English, adding anecdotes about the fort's colourful past. "The Tides of History," a 40-minute audiovisual presentation, takes visitors on a dramatic tour

through Halifax's military history. Visitors to Halifax are encouraged to find time for the Citadel, where they will discover why it held pride of place for much of the city's long life as a garrison town. And the view of downtown Halifax and the harbour is often reward enough for making the steep climb up Citadel Hill.

The Old Town Clock has

marked the time at the base of Citadel Hill since 1803. Unperturbed by such cataclysmic events as the Halifax Explosion in 1917, the clock has undergone restoration to ensure that it will remain, in the words of Joseph Howe, "a good example to all the idle chaps in town."

From the Citadel, looking east and north, you see Halifax's North End and the area demolished in the explosion. Nearby, there are some fascinating historical buildings.

LITTLE DUTCH CHURCH (TOP) OLD TOWN CLOCK (BELOW)

The Little Dutch (Deutsche) Church was originally built to accommodate German settlers who were brought to Halifax not long after its founding. Across the street is the beautiful St. George's Round Church, largely reconstructed after a disastrous fire several years ago. It is one of Prince Edward's many round-shaped buildings in the city. Several handsome 19th-century townhouses still stand along Brunswick Street. Further from the Citadel in the North End is the Hydrostone area, known to Canadian town planners as the first example of 20th-century urban renewal (and a much better precedent than what came later). By the MacKay Bridge is Seaview Park, site of Africville, which was razed by Halifax city hall in the 1960s in a relocation scheme meant to better living conditions for the Black community. The residents were opposed to the plan, a vital community was destroyed and Africville is mourned to this day.

ST. GEORGE'S ROUND CHURCH

Along the waterfront are the Historic Properties, a 1970s restoration project that revitalized the downtown core. The Privateers' Warehouse, one of 10 buildings from the Georgian and early Victorian periods, is the

85

MODEL OF RMS *TITANIC*, MARITIME MUSEUM OF THE ATLANTIC

most storied. Early in the 19th century Enos Collins, a wealthy Halifax merchant, used the building to warehouse booty that he seized during legalized privateering raids off the New England coast. Today, these buildings house a variety of shops and services. Handsmith sells lovely crafts made by artisans from across Canada. The Lower Deck offers lively Celtic entertainment. The food court offers casual dining, including a micro-brewery, pizza and seafood, with a view of the harbour.

More shops and restaurants can be found on the boardwalk along the harbour's edge to Cable Wharf, named for the transatlantic cable ships that once docked here. NovaScotian Crystal, home of Canada's only mouth-blown, hand-cut crystal, has a window that gives visitors a peek at the glass-blowers at work.

Boats operating from Cable Wharf are available for private charter. If you are interested in deep-sea fishing, make careful inquiries before booking your spot or you

may find yourself simply drifting in the harbour off Point Pleasant Park — hardly a deep-sea experience! The *Harbour Queen I* and the *Haligonian III* offer historical commentaries during their harbour cruises. A private ferry will take you to McNabs Island, where grassy trails lead to secluded coves, overgrown forts and rocky beaches. Further along the boardwalk from Cable Wharf is the Maritime Museum of the Atlantic. The museum houses over 20,000 maritime artifacts and features the exhibit that gives a complete account of the Halifax Harbour Explosion of 1917. There are exhibits on shipwrecks and lifesaving, the *Titanic*, the Navy, steamships and sailing ships. The William Robertson & Son ship chandlery has been restored, and there are lots of boats — about 70 in all.

PRIVATEERS' WAREHOUSE (ABOVE) MARITIME MUSEUM OF THE ATLANTIC (BELOW)

Since the blockbuster movie *Titanic*, the museum has

mounted a permanent display of its fine collection of artifacts from the ship *Titanic*. Halifax's connection to the disaster came about because the city was the nearest large port to the site of the sinking. It was from Halifax that efforts were organized to search for the wreckage and to recover the bodies of the victims. Funerals were organized, and many of the dead lie in graves in Halifax. Crew members on the ships sent out to the wreck site collected memorabilia (a deck chair, for example), and many of these items gradually found their way into the museum's collection.

PIER 21 NATIONAL HISTORIC SITE

Items in the exhibit also reflect the work of scientists from the Bedford Institute of Oceanography, who were more recently involved in expeditions to the wreck site, and who conduct research on the deep ocean environment.

Though modest in size, the *Titanic* exhibit is informative and appealing to visitors of all ages. It has become the museum's leading attraction, and is well worth a visit. Note that there is a visitor information centre at Sackville Landing behind the museum. Further south is Bishop's Landing, a complex of upscale restaurants, boutiques, residences and a spa.

Continue south and visit Pier 21 on Marginal Road. Now a National Historic Site, this was the last immigration shed in Canada; a million immigrants and refugees passed through here to their new country. Multimedia presentations, live performances and genealogical records tell their stories.

One of the easiest and least expensive ways for visitors to get out on the water is to take a trip on the Halifax Harbour ferry. In Dartmouth, Ferry Terminal Park affords outstanding views of the Halifax waterfront. The World Peace Pavilion on the Dartmouth waterfront displays historical rocks and bricks from countries around the world, including pieces of the Berlin Wall and the Great Wall of China.

The beginning of the Shubenacadie Canal is nearby.

HALIFAX HARBOUR FERRY

SHUBENACADIE CANAL (TOP)
POINT PLEASANT PARK (ABOVE)

Following the old Mi'kmaq canoe route cross-country from the Bay of Fundy, the canal took more than 30 years to build. Shortly after it was completed in 1861, the new Intercolonial Railway made it obsolete, but the canal workings remain a source of fascination. More of the canal, including locks 2 and 3, can be seen at Shubie Canal Park, off Waverley Road.

Near the MacKay Bridge in Dartmouth, the Bedford Institute of Oceanography is one of the world's largest oceanographic establishments. Models and tours explain to visitors the institute's research of fishery science, oceanography and hydrography.

On Main Street (Route 7) at Cherrybrook Road in Dartmouth, the Black Cultural Centre for Nova Scotia preserves the history and culture of Black Nova Scotians with a library, auditorium and exhibits on life dating back to the 1600s.

The Cole Harbour Heritage Farm is also worth a look. Right in the middle of the suburbs, this 1-hectare farm includes heritage buildings, farm animals, archival materials, gardens and a tea room. Special events are held here throughout the year.

On February 1, 1793, a 22-year conflict began with the French declaration of war against Britain. A year later, Prince Edward, son of George III and, eventually, father to Queen Victoria, arrived to take command of the garrison in Halifax. He set to work strengthening the town's fortifications. Martello towers were all the rage, and Edward built three of them. Two of these, one overlooking the western approaches of the harbour at York Redoubt, and the Prince of Wales Tower (which Edward named after his favourite brother) in Point Pleasant Park are national historic sites. Both locations are worth visiting, for their scenic as well as historical value. York Redoubt is a perfect spot for a picnic, affording a wonderful view of the harbour.

Point Pleasant Park covers 75 hectares in Halifax's South End and is leased by the city from the Crown for a shilling a year. From the park, ships entering the harbour or sailboats tacking across the Northwest Arm can be seen. A series of walking paths makes Point Pleasant ideal for an afternoon stroll, passing by a number of interesting ruins (see the map in the parking lot at the western entrance). From the Chain Rock Battery, a chain boom once stretched across the water to defend against enemy warships. During the First World War, mines were laid between the Point Pleasant Battery and McNabs Island, leaving a narrow channel lit by searchlights. A steel anti-submarine net was added later.

VICTORIAN CRAFTSMANSHIP

Returning from Point Pleasant Park towards the downtown, you pass through Halifax's South End. Here are many of the city's grandest homes and a wonderful collection of unique Victorian townhouses built of wood and painted bright colours.

From Young Avenue (which becomes South Park Street), you can explore the Victorian South End by turning east along any one of the streets that run between Inglis and Spring Garden. Of course, the Victorian streetscape is regularly interrupted by clumsy, unappealing post-1945 construction, including high-rise apartments, but many of the original buildings remain and there are wonderful architectural details to notice in these houses' porches, windows, gables and trim.

For visitors curious about Halifax's royal past, a small

**MUSIC BUILDING,
BEDFORD HIGHWAY**

PUBLIC GARDENS

park along the Bedford Highway has a wonderfully romantic origin and a beautiful small building to appreciate. Three months after Prince Edward arrived, his beautiful French mistress followed. Governor John Wentworth lent them his country estate along the shores of Bedford Basin. The only building still standing is a round ornamental garden temple that is similar in design to several buildings that had been constructed at Kew Gardens, Edward's childhood home. Visible from the Bedford Highway, the building is not open to the public, but visitors are welcome to stroll through Hemlock Ravine opposite the rotunda. The pond in the 75-hectare park is heart-shaped and known as Julie's Pond in honour of Edward's mistress. Legend has it that the paths that once meandered through the estate spelled out her name.

Many of Halifax's parks evoke a sense of Victorian times, when Halifax "society" took leisurely strolls through Point Pleasant Park and picnicked on McNabs Island. The Royal Nova Scotia Yacht Squadron held regular regattas. By the 1880s, skating parties were held regularly at the rink in the Exhibition Building. In 1882, the Wanderers' Amateur Athletic Association Club was established to foster the growth of cricket, football and hockey. After a purifying workout on the Wanderers' Grounds, participants could cross Sackville Street and take a relaxing stroll through the Public Gardens.

These formal Victorian gardens are the oldest in North America. Originally owned by a group of prominent Haligonians who constituted the Nova Scotia Horticultural Society, the 7-hectare gardens were opened to the public in 1867. In 1874, the society sold them to the city, which still maintains them. The Public Gardens were to serve a threefold purpose: they would improve the physical and mental health of the working classes, provide material for polite discourse among the more refined and be a source of civic pride for all.

The gardens are outstanding. Pathways wander among beautiful weeping trees, formal flower beds and subtropical plantings. They lead across classical bridges and past cast-iron fountains to the elaborate central bandstand. During the summer months, Sunday afternoon concerts are held there. On Saturday afternoons, brides, grooms and attendants can be seen posing for photographers. If you need a break from the demands of travel, the gardens are a fine oasis.

THE DINGLE

Across the Northwest Arm from Point Pleasant is Sir Sandford Fleming Park, or "the Dingle." Fleming, creator of Standard Time Zones and engineer for the Canadian Pacific Railway, donated the park to Halifax in 1908. The 38-hectare park features the Dingle Tower, a sandy beach, a frog pond and two walking trails.

Connected to the trails in Shubie Park in Dartmouth, the Trans Canada Trail winds from Sullivans Pond along Lake Banook and Lake MicMac for 7 kilometres. The paths are wide and wheelchair accessible.

ARMDALE YACHT CLUB, NORTHWEST ARM

Throughout the summer months, Halifax and Dartmouth host a wide range of festivals and events. What follows here is only a small sampling. Dates vary, so call the province's

Check-In information line (1-800-565-0000) or consult the *Nova Scotia Festivals and Events Guide* for details.

The Royal Nova Scotia International Tattoo, which draws military bands from around the world, runs for a week each July at the Metro Centre. The International Busker Festival, held in August on the Halifax waterfront and along city sidewalks, is very popular with both locals and visitors. Children especially enjoy the clowns and jugglers. The Atlantic Jazz Festival is a first-rate event. Held in July, mainstage and late-night concerts make for crowded downtown bars. The annual Africville Reunion brings together former residents of the Halifax community that was razed in the 1960s. Visitors are welcomed, and the reunion provides a good opportunity to learn about the Black community of Halifax.

At the city's fine restaurants, not surprisingly, seafood is a

AT THE AFRICVILLE REUNION

ubiquitous specialty. Check the dining section of the listings at the back of this book for recommended dining spots.

For a raucous tavern evening, try the Lower Deck in the Privateers' Warehouse, where Celtic bands are a regular feature. The Economy Shoe Shop on Argyle Street is a mecca for the cultural set.

CASINO ENTERTAINER (ABOVE)
HALIFAX FIREWORKS OVER THE HARBOUR (INSET)
***BLUENOSE II* IN HALIFAX HARBOUR (BELOW)**

LIGHTHOUSE ROUTE

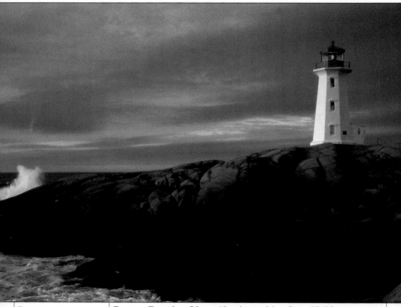

LIGHTHOUSE AT PEGGYS COVE

Peggys Cove is a 30- to 40-minute drive from Halifax on Route 333. About 15 km before Peggys Cove, the 18-hole Granite Springs golf course at Bayside welcomes card-carrying members of the Royal Canadian Golf Association and their guests. The course is usually in great shape, with tight fairways and interesting hazards that offer a stiff challenge.

Peggys Cove, with its vivid, pitched-roof houses perched atop a mass of granite overlooking the snug harbour, has been exposed on miles of film and acres of canvas. It has become the postcard profile of an east coast fishing village.

SWISS AIR MEMORIAL

It became the focal point of tragedy in 1998 when a Boeing MD-11, Swissair Flight 111, plunged into the ocean and all 229 persons aboard perished. Rescuers, families and the media flocked to Peggys Cove in the aftermath. Two memorials are found nearby.

Canadian journalist J. F. B. Livesay was one of the cove's early protagonists. He discovered the village in the 1920s, and his book *Peggy's Cove*, based on a summer visit in 1943, was published posthumously a year later. Livesay presented an unabashedly romantic view of the village: "The Cove on that first glance was still quite perfect, nothing to be added and nothing to be taken away, a little pulsing human cosmos set in the uneasy sea." He characterized the unwillingness of a local woman to purchase a washing machine as an emphatic rejection of modernity. Livesay did not mention that the same woman did own the only telephone in Peggys Cove, nor did he make any allowance for the discouragement that solid granite might offer someone who was considering additional plumbing!

What Livesay's prose did for Peggys Cove in the 1940s, the photographs of W. R. MacAskill had been doing since 1921. In that year, MacAskill's "Quiet Cove" appeared. Tourist promoters seized the opportunity afforded by MacAskill's beautiful photography. Peggys Cove was close enough to Halifax to offer visitors to the city a chance to encounter the "essential" Nova Scotia — the desolate boundary where land meets sea.

The successful promotion of Peggys Cove has led to a curious irony. You are exhorted to discover the unspoiled beauty of Peggys Cove in the company of dozens or even hundreds of other people. A mass of glacier-scarred granite cuts an impressive profile against sky and sea, but here you will also find air-conditioned coaches from all over North America. There is a busy restaurant and gift shop (The Sou'wester), and the old lighthouse now serves as a post office. The postcard you mail home will bear a postmark of the lighthouse itself.

But something truly elemental is still revealed at Peggys Cove — something about the human spirit in the face of adversity. William DeGarthe, one of many artists who have lived here

WILLIAM DE GARTHE RELIEF SCULPTURE IN PEGGYS COVE

and drawn inspiration from the rugged beauty of this place, immortalized Peggys Cove with a 30.5-metre sculpture of local fishermen and their families, carved into a huge wall of granite behind his home. If you visit on a day when a stiff onshore breeze sends waves crashing against the rocks (heed the warnings to keep your distance), you will marvel at the pluck of those who choose to live here.

For an impressive landward view of the cove, Peggys Cove Water Tours leave five times daily from the government wharf. The tours offer frequent sightings of seabirds, dolphins, whales and seals. From Peggys Cove Route 333 continues along through the picturesque villages that dot the eastern shore of St. Margarets Bay. Route 333 rejoins Route 3, which leads either back to Halifax or farther along the South Shore towards Chester and Mahone Bay. It passes popular Queensland Beach and eventually comes to the village of Hubbards, a popular vacation destination for Haligonians since the mid-1800s. The Shore Club's lobster suppers and Saturday night dances are legendary. There are cottages, inns and B&Bs within easy range of Hubbards Beach. Route 329 around the Aspotogan Peninsula is a scenic diversion that will reveal the quintessential Nova Scotia; it rejoins Route 3 at East River.

Nova Scotia's South Shore is a storied stretch of shoreline. In colonial times, privateers — American, French and Nova Scotian — plied these waters with letters of marque from their governments, licensing them to plunder enemy ships. Later, rum-runners unloaded their illicit cargoes in secluded coves and bays. Tall ships once

CHESTER WATERFRONT

crowded South Shore harbours, and today coastal towns like Chester and Mahone Bay have retained the romantic aura of earlier days. Their harbours are still boating havens.

The village of Chester lies across three fingers of a peninsula that overlooks Mahone Bay, a sailor's paradise. Local lore has it that there are 365 islands in Mahone Bay (one for each day of the year). However, 100-odd islands appear on the charts today. The village itself is a New England

coastal town that just happened to end up in Nova Scotia.

MAHONE BAY (TOP)
CHESTER LIDO (ABOVE)

Appropriately, Chester's first settlers (it was called Shoreham then) sailed from Boston in 1759. Much of the rest of the Mahone Bay area was colonized by Germans, French and Swiss. Although Chester is also increasingly the haunt of yachtsmen from Halifax, Toronto and beyond, its predominantly Cape Cod–style architecture and the Yankee accents of many of its summer residents still give the town an unmistakable New England flavour.

Despite its New England roots, Chester was unable to avoid the attention of American privateers. It is believed that the Blockhouse, a private dwelling near the government wharf on the village's Front Harbour, was part of the community's defenses. This was the site of a curious happening in 1782. Apparently, three American privateers were on their way to sack Chester when the commander of the local forces came up with an inspired plan. Since all the local men were away gathering firewood, this chap gathered a brigade of broom-wielding women from the village to march back and forth on the hill overlooking the harbour with the red linings of their cloaks exposed. The Americans, so the story

CHESTER RACE
WEEK (TOP)
CHESTER
PLAYHOUSE (INSET)

goes, were fooled into thinking there were British Redcoats guarding Chester and sailed down the coast to take out their frustrations on Lunenburg. Most Americans came to Chester with friendlier intentions. In 1822 the Reverend John Secombe, a Harvard graduate, sailed to the village from Boston with several friends. His home, now the Captain's House on Central Street, is a Chester landmark.

As the 19th century moved along, a growing number of wealthy Americans discovered Chester. They came to sail, fish and get away from it all. Students from Yale came to Chester to unwind following their studies, and the town's magnificent Front Harbour and Back Harbour provided a scenic refuge for yachtsmen and retired naval brass. American admirals joined their Canadian counterparts, as did bankers, doctors and oilmen from Boston, Baltimore and Pittsburgh. Their houses are among Chester's main attractions, especially those along the peninsula at the western boundary of Front Harbour. In the early days of the 20th century, American families would travel by steamer from Boston and Philadelphia to Yarmouth, Halifax or Digby, where they would catch a train or take another boat to Chester. Several gruelling days later, their chauffeurs

would arrive with their fancy cars. Of course, this annual pilgrimage changed Chester. Chesterites, who traditionally fished and farmed, began working as guides on the trout and salmon streams, and crewed on splashy sailboats. Visitors who

98

arrive at Chester by boat will find a range of yachting services without equal in Atlantic Canada. South Shore Marine, in nearby Marriotts Cove, is the region's largest marina. Chester Race Week, held in early August, is the height of the summer social season. Then, the Front and Back harbours are filled with sleek yachts. Some participants race to win; others are happy just to be a part of the hoopla. The parade grounds off South Street, site of the Yacht Club, a bandstand, a war memorial and a saltwater swimming pool (the Lido), provide the best vantage point for non-sailors who are interested in viewing the races.

A 45-minute ferry trip (for pedestrians only) from the government wharf takes you to Big Tancook, the largest island in Mahone Bay, and then to Little Tancook. The ferry is a great way to enjoy the beauty of the bay. The islands have many lovely walking trails where you might see unique flora.

Chester offers a number of landward diversions. Just outside the village, an 18-hole golf course is characterized by its short, tight fairways and wonderful views of the ocean and nearby islands. Live theatre and concerts are presented at the Chester Playhouse year-round. Next door at Nicki's Inn you might enjoy a fine dinner before the theatre. Those who like to shop should visit the Warp and Woof on Water Street. Nova Scotia's oldest gift shop sells local art and prints, handcrafts and table accessories.

Between Chester and the nearby town of Mahone Bay on the old road, Route 3, the Seaside Shanty at Chester Basin serves up a great chowder lunch. You soon pass Oak Island (now joined to the mainland by a causeway), reputed to be the hiding place of Captain William Kidd's treasure. Since 1795, when a pit was discovered on the island, fortune-seekers have sought in vain for the booty. And for just as long, people have tried to explain the ingenious method by

PEGGYS COVE

TANCOOK FERRY
(ABOVE)
THREE CHURCHES AT
MAHONE BAY
(BELOW)

which the famous pirate is thought to have hidden his treasure in an elaborate network of underground tunnels. The story is well told by Mark Finnan in *Oak Island Secrets*, and by Graham Harris and Les MacPhee in *Oak Island and its Lost Treasure*; both are available in local bookstores and gift shops. The Oak Island Resort and Spa, a recently renovated oceanfront hotel, is a good jumping-off point from which to explore the area.

The road dips and winds its way along the shore until a long, sweeping bend brings one of Nova Scotia's most recognizable landscapes into view. Colourful buildings and wharves, monuments to Mahone Bay's seafaring past, line the waterfront of the town's near-perfect harbour. Sailboats and other pleasure craft are moored offshore, and three fine 19th-century churches — United, Lutheran and Anglican — stand side by side at the head of the harbour. These heritage churches are the venue for classical music concerts, Music at the Three Churches, every second Friday night in summer.

The area's original inhabitants were Mi'kmaq. The Mushamush River on the edge of town bears the name of an early encampment. The pretty drive to Indian Point (turn left before the bridge) is worth the few minute's detour.

The present town was established by "Foreign Protestants" in 1754. The Settlers' Museum, on Main

CLASSIC BOAT FESTIVAL, MAHONE BAY

Street, tells their story. Mahone Bay was also a haven for French fishermen and pirates. The name Mahone is believed to be derived from the French *mahonne*, a low-lying vessel that kept French pirates hidden from their prey.

Mahone Bay had its own encounters with American privateers. During the War of 1812, the *Young Teazer* was chased into Mahone Bay by a British warship. One of the privateer's crew was a British deserter. Rather than risk capture, he set fire to the ship's powder magazine; 28 died in the explosion that followed. Today, the Teazer, on Edgewater Road (Route 3), is an upscale gift shop.

Mahone Bay was once a flourishing shipbuilding centre. Many Main Street businesses now occupy buildings formerly used in the trade. On the second floor of the Settlers' Museum, the town's shipbuilding heritage is revealed. It is also visible in the architecture of Mahone Bay. A walking-tour brochure is available at the museum and will steer you towards some of the beautiful Cape Cod, Georgian and Victorian homes that used to belong to local shipbuilders. After the three churches, Mahone Bay Bed & Breakfast, with its lovely wrap-around porch, is probably the most photographed structure in Mahone Bay. It is one of many heritage bed and breakfasts in the area.

In mid-summer, the town holds its Classic Boat Festival. Inaugurated in 1990, the festival is one of Nova Scotia's best. The quality of craftsmanship of many of the boats displayed at the festival upholds Mahone Bay standards. The Great Scarecrow Festival and Antiques Fair held in early October swells the small town with hundreds of amateur photographers and treasure seekers.

Fine shops abound — the kind of shops that

LUNENBURG WATERFRONT

have given way to malls in so many other places. Birdsall-Worthington Pottery on Main Street has an international reputation for its distinctive wares made of Nova Scotia clay. Across the road is Amos Pewter, where boats were once built. An interpretive workshop allows visitors to see artisans at work fashioning pewter items — vases, candleholders, goblets, annual Christmas collectible ornaments, earrings, pins and pendants. Still on Main Street, but away from the water, Suttles and Seawinds is one of Mahone Bay's most successful enterprises. Vicki Lynn Bardon is responsible for the collection of colourful, quilt-inspired home décor and gift items. The jewel-hued quilts in the adjacent Barnstorm must be seen. The traditional craft of rug hooking is fostered by two studios exhibiting and selling beautiful rugs, kits and supplies. Mahone Bay is a favourite antiquing destination. You will find shops specializing in everything from country furniture and collectibles to vintage jewellery and Asian antiques.

Several local restaurants attain the same high standard as Mahone Bay's shops. The Innlet Café, with a harbour view that includes the three churches, emphasizes stylish seafood dishes in casual surroundings. The Cheesecake Gallery serves artful entrees amidst local art. For good pub fare and 13 beers on tap (and sometimes Saturday night bands), try the Mug & Anchor. The Biscuit Eater is an internet café with good coffee, good books and good vibes (not to mention great biscuits).

With the possible exception of Annapolis Royal, Lunenburg is the province's prettiest and most interesting town. Its architectural integrity has been preserved to a remarkable degree. Lunenburg's "Old Town" — first laid out by the province's chief surveyor in 1753 — has been designated a National Historic District by the Government of Canada and a World Heritage Site by UNESCO.

Lunenburg's beautiful harbour, its outstanding architecture, its seafaring tradition and its proximity to Halifax have attracted many visitors over the years. Some have stayed. Lunenburg is home to a vital artistic community and has long been at the centre of Nova Scotia's fishing industry. The demand for wooden ships has declined, but waterfront companies continue to outfit and repair local boats.

MADER'S WHARF, MAHONE BAY

Lunenburg represents the second attempt made by British authorities to colonize Nova Scotia (Halifax was the first). This site had a number of advantages. It offered the best agricultural land along Nova Scotia's Atlantic coast, some of which was already cleared — though not nearly as much as was promised.

There was a fine harbour, the narrow peninsula could be easily defended by a palisade, and the site was close to Halifax and far from the French settlements at Ile-Royale (Cape Breton) and along the Bay of Fundy.

In 1753, a group of German-speaking "Foreign Protestants" (French, German and Swiss) arrived by boat from Halifax. These labourers and farmers had been recruited by British authorities to populate their colony. Surveyor General Charles Morris measured off blocks and streets in a gridiron pattern along the slope overlooking the harbour. The Old Town was a 48-block rectangle with rows of six blocks running parallel to the shore and columns of eight blocks running up the hill. A central core of four blocks was reserved for public purposes.

DORY BUILDING AT LUNENBURG

The settlers overcame the adversities of hostile French and Mi'kmaq in the area, and their endeavours eventually flourished. Surpluses of timber, boards and root vegetables were sent to Halifax. Settlement reached southwest as far as West Berlin, and northeast to Mahone Bay and beyond. Prime land along the banks of the LaHave River drew people farther and farther upriver, from Bridgewater to New Germany.

It was inevitable that some of the new settlers would turn to the sea for their livelihood. Towards the end of the 18th century, the inshore fishery began to flourish. Cod, mackerel, dogfish, salmon, herring and gaspereaux were easily caught from small boats close to shore.

Lunenburg's waterfront still reflects the importance of its shipbuilding industry and the fishery. At the eastern end of Montague Street, Scotia Trawlers has been outfitting and repairing fishing vessels since acquiring the Smith and Rhuland boatyards in 1976. Smith and Rhuland,

FISHERIES MUSEUM OF THE ATLANTIC, LUNENBURG

established in 1900, built both the *Bluenose* (1921) and the *Bluenose II* (1963). Lunenburg shipbuilders were renowned long before the *Bluenose* was launched, but it was this 285-ton racing schooner, never defeated in Nova Scotia waters, that won them international recognition. In addition to the *Bluenose II*, the same shipyard also

ADAMS & KNICKLE, LUNENBURG

launched replicas of HMS *Bounty* (1960) and the *Rose*.

The fishery spawned other industries. The buildings of the old Adams & Knickle outfitting company can still be seen. Farther west on Montague Street, the Fisheries

LUNENBURG ARCHITECTURE (BELOW) LUNENBURG ACADEMY (BOTTOM)

Museum of the Atlantic occupies buildings that were once a part of the National Sea Products processing plant (now located at Battery Point). The museum, one of Nova Scotia's best, has many excellent exhibits relating to Lunenburg's fishing and shipbuilding heritage. The aquarium of Atlantic fish is especially popular with children; adults may find the rum-running display more to their taste. An exhibit on the Banks fishery and the Age of Sail includes meticulously crafted models. Various demonstrations take place throughout the summer. Moored alongside the museum's wharf, the *Theresa E. Connor*, a salt-bank schooner, and the *Cape Sable*, a steel-hulled trawler, welcome visitors aboard. The *Bluenose II* may also be here (she sails out of Halifax and other Nova Scotia port towns as well).

In recent years, careful planning has preserved Lunenburg's architectural character. Before that, good fortune was largely responsible. Lunenburg's failure to industrialize in areas other than the fishery is one

explanation for the absence of major fires in the downtown area. And significant redevelopment in the Old Town was averted when the "New Town" was established in 1862. With a few minor exceptions, Old Town remains remarkably similar in both form and function to Morris's 1753 plan. Public buildings still stand where they did in the settlement's early days. St. John's Anglican Church, built between 1754 and 1763, was the tragic victim of a Halloween fire in 2001. The second-oldest Anglican Church in Canada, it has been faithfully restored to its former magnificence. Lunenburg's courthouse was built in 1775, and is now used by St. John's parish as a church hall. Predictably, the new courthouse, built in 1902, also stands on the Grand Parade in the centre of town.

There are a number of other 18th-century structures. Typically, these are one-storey Cape Cod–style houses or two-storey dwellings in the British Classical tradition. Knaut-Rhuland House Museum, a designated heritage property (c. 1793) on Pelham Street, has one of the most intact original Georgian interiors in Nova Scotia.

Nineteenth-century buildings dominate Old Town. Although architecturally conservative, Lunenburgers permitted themselves one extravagance in the latter half of the 19th century: Scottish dormer windows were added to British Classical houses. Over time, these were moved down the slope of the roof until they hung over central doorways. The "Lunenburg Bump" can be quite ostentatious, and probably was a reflection of the town's success in the salt fish trade.

Built just before the turn of the 20th century, the second Lunenburg Academy (the first was destroyed by fire in 1893) is one of the town's architectural gems. It stands outside Old Town, atop Gallows Hill, and the four towers that jut from its Mansard roof are visible for miles. Young Lunenburgers are still educated at the academy.

Lunenburg hosts a series of first-rate festivals during the summer. Its growing reputation as a centre for arts and crafts is reflected in the quality of work displayed at the Lunenburg Craft Festival (mid-July) and the Nova Scotia Folk Art Festival (early August). At the Lunenburg Fishermen's Reunion and Picnic in August fishermen's competitions, including dory racing and scallop shucking, are hotly contested by highly skilled participants. A highlight of the summer festival season, the Lunenburg Folk Harbour Festival (August) features top North American performers, as well as some from further afield, and attractive waterside venues.

BLUE ROCKS, NEAR LUNENBURG

The town boasts a number of fine shops and galleries, and across the harbour you can shoot nine holes of golf at the Bluenose Golf and Country Club while enjoying the spectacular view. There are several good restaurants

OX TEAM AT WORK, ROSS FARM

LAHAVE RIVER

serving, not surprisingly, lobster and fish dishes. Fleur de Sel on Montague Street provides an elegant, upscale interpretation.

To the south of Lunenburg, the privately run Ovens Natural Park has a series of coastal caves. A cliff-side hiking trail leads down a concrete stairway to the mouth of Cannon Cave — so named because of the dramatic boom created by the surge of waves into the narrow cavern. Zodiac tours of the caves are available between late June and early September (weather permitting).

Follow the coastline south to the LaHave River, and then go upriver on Route 332 to Bridgewater, a thriving town that prides itself as the main street of the South Shore. Bridgewater offers its visitors numerous services and conveniences, including restaurants, accommodations, bustling malls, banks, a regional hospital, a library, museums, recreational facilities and a visitor information centre.

Built in 1860, the Wile Carding Mill displays machines that once carded wool for spinning and weaving. The DesBrisay Museum relates the history and development of Lunenburg County through documents, exhibits and artifacts, including a beautiful Mi'kmaq quillwork cradle. Bridgewater hosts its rural neighbours each July at the South Shore Exhibition and International Ox Pull. A pleasant drive down the western banks of the LaHave (Route 331) leads to the dock where a cable ferry provides a transportation link across the river. Nearby is the Fort Point Museum, a former lighthouse keeper's house, and site of the Fort Sainte-Marie-de-Grâce National Historic Site, where Isaac de Razilly, the first governor of New France, landed with his settlers in 1632. At Rissers Beach, supervised swimming, picnic areas and change facilities are provided.

More excellent beaches and inviting villages can be found at such shoreline communities as Petite Rivière, Green Bay, Broad Cove and Cherry Hill.

Situated at the estuary of the Mersey River, Liverpool was settled by New England Planters in the 1760s. These

PERKINS HOUSE

settlers were invited to Nova Scotia by Governor Charles Lawrence to take up lands made vacant by the expulsion of the Acadians and to bolster the loyal British population of the province.

Much of Liverpool's colonial past has been popularized in the historical fiction of Thomas Raddall. Raddall was far and away Nova Scotia's best-selling novelist, with millions of copies sold in the United States, Great Britain and Canada. In *His Majesty's Yankees,* he told the powerful story of a fictional Liverpool family caught up in the events surrounding the American Revolution. To give his novel life, Raddall relied heavily on the diaries of an 18th-century Liverpool merchant, Simeon Perkins.

Perkins' diaries give a unique account of colonial Nova Scotia. They describe the dilemma faced by the Planters, who had spent most of their lives as New Englanders, when the American Revolution polarized loyalties. Perkins was among those community leaders who eventually called for armed resistance to the attacks of American privateers.

Today, Perkins House on Main Street is one of Liverpool's chief attractions. Built in 1766, the house was acquired by the Queens County Historical Society in 1936 and is now a part of the Nova Scotia Museum. Like Raddall's novels, Perkins House and the adjacent Queens County Museum tell a romantic story of Liverpool's tumultuous early days. Much is made of privateers — hardly surprising in a town that styles itself as the "Port of the Privateers." Liverpool hosts a Privateer Days celebration at the end of June. The town also stages a summer program of concerts and plays at the beautiful Astor Theatre, once Liverpool's town hall. This is also the venue for the Liverpool International Theatre Festival, a biennial springtime series of high-calibre performances.

Logging has been the backbone of Liverpool's economy almost from the beginning. Some of the lumber was used to build ships, which often took on additional lumber for export to Great Britain.

PERKINS HOUSE

107

LOYALIST DAYS, SHELBURNE

In the 1920s, the forest industry in Queens County was given a major boost by the decision of Yarmouth-born financier Izaak Walton Killam to build a pulp and paper mill at Brooklyn, on the north side of Liverpool Bay. Completed in 1929, the Mersey Paper Mill got off to a slow start, but soon picked up speed. When Killam died in 1955, he held approximately three-quarters of the company's common stock and his estate was valued at around $200 million. The Killam trusts are still used for university endowments and the construction of public buildings across Canada. Bowater Mersey continues to be the major employer in the Liverpool area.

The Sherman Hines Museum of Photography and Galleries, located in Liverpool's historic town hall, is the only photographic museum east of Montreal. It features artifacts and vintage photographs by the likes of Karsh and MacAskill. Another one-of-a-kind attraction, the Rossignol Cultural Centre on Church Street is a museum and gallery complex that illustrates many natural and social aspects of the area's past. The former Liverpool train station is now the Hank Snow Country Music Centre, honouring the Queens County–born country music legend. The centre has rotating displays and memorabilia from well-known Nova Scotia musicians, interactive exhibits, railway memorabilia, workshops and a gift shop. In August, the Friends of Hank Snow Society hosts a weekend of classic country music at the exhibition grounds in Bridgewater.

HANK SNOW MUSEUM

Nova Scotia's fourth-oldest surviving lighthouse is the centrepiece of Fort Point Lighthouse Park. Once a welcome sight for seafarers entering Liverpool's busy harbour, the lighthouse now contains an exhibit area with models, interpretive panels and an audiovisual presentation. Lane's Privateer Inn offers good accommodation and dining in a restored 208-year-old property with lovely grounds on the edge of the Mersey River. South of Liverpool, Route 3 leads to White Point Beach Resort; its wide-ranging facilities include a playground, pool, spa, nine-hole Canadian PGArated golf course, tennis courts, freshwater paddling and, of course, a long stretch of fine, white, sandy beach (warm-water enthusiasts will prefer the pool for swimming). Farther along Route 3 are some of the province's best beaches. Summerville Beach Park, with its saltwater lagoon, is a great spot for a picnic and swim. The Quarterdeck Beachside Villas & Grill is situated along this white-sand beach. The villas offer all the amenities including full kitchen facilities, jacuzzis and fireplaces.

FORT POINT LIGHTHOUSE PARK

For a more secluded setting, drive on to Carters Beach at Port Mouton. The beach is actually three crescent-shaped stretches of the finest white sand imaginable. It's worth the trouble to ford the small stream that separates the last two of these beaches from the first. Here, you will find magnificent dunes and unmatched views of Port Mouton Bay.

The endangered piping plover has also taken advantage of the relative seclusion of this coastline. Kejimkujik National Park's Seaside Adjunct protects key nesting areas between Port Mouton and Port Joli. Two hiking trails lead to isolated beaches, sections of which are closed from late April to late July, so that nesting birds remain undisturbed. Both hikes offer spectacular coastal views. There are still more wonderful beaches at Lockeport, just off Route 3. Crescent Beach, one of five in the area, is a fully-serviced 1.5-kilometre-long stretch of fine, white sand. It is a short drive from here up the indraft of Jordan Bay and across the peninsula to Shelburne.

Shelburne is Nova Scotia's Loyalist town. Drawn by the outstanding harbour, one of the largest in the world, thousands of Loyalists settled along the shores of the Roseway River estuary in 1783. Within a year, nearly 10,000 people were there, making Shelburne the largest town in British North America.

PIPING PLOVER

CARTERS BEACH

A number of Loyalist-era structures have survived in Shelburne. Ross-Thomson House and Store, now part of the Nova Scotia Museum, was built in 1785. The store was soon occupied by business partners and brothers Robert and George Ross (Robert Thomson would become their clerk). The old store has since been refurbished with 18th-century furnishings and merchandise. The comfortable, solid building, no doubt the work of a shipbuilder, is impressive in itself.

The Cooper's Inn, also on Dock Street, is one of several waterfront restoration projects that grew out of the visit of the Prince and Princess of Wales to Shelburne in 1983. The former owners received an award from Heritage Trust Nova Scotia for their work on this 18th-century Loyalist home (c. 1785).

LOYALIST REENACTORS

South on Dock Street, the Shelburne County Museum tells more of the Loyalist story. A walking tour brochure available at the museum points out several other Loyalist buildings in town. Most points of interest are along the waterfront, on or near Dock Street. Treat yourself to a wonderful meal prepared by chef Roland Glauser at Charlotte Lane.

Like other fishing communities along the South Shore, Shelburne also has a rich shipbuilding heritage. The town is renowned for its dories. In 1877 Isaac Coffin Crowell, a native of nearby Barrington, invented and patented a metal clip for joining the floor futtocks with those on the sides of the dory. In Lunenburg, dory builders continued (and continue) to use naturally crooked tamarack roots for the

BARRINGTON MEETING HOUSE

job. A debate still rages as to whose method is better, but Crowell's clip allowed Shelburne builders to undersell their Lunenburg competitors.

At one time, Shelburne had seven dory shops. The Dory Shop Museum, a going concern from 1880 to 1970, demonstrates the building and outfitting of a Shelburne dory and explains the crucial role that these boats played in the fishery. Now part of the Nova Scotia Museum, the Dory Shop has a dory builder at work several days a week.

Between Shelburne and Yarmouth lies Barrington. Just four years after Barrington was founded by Planter families from Cape Cod in 1761, the new township had a New England-style meeting house. Now part of the Nova Scotia Museum, the unadorned structure that served both religious

LOYALIST DAYS, SHELBURNE

and secular purposes is Canada's oldest extant nonconformist place of worship.

Nearby, the Barrington Woolen Mill, built in 1884, is also operated by the museum. The mill houses original machinery and includes exhibits on sheep raising and wool processing. The Seal Island Lighthouse Museum was constructed in Barrington to commemorate the light and its keepers, who steered countless sailors past Seal Island's notorious shoals for 160 years. Built in 1830, the lighthouse was automated in 1990. The exhibits relate to lighthouse life. There is a good view of Barrington Bay from the top of the five-storey lighthouse tower.

Reached by causeway from Barrington Passage, Cape Sable Island in Barrington Bay is also steeped in maritime lore. The island was home to Ephraim Atkinson, who first built the boat that became the workhorse of the North Atlantic lobster fishery. Typically, the Cape Islander is about 12 metres long with a 3- to 4-metre beam. You'll find them in working harbours throughout Atlantic Canada. Learn more about the Cape Islander and this storied fishing community at the Archelaus Smith Museum in Centreville.

At West Pubnico, the oldest Acadian settlement still inhabited by descendants of its founders, Historic Acadian Village (Village Historique Acadien) honours the perseverance and generosity of the Acadian people. Original structures and artifacts donated by local residents were used to create vintage Acadian buildings, including houses, a forge, a barn and a lobster peg mill. Guides in period costume welcome visitors to a reception centre, a restaurant serving traditional Acadian dishes, and an arts and crafts shop.

Take a stroll through the town of Yarmouth and you'll be struck by the houses. On the slope rising up from the ferry terminal are lavish 19th-century homes — Georgian, Gothic and Italianate, among others. Some have costly frills, like the one on Parade Street, not far from the Yarmouth County Museum, which is trimmed with wooden rope and comes complete with portholes.

Fish-processing plants along the waterfront attest to a fairly healthy fishery (a rarity in Nova Scotia these days) and the town is well-serviced, but there are few clues as to where the extravagant wealth came from that built these homes. That is because Yarmouth's century

111

YARMOUTH COUNTY MUSEUM

was the 19th — first as Nova Scotia's most prosperous "wood, wind and sail" community, and then as a thriving industrial centre.

The Yarmouth County Museum is a good place to begin a tour of the town. Here, there are many paintings of the fleet, commissioned by Yarmouth captains in ports like New York, Belfast and Hong Kong.

During the middle of the 19th century, Yarmouth families like the Killams and Lovitts, who traced their roots back to the New England Planters who first settled Yarmouth in the 1760s, became powerful shipping magnates. Their ships, flush with lumber and salt fish, made for the West Indies. There they laded rum, sugar and molasses bound for Boston, then returned to Yarmouth with manufactured goods. They reinvested the profits in shipping. For a time, Yarmouth boasted the largest per capita concentration of registered shipping tonnage in the world.

By the 1860s, huge ships were being built for the international bulk trade. Yarmouth's wealthiest families entered into partnerships to finance their construction. All along the French Shore — the string of Acadian communities between Yarmouth and Digby shipyards were kept busy.

The Killam Brothers Building, part of the Yarmouth County Museum and located along the waterfront, attests to the wealth of the ship owners. Look for the hand-worn grooves in the cash tray of the huge, stand-up chestnut desk.

And then, so the story usually goes, sail was replaced by steam, and it was over. The worldwide slump in trade in 1873 is often cited as the turning point. The golden age of wooden ships and iron men had passed. Yarmouth's mercantile class was left to languish in the face of progress.

But that's not what really happened. A visit to Yarmouth's excellent Firefighters Museum on Main Street provides some insight into the real story. Among the exhibits is a horse-drawn hose reel that was built in Yarmouth by the Burrill-Johnson Iron Company in 1891. The threat of fire was real because Yarmouth industry boomed until the turn of the century. In addition to the Burrill-Johnson foundry, which had been expanded during the 1880s to supply more products to national and international markets, the Yarmouth Duck and Yarn Company was started in 1883. It was one of several cotton mills established in the Maritimes to take advantage of the federal government's National Policy.

That policy, implemented in 1878, sought to stimulate the Canadian manufacturing sector by slapping tariffs on foreign manufactured goods, while allowing certain raw materials, including cotton, to enter the country duty-free. So, Yarmouth merchants did not suddenly abandon shipping in a fit of panic. Rather, they scaled back operations in light of the advent of steam and sought to take advantage of the new technologies by investing in land-based manufacturing. The National Policy provided the economic stimulus, and the newly completed Western Counties Railway linked Yarmouth to the national market.

But regional manufacturers could not compete with their central Canadian counterparts. The transfer of local capital to larger Ontario and Quebec interests was a problem experienced in all of Nova Scotia's industrial towns. Yarmouth's decline was as dramatic as its rise. By 1900 little industry was left. The cotton mill was still around, but was soon controlled by outsiders.

Today, there are some wistful reminders of Yarmouth's heyday. But there is a bright side to the story. The town still thrives as the service centre for southwestern Nova Scotia and a key entry point for the province. Bay Ferries operates a speedy car ferry, the *Cat*, to Yarmouth from Bar Harbor, Maine, on weekdays and from Portland, Maine, on weekends.

The Yarmouth Arts Centre (Th'YARC) stages a variety of entertainment, including summer theatre, in its 380-seat theatre on Parade Street. Dory races are a highlight of Seafest, a week-long community festival held each July.

For the most part, Yarmouth offers hotel/motel-style accommodation, but there are notable exceptions. Harbour's Edge Bed & Breakfast is an elegantly appointed heritage property. The beautifully restored Charles C. Richards House is another notable B&B. The impressive Guest-Lovitt House B&B with its widow's watch speaks of Yarmouth's former shipping wealth. The Manor Inn, in nearby Hebron, features all the amenities (dining room, pub, tennis courts and more) on about 4 hectares of attractively landscaped waterfrontage. Still in the Yarmouth area, Trout Point Lodge in Kemptville features a rustic décor (with all amenities) on a large river- and lake-side acreage.

Rudder's Seafood Restaurant and Brewpub is the centre of activity on the Yarmouth waterfront; it offers good food, house-brewed beer and lively entertainment.

CAT FERRY IN YARMOUTH HARBOUR

Yarmouth's lobster fishery still flourishes. Along the drive out to the lighthouse at Cape Forchu between the spring and fall lobster seasons, there are thousands of traps piled along the roadside.

EVANGELINE TRAIL

CAPE BLOMIDON

The Annapolis Valley is an area of peaceful beauty. The North and South Mountain ranges provide shelter from heavy winds and Fundy fog. The valley is blessed with more sunshine than anywhere else in Nova Scotia. The fertile soil has been farmed since the Acadians settled the land early in the 17th century. Stately elms and beautiful willows (an Acadian favourite) impart a sense of timelessness to the valley. Is it any wonder that you can find a village named Paradise here?

The Annapolis Valley is an ideal setting for a tragic romance. And history obliged with a suitable cast of characters, the Acadians — French farmers who were Nova Scotia's earliest European settlers. Unable to retain their neutrality in the struggle between France and Britain for supremacy in the New World, the peaceful Acadians were expelled in 1755 for refusing to take an unconditional oath of loyalty to the British Crown — their lands, houses and livestock were all confiscated. All that was needed was for someone to write their story.

Henry Wadsworth Longfellow's epic poem *Evangeline* was published in Boston in 1847. It was immensely popular, running through five editions in its first year. Other publications followed, which further aroused the curiosity of New Englanders in the "Land of Evangeline."

A rail link between Halifax and Yarmouth, completed in 1891, provided a convenient way of getting here. The Yarmouth Steamship Company added a new ship to its Boston run, and the Windsor and Annapolis Railway inaugurated the "Flying Bluenose." Since then, the valley has been a popular destination for visitors from New England and beyond.

Approaching the Annapolis Valley from Halifax, Highway 101 passes near Mount Uniacke, where Richard John Uniacke built an impressive Georgian mansion, Uniacke House, in 1813. After fighting on the rebel side of

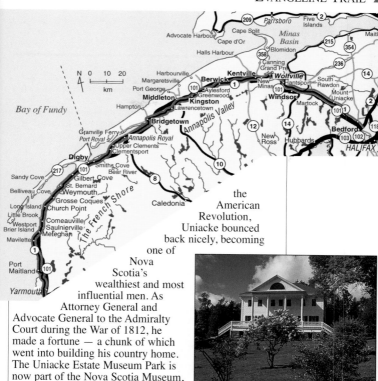

UNIACKE HOUSE

the American Revolution, Uniacke bounced back nicely, becoming one of Nova Scotia's wealthiest and most influential men. As Attorney General and Advocate General to the Admiralty Court during the War of 1812, he made a fortune — a chunk of which went into building his country home. The Uniacke Estate Museum Park is now part of the Nova Scotia Museum, and features many original furnishings and Uniacke family portraits. Many kilometres of walking and hiking trails have been developed throughout the landscaped grounds and natural woodlands.

Continuing the journey toward Windsor, the lush valley landscape makes a dramatic appearance. Spread out before you are the rich farmlands that skirt the Avon River. If the tide is out, the river is an expanse of red mud flats. Remnants of Acadian dykes are here, although it is impossible to distinguish the originals from later reconstructions.

Windsor is a service centre for Hants County farmers. The town was also home to Thomas Chandler Haliburton, the Nova Scotian humourist who created the character Sam Slick, the Yankee clockmaker with the acerbic wit. Haliburton House, a provincial museum, features Victorian furnishings and an attractive 10-hectare estate. Shand House, another provincial museum, is a state-of-the-art Victorian home with all of the modern conveniences of the time. Windsor is the home of Howard Dill, the farmer who developed the "Atlantic Giant" pumpkin that has produced pumpkins weighing more than 650 kilograms. Visitors flock to the Dill farm on College Road, particularly in late summer and early fall, to marvel at the monster vegetables.

The Dill farm is also the site of Long Pond, where students at King's College School played the first-ever game of hockey. Downtown, the Windsor Hockey Heritage Centre tells the story of how Canada's great winter sport began.

Close by, at Falmouth, the Saint Famille Winery, which provides tours, and the well-kept greens and fairways of the Avon Valley Golf and Country Club attest to the fine

Annapolis Valley weather.

Hantsport, once a prosperous shipbuilding centre, is now home to a busy pulp and paper products plant, and serves as a depot for the export of gypsum. As you travel west, fields and orchards appear, reminders that agriculture has always been the mainstay of the area. During harvest season, roadside stands and U-picks do a brisk business as locals and visitors load up with fresh fruit and vegetables.

In late May, the Annapolis Valley is in full bloom — orchards and orchards of apple trees are laden with delicate pink and white blossoms. Since 1932, valley residents have celebrated the start of the growing season with an Apple Blossom Festival. Before the mid-19th century, there was not much of an apple industry in the area. Poor roads and contrary winds made the shipment of perishable goods a dubious enterprise. Railways and steamships changed all that. By the 1880s, apples from the Annapolis Valley were being regularly shipped to Great Britain. In 1905, the Nova Scotia Fruit Growers' Association convinced the federal government to locate an experimental farm in Kentville.

SAINT-FAMILLE WINERY, FALMOUTH

Valley farmers successfully lobbied rail and shipping interests for favourable rates that strengthened their position in the British market. For their part, the British co-operated by consuming more apples than any other people in the world. By the 1930s, Britain regularly consumed three-quarters of Nova Scotia's commercial crop.

When that market suddenly dried up with the outbreak of war, the problem was thought to be temporary. It was not. A sluggish post-war economy forced Britons to severely limit the number of pounds that they could convert for purchases made in dollars, and apples were not a high priority. Currency restrictions were eventually relaxed, but the British market for Annapolis Valley apples never recovered. Now, much of the crop is bought by multi-national corporations for processing; relatively few apples are grown for export.

But there are plenty of apples for the local market. In early fall, roadside stands brim with apples — old favourites like Cortland, McIntosh,

Gravenstein and Delicious, and newer Royal Gala and Jonagold. Visitors with their own favourite apple recipes can spend an afternoon at one of the valley's many U-pick orchards. Between Windsor and Wolfville is the Grand Pré National Historic Site. Hundreds of

Acadians were deported from the area in 1755, and the village of Grand Pré became the setting for Longfellow's *Evangeline*. The grounds of the historic site are beautiful, with gardens and winding paths shaded by old willow trees. A memorial church built in 1922 houses an exhibit, and a new interpretive centre explains the history of the expulsion. Bilingual tours are provided. There is also a thriving winery (the first in Nova Scotia) in the village of Grand Pré with a restaurant and Inn on site. Nearby in the Gaspereau Valley is Gaspereau Vineyards — a newer winery operated by the Jost family, who started the wine-making industry in Nova Scotia at Malagash.

Wolfville is the cultural and academic centre of the Annapolis Valley. Acadia University, established as Acadia College in 1838, is situated on one of Canada's prettiest campuses. A 2.4-hectare native botanical garden is part of the university's new K.C. Irving Environmental Science Centre.

In addition to being the valley's cultural centre, Wolfville is also one of its loveliest towns. Beautiful Victorian homes line elm-shaded streets. The visitor information centre at Willow Park, on Main Street, will provide you with a brochure for the Heritage Home Walking Tour.

ACADIA UNIVERSITY, WOLFVILLE

GRAND PRÉ

Several of Wolfville's grandest homes are now among the province's best tourist accommodations. The Blomidon Inn features 26 rooms in a lavish 1877 mansion. The entrance and public spaces are especially impressive, as are the Blomidon's best rooms. The Tattingstone Inn is a special place — you'll find four-poster beds and marble-tiled bathrooms, but also a swimming pool and tennis court. There is a carriage house and a cottage for honeymooners. Victoria's Historic Inn and Carriage House Bed & Breakfast (1893) is another registered heritage property. The main house includes three honeymoon suites, complete with jacuzzis.

Wolfville offers fine dining as well. Two restaurants in particular — the Tempest and Acton's, where a popular lunch buffet features fresh Valley produce and Fundy seafood — make dining out in Wolfville a pleasure.

There are a number of interesting shops in town. Box of Delights is a good general bookstore with the valley's best selection of local titles. Blomidon Inn's House of Gifts has a wide selection of hand-crafted items and kitchen wares.

Wolfville's Robie Tufts Nature Centre provides summer visitors with a rare spectacle. From May to late August, chimney swifts gather here for a startlingly acrobatic descent down a chimney. (Tufts's bird books are available at most Nova Scotia bookstores.)

Randall House, another grand Wolfville home, features a collection of historical materials relating to the Planters — New Englanders invited to Nova Scotia to take over the lands made vacant by the Expulsion of 1755 — who settled Mud Creek before it became Wolfville. Across the street, a path leads to a series of dykes that are ideal for walking and offer great views of the town and surrounding countryside.

In an area renowned for its agriculture, it may surprise you to learn that many of Wolfville's elegant homes, including the Blomidon Inn, were built with wealth earned from the shipping trades. Nearby Kingsport, Hantsport and Port Williams were all important shipping centres. After 1928, some

NEW ENGLAND
PLANTER HOUSE,
NEAR WOLFVILLE

independent growers shipped local apples directly from Port
Williams. Three kilometres away, at Starrs Point, Prescott
House was built in 1815 by Charles Prescott, a businessman
and horticulturist who introduced several varieties of apples,
including the Gravenstein, to Nova Scotia. The house is
filled with period furnishings, and the perennial garden and
grounds are especially attractive. Today, visitors can enjoy a
sunny early-fall afternoon picking their fill of apples at U-
picks in Starrs Point and many other locations throughout
the valley.

Back at Port Williams, Route 358 continues north across
Acadian dykes, through Canning (where there is yet another
winery — Blomidon Estate) then on to a look-off. From
high atop Cape Blomidon, you can survey the Minas Basin
and six river valleys. In autumn, the view is made even more
beautiful by the fall foliage that spreads out beneath you.

At the end of Route 358, hikers can carry on to the end
of Cape Split (the continuation of Cape Blomidon) along a
13-kilometre marked trail that yields spectacular views of
the Bay of Fundy. Further along Route 358 is Blomidon
Provincial Park, which has many hiking trails offering
amazing views of the Minas Basin and opportunities for
rockhounding for the amethysts and agates that are
constantly being exposed along the cliffs and beaches by
the massive Fundy tides.

Kentville services the richest farming area in the valley
and has been a long-time leader in the apple industry. The
Agriculture Canada Research Station assists fruit growers

CAPE BLOMIDON

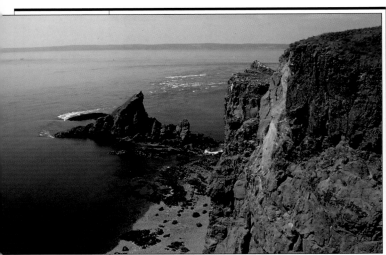

TIDE RIPS AT CAPE SPLIT

with an ongoing program of scientific research. Blair House is an on-site museum with exhibits relating to the history of the apple industry and the research station's involvement in it. In town, the Old Kings Courthouse Heritage Museum on Cornwallis Street devotes much of its space to the social history of the area — especially to the arrival of the New England Planters in the 1760s. A good walking tour brochure is available from the visitor information centre. The tour lasts about three hours and will take you past several outstanding heritage homes.

Back towards Wolfville, the Ken-Wo Golf Club is one of the valley's best courses. The sheltered fairways are well maintained, and the casual atmosphere makes green-fee players feel more than welcome.

Villages and towns run into one another as you continue west through the valley along Route 1. Road-weary travellers can choose from the many rural bed and breakfasts in places like Berwick, Middleton and Lawrencetown. Century Farm Inn and Falcourt Inn in the Middleton area are gracious old establishments. At

OAKLAWN FARM ZOO

Aylesford, families will enjoy the Oaklawn Farm Zoo, which features over 100 species of mammals and birds. The 18-hole Paragon Golf Course at Kingston is usually less crowded than other courses in the valley, and is almost always drier (a nuisance at the height of summer, but a blessing at

other times). Its wide-open fairways make it a forgiving course for novices.

A short side trip over North Mountain takes visitors to picturesque fishing villages hugging the shores of the Bay of Fundy. At places like Halls Harbour, Harbourville, Margaretsville or Hampton, fishing boats dramatically demonstrate the rise and fall of the tides, as they alternately ride high at their moorings or sit on the mud flats awaiting the next high tide. Stop for fresh lobster at the pound in Halls Harbour. If you have time, take a detour through Bridgetown and see for yourself why it is billed as "the prettiest little town in Nova Scotia." A self-guided walking tour highlights Bridgetown's heritage homes and history. Bridgetown was the setting for Ernest Buckler's *The Mountain and the Valley*, probably the best work of fiction to come out of Nova Scotia.

LOW TIDE, BAY OF FUNDY (TOP)
THE HABITATION AT PORT ROYAL (INSET)

The communities along the shores of the Annapolis Basin are a treasure trove of history. All Nova Scotia school children know the story of the arrival of Sieur de Monts and Samuel de Champlain to Port Royal at the beginning of the 17th century. They also learn how a second Port Royal, established on the opposite shore of the basin in 1635, became Annapolis Royal in 1710 and served as the seat of British colonial government in Nova Scotia until Halifax was established in 1749. Here was the first successful European settlement in what is now Canada — and the genesis of British rule in Nova Scotia.

Off Route 1, about 10 kilometres southwest of Granville Ferry, is the reconstructed Port Royal Habitation. Close to here, de Monts and Champlain established a fur-trading post in 1605. The reconstruction is based on Champlain's sketch of the site. Like Normandy farms of that time, buildings form a rectangle around a central courtyard.

A good deal is known about the French stay at Port Royal through the writings of Champlain, Marc Lescarbot and Father Pierre Biard. Lescarbot, a disenchanted lawyer with literary aspirations and an ebullient personality, wrote extensively about his year at the habitation. His frivolous Neptune pageant, now celebrated as Canada's first theatrical presentation, was played out along the shores of Port Royal in November 1606. Even Champlain, no great fan of Lescarbot, was entertained.

The winter that followed was a relatively mild one, made even more bearable by Champlain's *Ordre de Bon Temps* (Order of Good Cheer). Champlain sought to ward off the ravages of scurvy and the monotony of winter by promoting

PORT ROYAL
(ABOVE AND BELOW)

feasting and fellowship among the order's members.

In 1607, de Monts' fears were realized when his monopoly was revoked; the habitation was abandoned until 1610. Father Biard, a Jesuit priest, arrived the following year. His frequent clashes with the Biencourts, the father and son who now ran the habitation, and the difficulties he encountered in his mission work with the Mi'kmaq, were well suited to Biard's acid pen. When Port Royal was sacked by a group of Virginians led by Samuel Argall in 1613, Biard may well have breathed a sigh of relief had he not been wrongfully accused of complicity in the raid by the younger Biencourt. (Elizabeth Jones provides a lively narrative history of the Port Royal years in *Gentlemen and Jesuits*.)

The present-day habitation evokes Canada's first European settlement. Costumed interpreters, employed as 17th-century artisans, go about their tasks. Visitors can imagine Marc Lescarbot scribbling away in his reconstructed dwelling. Other buildings at the site, which include the Governor's House, the Priest's Dwelling, the Chapel, the Blacksmith's Shop and the Trading Room, may well inspire 17th-century reveries.

At Granville Ferry, pause long enough to look across the river at the Annapolis Royal waterfront. On a calm, clear day this is one of Nova Scotia's special views. Also worth a look is the fine collection of Georgian furniture, ceramics, glass and silver housed at the North Hills Museum in Granville Ferry.

At the Annapolis River Causeway, there is a prototype tidal power installation. An on-site interpretive display shows how the generators work, but the power house itself is underground and off-limits to the public. From here, Route 1 leads directly to Annapolis Royal.

Beautiful Annapolis Royal, on the shores of the Annapolis Basin, is a showcase of heritage restoration. A reconstruction project launched in 1979 spruced up some of the town's fine old buildings, attracting both business and tourists. Before the project, visitors to Annapolis Royal had to leave town to get a good meal. Today, there are several good local restaurants. Leo's Café is situated in the Adams-Ritchie House, built by a New England merchant in 1712. The fine dining at Garrison House Inn has been recommended in *Where to Eat in Canada*. The Queen Anne Inn is one of several grand old mansions that now accommodate tourists in fine style. Since 1984, the restored King's Theatre has featured the Annapolis Royal Arts Festival, a September celebration of local, regional and national talent. The same venue hosts a summer theatre festival during July and August. The work of local artists and artisans, many of them recent arrivals to Annapolis Royal, can be seen in waterfront shops and galleries.

In the centre of town, the Fort Anne National Historic Site represents the fourth and last fort built by the French at this location. Governor Subercase's powder magazine (1708) is the only extant building from the French era. The story of the struggle for supremacy between the French and English is told in the museum building, which was constructed as officers' quarters by the Duke of Kent in 1797. A stroll along the earthworks affords some beautiful views of the Annapolis Basin.

The Annapolis Royal Historic Gardens were opened in August 1981 as part of the heritage restoration project. Abutted by reclaimed marshland and a 20-hectare wildfowl sanctuary, the stunning 4-hectare gardens display much of the area's natural history. Among the more than 200 varieties in the Rose Garden are several that were grown by Acadian settlers in the area in the 17th century (the roses are at their peak from late June until August). Next to

FORT ANNE, ANNAPOLIS ROYAL

the replica of an Acadian cottage, willow and apple trees shade an Acadian potager, or vegetable garden, wherein can be found the makings of an outstanding pot of soup. Other highlights include the Governor's Garden, which was modelled

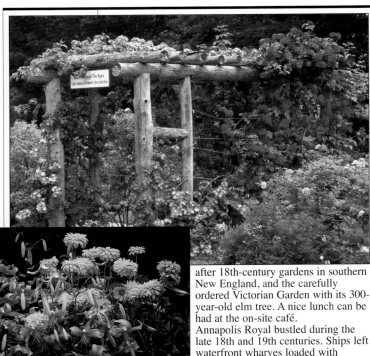

HISTORIC GARDENS, ANNAPOLIS ROYAL

O'DELL HOUSE MUSEUM, ANNAPOLIS ROYAL

after 18th-century gardens in southern New England, and the carefully ordered Victorian Garden with its 300-year-old elm tree. A nice lunch can be had at the on-site café.

Annapolis Royal bustled during the late 18th and 19th centuries. Ships left waterfront wharves loaded with apples, potatoes and lumber, and returned with sugar, molasses and rum from the West Indies. Packet boats from Digby, Saint John and Boston made Annapolis Royal a regular port of call. The town was a popular overnight stop.

Today, the O'Dell House Museum, dating from the 1860s, recreates the cosmopolitan atmosphere of a busy 19th-century inn. It catered to well-off travellers, the nicer rooms going for $1.50 a night. The museum also houses collections of Victorian costume and furnishings, artifacts of childhood, as well as the ubiquitous relics of a shipbuilding past. Sinclair Inn National Historic Site, built in 1710, offers a fascinating insight into construction techniques spanning nearly three centuries, from the Acadian clay walls to modern wood paneling. Several other outstanding Georgian and Victorian structures are along or just off St. George Street. The deGannes–Cosby House, built in 1708, is thought to be the oldest wooden house in Canada. "Stroll Through the Centuries," a brochure put out by the Historical Association of Annapolis Royal, provides an interpretive walking tour of the town. During the summer months (except Sundays), the association offers regular guided tours from its headquarters at the lighthouse on Lower St. George Street.

From Annapolis Royal, Route 1 meanders along the shore of the Annapolis Basin towards Digby. (Alternatively, Highway 101 provides a faster, but less scenic, route.) At Upper Clements, the 10-hectare Upper Clements Park is popular with children. The flume ride, roller coaster and carousel are special favourites, as is the large water side. Across the highway, the Upper Clements Wildlife Park offers visitors a chance to see native Nova Scotian animals — lynxes, cougars, porcupines, foxes, groundhogs, skunks, deer and moose — along winding, wooded trails.

To the southwest, Route 1 eventually crosses Bear River into Digby County. The work of Nova Scotia artisans, many from Bear River, is showcased at Flight of Fancy on Main Street. Featured downstairs are striking bird paintings on stone, Mi'kmaq crafts, sculptured hardwood burls, pottery, weaving, jewellery, stained glass and carved birds. The upstairs gallery displays paintings, photographs and sculptures by well-known Nova Scotia artists. Bear River is stunning in autumn when the hardwood hills on either side of the river are ablaze with colour.

Back on the main drag is the community of Smiths Cove. Outstanding views of the Annapolis Basin and Digby Gut can be enjoyed from Smiths Cove. From there, it is a short drive to Digby, home of the world's largest scallop fleet. Scallops and Digby chicks (smoked herring) are served in local restaurants. From the deck of the Fundy Restaurant on Water Street, you can enjoy Digby seafood with a view of the boats that caught your meal. Golfers rave about Stanley Thompson's championship course at the Digby Pines Resort. The par-71, 18-hole course plays through mature stands of spruce and pine while affording some beautiful views of the Annapolis Basin. The hotel, built in 1929,

ACROSS THE ANNAPOLIS BASIN TO DIGBY GUT (TOP) FISHING BOATS, DIGBY (BOTTOM)

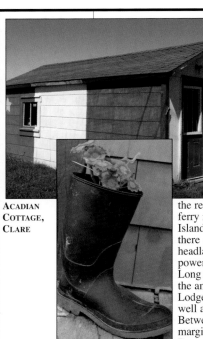

ACADIAN COTTAGE, CLARE

features a Norman-style chateau and 30 cottages strung out along a bluff that rises from the shores of the basin. There are a number of excellent inns and bed and breakfasts in the Digby area. Thistle Down Country Inn has 12 spacious room, views of the scallop fleet and a gracious dining room. Whale- and seabird-watching tours are just some of the reasons to enjoy a drive and two short ferry rides along Digby Neck to Long Island and Brier Island. Along the way there are spectacular panoramas of rocky headlands that have been carved by the powerful Fundy tides. At Tiverton on Long Island, a scenic hiking trail leads to the amazing Balancing Rock. Brier Island Lodge offers food and accommodation as well as breathtaking ocean views.

Between Digby and Yarmouth, along the margin of Baie Ste-Marie (St. Marys Bay), runs a string of Acadian villages. There is no mistaking Nova Scotia's Acadian Shore. Every few kilometres, a steeple soars from one of the magnificent Catholic churches. Colourful houses adorned with curious whirligigs and gizmos line the road at Mavillette or Grosses Coques. Yet for generations after their arrival from France, the original Acadian settlers ignored this area. Most preferred the fertile land of the Annapolis Valley.

The British paid no heed to Acadian preferences in 1755. The Acadians were deported, their houses and barns put to the torch, and the lands they had farmed for 100 years were

BRIER ISLAND, AT THE ENTRANCE TO ST. MARYS BAY

seized by the Crown. Soon after, the governor began granting these lands to new settlers, the so-called Planters, many of whom came from New England and whose loyalty he trusted.

Some Acadians managed to escape deportation. They withdrew to the forests or fled to remote corners of the province, where they lived as refugees. Many died during that first winter, while others were caught and imprisoned at Halifax, Windsor or Annapolis Royal. Still, there was a group of Acadians in Nova Scotia who somehow persevered. When the Treaty of Paris ended the war between France and England in 1763, these people began to look for a home. Others returned from exile. Sadly, the Annapolis Valley was lost to them.

Eventually, Lieutenant-Governor Michael Francklin responded to their plight. Land was surveyed along St. Marys Bay. In 1768 the Township of Clare, named after the Irish county, was created for settlement by the Acadians. The villages of St. Bernard, Belliveau Cove, Grosses Coques, Church Point and Little Brook fall within the boundaries of that original grant. As families grew and others returned from exile, Acadian settlement extended southward to Salmon River. Today, this entire stretch is part of the Municipality of Clare.

L'ÉGLISE SAINT BERNARD

Life along the shore was much different from the life the Acadians had known in the Annapolis Valley. They still kept gardens, although the soil was poorer, but the forest and the sea were irresistible forces. Acadian farmers became woodsmen, shipbuilders and fishermen — jacks of all trades. Today, their self-reliance is revealed by a drive along Route 1, sometimes called "the longest main street on earth." Family-run businesses crowd the shore. U. J. Robichaud and

WEDGEPORT ACADIAN DANCERS

L'ÉGLISE SACRE
COEUR,
SAULNIERVILLE

Sons run a lumber business at Meteghan Centre. A. F. Theriault and his sons have a shipyard at Meteghan River. Comeau and Deveau are two French names that you will frequently see. Comeau's Sea Foods in Saulnierville is a huge operation. The Deveaus have a fish operation at Belliveau Cove and an insurance business at Meteghan. Few businesses along the Acadian Shore are run by outsiders.

The Acadian Shore has long served as a centre for Acadian culture in Nova Scotia. Both in terms of size and population density, it is the largest Acadian region in the province. In villages all along Baie Ste-Marie, people gather each July to celebrate their Acadian heritage during the Festival Acadien de Clare. Festivities are fuelled by Acadian music and food. (For a special treat try rappie pie, a savoury casserole of potato and chicken, at the Cape View Restaurant, overlooking Mavillette Beach.) Mavillette, one of several wonderful beaches in the area, has 5 kilometres of magnificent shore.

In 1890, a group of Eudist priests established Collège Sainte-Anne at Church Point. Over the years, Saint-Anne, which became a university in 1977, has made enormous contributions to Acadian culture in Nova Scotia. *Évangéline*, a musical drama based on Longfellow's poem, is staged here from mid-July to mid-August. English translation is available (though not necessary to the understanding of the action) and there is one performance a week in English. The Magasin Campus (campus bookstore) has a wide selection of books on Acadian themes.

A large, fairly homogeneous Acadian population has benefited the people of the Acadian Shore in other ways. The area also has a long tradition of political representation by Acadians, both at the federal and provincial levels. And recent studies have shown that the French spoken in this part of the province has retained more 17th-century features than that spoken elsewhere in Nova Scotia.

But the most visible expressions of the cultural vitality along the shore are the beautiful churches. Acadians pride themselves on their Catholic faith, and parishioners of modest means went to great pains to demonstrate this pride. Hidden behind the graceful exteriors of these churches are surer signs of Acadian faith, workmanship and resourcefulness. Two churches — St. Mary's Church at Church Point and St. Bernard's Church at St. Bernard — should not be missed.

The plans for Sainte Marie were drawn up in France, but construction of the church was left in the skillful hands of

Leo Melanson, a master carpenter from nearby Little Brook. Between 1903 and 1905, he and many others laboured. They must have been in awe of their achievement.

Sainte Marie is the largest wooden church in North America. Its steeple rises 56 metres above the community of 318 people. It is anchored by 36 tonnes of stone ballast to keep it from blowing off in hurricane-force winds.

Other things impress. The interior of the church belies its size. A wooden floor softens the stained glass light, lending a warm and comfortable feeling to the entire nave. The "stone" pillars that support the roof are not stone. They are huge tree trunks that have been lathed and covered in plaster. Overhead, the "marble" arches are wooden as well.

The parishioners of St. Bernard were not to be outdone. They hired an architect from Moncton, New Brunswick, who had visited France. He sent down the plans, but the work was left to locals. Between 1910 and 1942, they built a huge stone church that seats over 1,000.

Visitors to the Acadian Shore will receive a warm welcome in French or English. All but a handful of the Acadian population speak both languages. However, it is through French, like their magnificent churches, that the Acadians of Clare express pride in their culture.

The Evangeline Trail continues on to Yarmouth.

SAINTE MARIE, CHURCH POINT

GLOOSCAP TRAIL

UNUSUAL ROCK FORMATIONS AT CAPE D'OR

SPRINGHILL MINERS' MUSEUM

Spectacular views of the Bay of Fundy, where the world's highest tides twice daily move 115 billion tonnes of water, await the visitor to the Glooscap Trail. Named for the mythic cultural hero of the Mi'kmaq and other northeastern Native tribes, the Glooscap Trail starts at Amherst, the border point with New Brunswick, and follows the shores of the Bay of Fundy to Windsor.

Along the shores of Cobequid Bay, the tide can rise 2.5 centimetres in a minute, and in some areas the difference between low and high tide has been recorded at 16 metres. The explanation for these extreme tides lies in the bay's funnel shape, which serves as an amplifier. The bulge of water that floods up the Fundy is less than a metre high at the edge of the continental shelf, but at its mouth it meets a slow-moving wave that continually sloshes up and down the bay. This wave, reinforced and pushed by the tide, moves up the bay, where it is squeezed by the rising ocean bottom and the narrowing Fundy shores.

This action produces some dramatic effects. Tidal bores

occur when a wave of water moves upstream and collides with the current, making it appear as though rivers are flowing backwards. Depending on the phase of the moon and other factors such as wind direction, the tidal bore can be either a barely detectable ripple or a wall of water a metre high. Tidal bores can be viewed along a number of rivers in the upper Fundy region, including the Salmon River near Truro; the Shubenacadie River at various locations, including South

Maitland Village Park where an observation deck has been built on the remains of an old railway bridge; and from the Maccan and River Hebert bridges. Several companies offer upriver rafting trips on the Shubenacadie. These are safe, but can be very exciting, as the small craft go downriver, then return on the crest of the incoming tide.

Join the Glooscap Trail at Amherst, where the shells of old factories and some truly grand homes, especially along Victoria Street, stand as evidence of past industrial glory. Some of these grand old homes are now bed and breakfasts; the Regent B&B is notable. The Cumberland County Museum tells some of Amherst's industrial and labour history. Amherst was one of the towns able to take advantage of the steam-based technologies that fueled the new industrialism of the 19th century. Amherst boomed, as textile milling, boot and shoe manufacturing, gas-boiler production and railway car construction drew hundreds of people to the town. The Amherst area is a bird-watcher's paradise. The Amherst Marsh, part of the Tantramar Marsh, is an important breeding site for over 100 species and migratory bird stopover. At Amherst Point, just south of town, there is a migratory bird sanctuary.

There is a choice of routes from Amherst to Parrsboro. One can either follow Route 302, the Fundy Shore Scenic Drive, along a sparsely populated section of the Fundy Shore, or Highway 2, to enjoy a stop at Springhill, which remembers the bustle and tragedy of its coal mining history and celebrates the success of its contribution to the continent's entertainment industry. Over the years, more than 400 people have died in local mines. The "Springhill Bump" of 1958, remembered more for the miraculous survival of 18 men who spent a week trapped underground than for the 75 who did not make it, brought an end to large-scale mining in the town. But it did not bring an end to tragedy. In 1975, fire ravaged the town's main street business district. Today, retired miners give underground tours at the Springhill Miners' Museum, where exhibits include poignant accounts of the mining accidents. The museum is built on the site of a small mine that closed in 1970.

ANNE MURRAY
CENTRE

The Anne Murray Centre pays tribute to the Springhill-born recording artist and offers a surprisingly candid look at her life — including report cards and baby pictures. Fans of "Canada's Country Sweetheart" should definitely drop in. Those who choose to take the Fundy Shore Scenic Drive following Route 302 to Apple River will see a part of the province that has long been recognized as a treasure trove of fossils. The Fossil Centre at Joggins, an old coal mining town on Chignecto Bay, offers guided tours of the famous fossil cliffs. Fossil finds, usually plant material, date from the time when Nova Scotia's vast coal deposits were formed about 300 million years ago. The cliffs themselves are off-limits, but they erode so quickly that new fossils are always falling to the beach. As you search the beach beneath the cliffs, take an

OTTAWA HOUSE,
PARRSBORO

occasional peek behind you; you will be surprised to see how quickly the tide is falling — or rising! At Apple River, continue on Route 209, passing Cape Chignecto Provincial Park, Nova Scotia's newest and largest provincial park — 4,000 hectares of coastal wilderness trails, dramatic cliffs and old-growth forest. This is Nova Scotia's premier hiking destination. There is a picnic area overlooking the Bay of Fundy. A new day park offers short hikes and views of the famous "Three Sisters" rock formation. The Bay of Fundy, like most large bodies of water, has its share of marine folklore, and one of these stories, the saga of the *Mary Celeste*, is recounted on a cairn at Spencers Island where the "ghost ship" was built. In December 1872, the brigantine was discovered at sea with sails set and everything in order but no one was on board. It would turn out to be one of the great sea mysteries of all time. More seafaring history of the area can be found at the Age of Sail Centre in nearby Port Greville. The Old Shipyard Campground, along the beach at Spencers Island, is the base for sea-kayaking tours around the bay.

AGE OF SAIL
HERITAGE CENTRE,
PORT GREVILLE

Along the stretch of coastline between Advocate and Parrsboro, the scenery rivals the coastal views along Cape Breton's Cabot Trail. Across the Minas Channel, Cape Split

and North Mountain loom large on a clear day, and Cape d'Or is just as spectacular. There is a look-off at the Cape d'Or lighthouse (just off Route 209) with an unforgettable view — east toward the Minas Basin, south across the Minas Channel and west to the Bay of Fundy.

In Parrsboro, the Fundy Geological Museum houses a display on the effects the giant Fundy tides have had on the people and the land. Museum exhibits also detail the geological and fossil history of the area.

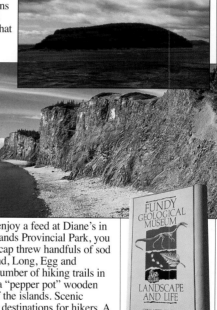

Good opportunities for rockhounding are plentiful in the Parrsboro area. The town holds Nova Scotia's Gem and Mineral Show each August. Zeolites — semi-precious stones such as agate and amethyst — are common finds along the beaches and cliffs of the Minas Basin. Eldon George, Parrsboro's most famous rockhound, has a rock shop at the edge of town. In April 1984, George found a rock with some very tiny — and soon to be highly celebrated — dinosaur footprints on its surface.

DINOSAUR, FUNDY GEOLOGICAL MUSEUM

FIVE ISLANDS PROVINCIAL PARK

Parrsboro's Ship's Company Theatre stages innovative productions at a theatre built around the original MV *Kipawo*, a beached ferry boat that once serviced Parrsboro, Kingsport and Wolfville. The acclaimed company features many plays by Maritime writers during a season that runs from mid-June to Labour Day. Gillespie House Inn is one of several good B&Bs in Parrsboro.

The road from Parrsboro to the Trans-Canada Highway at Glenholme offers an opportunity to visit several quaint and historic hamlets such as Economy, Bass River, Portapique and Great Village. This shore is clam country. Try your hand at digging some or enjoy a feed at Diane's in Five Islands. If you stop at Five Islands Provincial Park, you can see where the legendary Glooscap threw handfuls of sod at Beaver, creating Moose, Diamond, Long, Egg and Pinnacle islands. There are also a number of hiking trails in the park. Five Islands Lighthouse, a "pepper pot" wooden structure, also has a terrific view of the islands. Scenic waterfalls in the region are popular destinations for hikers. A novel opportunity to observe the evolution of nature can be enjoyed at Economy Falls, where a major rock fall changed the appearance of that popular attraction in late 1997. For

WENTWORTH FALLS

enjoying a respite from town life, the cottages at Four Seasons Retreat near Economy are ideal.

Truro is the commercial crossroad in the centre of the province and is known as "the Hub of Nova Scotia." Truro is a good stopping place. You won't miss the 13-metre-tall statue of Glooscap at Exit 13A off Highway 102. It marks the entrance to the Glooscap Heritage Centre where Mi'kmaq culture is interpreted through exhibits, displays and a multi-media presentation. Truro has

RAFTING ON THE SHUBENACADIE RIVER

many shops, restaurants and accommodations. It is also a hub for golf, with several good courses in the area, including the Truro Golf Club, the oldest club in the province. Victoria Park is a surprising 405-hectare oasis in the middle of town with shaded walking trails, waterfalls and Jacob's Ladder — about 200 wooden steps that are a challenge for even the fittest legs. From Truro, there is the option of heading towards Halifax or continuing along the Fundy Shore to Maitland. Route 2 towards Halifax passes Stewiacke where the pastoral 18-hole Fox Hollow golf course provides tee times for visitors. A bit further along Route 2 is the Shubenacadie Wildlife Park, where most of Nova Scotia's native birds and animals can be seen in natural surroundings. An impressive recent addition to the park is a marsh and wetland interpretative centre.

The village of Maitland, located at the mouth of the Shubenacadie River, flourished during the Age of Sail. At one time, 11 shipyards bordered an 11-kilometre stretch of shore near Maitland. Fortunes were made and lavish homes were built. Close to 50 of these have survived, prompting the provincial government to designate Maitland as Nova Scotia's first Heritage Conservation District. A walking tour brochure is available at the local visitor information centre. A former shipbuilder's home, Cresthaven by the Sea Inn is a good base from which to explore the Bay of Fundy. The Frieze and Roy General Store, established in 1839, is the oldest continuously operating store of its kind in Canada. It offers everything from fishing gear to crafts.

On October 27, 1874, more than 4,000 people gathered in Maitland to see the launching of the *William D Lawrence*, the largest full-rigged ship ever built in Canada, and named after the man who built it. The village commemorates the event with a Launch Day Festival in September. The *William D Lawrence* was nearly 2,500 tonnes and turned a handsome profit for her owners. At Lawrence House, designated a National Historic Site in 1965, the signs of wealth are everywhere. English iron-work radiators are topped with Italian marble. At the back of the house, you can see the huge blocks that were used to step the masts of Lawrence's ships. Not surprisingly, William Lawrence, elected to the Nova Scotia Assembly in 1863, strongly opposed Confederation, and fought for the repeal of the Union Act. The Intercolonial Railway, the linchpin of Confederation and a symbol of future prosperity, would not run through Maitland.

MINAS BASIN AT WALTON

Continuing west from Maitland, along coastal Route 215 toward Windsor, one soon begins enjoying the scenic Noel Shore, one of the prettiest spots in the province when the horse chestnuts are in bloom in late June. At Burncoat Head, during the Saxby Tide in 1869, the highest tides in the world were recorded. Gale-force winds helped generate a high tide of 16.5 metres.

SUNRISE TRAIL

The Sunrise Trail follows the North Shore from Amherst to the Canso Causeway. With its picturesque towns, gentle farmland and seaside views, this route is a recommended alternative to the Trans-Canada Highway. Several fine beaches and the warm waters of the Northumberland Strait help make it a popular summer holiday destination.

From Amherst, Route 366 takes you to Tidnish, a less-travelled provincial gateway where the visitor information centre displays information on the Chignecto Ship Railway, the ambitious 19th-century venture that was to transport ships from the Bay of Fundy to the Northumberland Strait by rail. A 4-kilometre walking trail follows the remnants of the railbed to Tidnish Dock Provincial Park.

Not much farther, near Lorneville, is the Amherst Shore Country Inn. The inn offers four rooms and four suites, as well as a rustic seaside cottage and memorable

SEAGULL PEWTER, PUGWASH

dining. In Port Howe, Chase's Lobster Pound offers fresh live and cooked lobsters. Pugwash, with street signs in both Gaelic and English, is one of several North Shore communities with a rich Scottish heritage. The village holds a Gathering of the Clans Festival in early July.

During the 1950s and 60s, wealthy Cleveland industrialist Cyrus Eaton hosted a number of Thinkers Conferences at his Pugwash estate, to which he invited Western and Soviet intellectuals. Albert Einstein was among the attendees.

Today, Pugwash is home to Seagull Pewter, Canada's largest manufacturer of pewter giftware, who ship to worldwide markets. Seagull Pewter has a large retail shop on the main road. Just outside town, serious golfers can enjoy 18 challenging holes on the Northumberland Links. The open, tree-lined fairways are well-maintained. Several holes play along the water, and the views of the strait can be quite a distraction.

The views are just as striking at the Sunrise Beach Golf & Country Club, overlooking Brule Harbour near Tatamagouche. But unlike the Pugwash course, this wide-

open, nine-hole round of golf is well suited to beginners. In addition to a modest fishery, Tatamagouche is a service centre for local dairy farms. Appropriately, Highland cattle are beginning to catch on in the area as well. And the favourable climate sustains some other, more exotic enterprises. The Josts, one of several German families to settle along the North Shore since the Second World War, have a winemaking operation in nearby Malagash. Tours of the vineyards are provided and visitors are invited to sample Jost wines at the on-site retail store. Good-quality, inexpensive wines, including some award-winning ones, are available for purchase. There are excellent housekeeping cottages with all amenities and a private beach at Malagash and, for railway buffs, the Train Station Inn at Tatamagouche is a treat.

Farther along, two restored mills give a glimpse of earlier times. The Balmoral Grist Mill Museum, at Balmoral Mills (Route 256), grinds wheat, oats and buckwheat into flour using 19th-century milling techniques. The Sutherland Steam Mill, in nearby Denmark (Route 326), began sawing logs into lumber in 1894 and is now part of the Nova Scotia Museum; visitors can find out how it was done. On Route 311 between Balmoral Mills and Denmark is Earltown and Sugar Moon Farm, a year-round maple sugar camp and pancake house. On the way to Earltown, you may see Nova Scotia's first herd of buffalo grazing by the roadside.

The Northumberland Strait is a choice area for the lobster fishery. The season runs from early May to late June, when communities like River John bustle. The village holds frequent lobster suppers during the season, and visitors are invited to take part. The Lismore Sheep Farm and Wool Shop is a working sheep farm where you can see some sheep and learn about wool. You can also buy wonderful wool and sheepskin items from comforters to slippers.

BALMORAL GRIST MILL

The good beaches — such as the one at Caribou, northwest of Pictou — attract cottagers to this shoreline. For a shorter stay, you might choose the Pictou Lodge Resort on Braeshore Road, just east of the town of Pictou and 4 kilometres from the Prince Edward Island ferry. Built in the mid-1920s as an exclusive retreat, the lodge was originally managed by the Canadian National Railway. Its log construction is typical of many CNR resorts, including the Jasper Park Lodge in the Canadian Rockies. The cabins include several dating from the 1920s, plus many more modern units. Ocean views can be spectacular, especially at sunset from the sunporch bar. If you're lucky enough to be there in July you might catch the Kites & Kayaks festival.

Pictou's Scottish culture, scenic harbour and fine architecture make it the North Shore's most popular destination for visitors. And for those Nova Scotians who take great pride in their Scottish heritage, Pictou is a kind of Plymouth Rock. The *Hector*, which landed Nova Scotia's first Scots on the shores of Pictou Harbour in 1773, has been called the "Scottish Mayflower." For a Nova Scotia Scot, having ancestors aboard the *Hector* accords special status.

Today, the showpiece of Pictou's waterfront is the ship *Hector*, at the Hector Heritage Quay. The 33-metre-long full-rigged ship was reconstructed on-site and is now a floating heritage exhibit. Although no plans of the original *Hector* exist, engineers went to some trouble to ensure that the reconstructed ship closely resembled its predecessor. The saga of 18th-century Scottish immigration and the *Hector* voyage is told in the adjacent interpretation centre. The site also includes a carpentry shop, a blacksmith shop and a gift shop, and nearby a pub for a wee dram.

FIDDLER, HECTOR FESTIVAL

During August, the Hector Festival celebrates the arrival of the ship and the town's Scottish heritage, and features Scottish music, dance and food, with Celtic musical performances at the deCoste Centre on Water Street. This venue also serves as northeastern Nova Scotia's centre for the performing arts throughout the year. New Scotland Days, held in September on the anniversary of the arrival of the *Hector*, features lots of bagpipes, highland dancing and wooden boat-building demonstrations.

Next to the Hector National Exhibit Centre, on Old Haliburton Road, is the restored McCulloch House (now a museum) which was built in 1806 with bricks brought over from Scotland.

Pictou's architecture is another Scottish legacy. Throughout the town you can see 19th-century neoclassical buildings, mostly of stone. Typically, these have gabled walls that extend above the plane of the roof at either end of the house. The Scottish dormer, recognizable by its bay window, is another prominent feature. Fine trim and mouldings lend elegance to houses that would otherwise appear stark. Some Pictou streets, especially those with row houses, could easily run through towns in western Scotland. Walking tours of the town are available Sunday mornings throughout the summer.

The tourist bureau, located at the rotary just outside town, can direct you to to the town's historic buildings. Several are open to visitors. The Consulate Inn (c. 1810), so named because it housed the American Consulate during the last half of the 19th century, offers bed and breakfast–style accommodation in the downtown area. The Customs House Inn has carefully restored rooms in an 1870s brick and sandstone building that also houses a pub. The Braeside Inn, though built this century, also impresses from its hilltop perch overlooking the harbour. The inn offers fine harbour views from its two large dining rooms (seafood is a specialty) and from several of its 20 guest rooms.

Pictou's architecture and landscape also reflect its historic importance as a shipbuilding centre. Visitors who arrive on the right day may still see a large vessel in dry-dock at the shipyard. The lobster fishery also makes this a working harbour. Here, and in countless other villages along the strait, fishermen spend May and June mornings setting and unloading traps. Since 1934, the town has celebrated this fishery with the Pictou Lobster Carnival, held in early July. Local boat races, a lobster dinner and concerts featuring the best of Nova Scotia's musical talent highlight the festival.

While in town, you can also visit Grohmann Knives, known to outdoor enthusiasts as the manufacturer of the world-renowned D. H. Russell belt knife. Grohmann offers free factory tours (some restrictions apply), and the gift shop often has good buys on seconds. Nearby gift shops and galleries offer a range of crafts from local artisans.

The Pictou Golf Club, overlooking the harbour, is a fairly easy nine-hole course despite all the downhill, uphill, and sidehill lies that you'll encounter. The Jitney Trail, spanning the southern portion of Pictou Harbour, is a scenic 3-kilometre pathway connecting the waterfront to the original landing site of the *Hector*.

Melmerby is the most popular of several good warm-water beaches in the Pictou area. Take Exit 25 off Highway 104 (the Trans-Canada) to get to this 2-kilometre stretch of broad, sandy beach. Melmerby is supervised and offers a canteen, shower and change facilities.

Most of the area's heavy industry sprang up in the towns across the harbour, to the southeast of Pictou. Coal mining transformed the landscapes of Westville and Stellarton. Canada's first integrated metalmaking and metalworking complex did the same to New Glasgow and Trenton. These towns, with their long history of industrial activity, have fascinating stories to tell, including the 1992 disaster at the Westray coal mine.

There was nothing exceptional in the rise of the Pictou County coal industry; similar growth was taking place in Cape Breton and Cumberland County. It was the metals industry that relied heavily on the entrepreneurial spirit of the Pictou County elite. When shipbuilding became unprofitable in the 1880s, New Glasgow's wealthy merchant families began looking for somewhere else to put their money. What they founded — the Nova Scotia Steel and Coal Company — changed Pictou County. The populations of New Glasgow and Trenton exploded as people came to work in one of the country's foremost industrial enterprises. During the First World War, "Scotia" employed close to 6,000 miners and steelworkers. Many other Pictou County operations were busy converting Scotia's steel into a wide range of secondary metal products.

But Scotia's story is a familiar one. During the 1920s, increased freight rates, competition from central Canada, and outside ownership led to a rapid decline. Pictou County industry has been teetering on the brink ever since. There were, however, some hardy survivors. Maritime Steel and Foundries Limited marked its 100th anniversary in 2002. Maritime Steel produces steel castings that are exported around the world. The story of industrial boom and bust is told at the Nova Scotia Museum of Industry, just off the Trans-Canada Highway at Stellarton. Exhibits include two of the world's oldest steam locomotives. Children, especially, enjoy working on the museum's toy train assembly line. Stellarton is also where the Sobey grocery giant was born, and today is the home of the corporate office of what is now the second largest grocery retailer in Canada.

MUSEUM OF INDUSTRY IN STELLARTON

The community that was to become New Glasgow was settled by Scots in 1784, and by 1809 the town had been named after Glasgow in Scotland and then officially incorporated in 1875. Enterprise and the entrepreneurial spirit were evident even in 1809, when James William Carmichael and George Amos established a trading post. New Glasgow is still true to its roots and, today, is the commercial and service centre for northern Nova Scotia.

The Festival of the Tartans, a celebration of Scottish music and heritage, is held here annually in mid-July. In early August the New Glasgow Riverfront Jubilee features East Coast and Canadian musical talent . Later in August, there is the new Race on the River, the Pictou County Dragon Boat Festival. New Glasgow's Abercrombie Country Club is a challenging 18-hole course that punishes wayward tee shots. It is essential to book tee-times in advance. More golf is within 10 minutes of New Glasgow at Glen Lovat and Linacy Greens.

Antigonish, along the eastern section of the North Shore, is home to St. Francis Xavier University and the Antigonish Highland Games. The games, held in mid-July, include piping, Highland dancing, heavy events and track and field, making for one of Nova Scotia's best Scottish festivals. Festival Antigonish presents live professional theatre in the 227-seat Bauer Theatre on the St. FX campus throughout the summer months. Within walking distance of the campus is the elegant Antigonish Victorian Inn. The Antigonish Golf Club is the North Shore's best 18-hole bet for spur-of-the-moment golf. It is rarely crowded on summer weekdays and provides a stiff test, playing 6,100 yards from the men's tees.

AT THE ANTIGONISH HIGHLAND GAMES

If you have time to dawdle, take Route 337 north from Antigonish along the western shore of St. Georges Bay. Like many of the roads along the North Shore, this drive takes you off the beaten track. The views from the Cape George Lighthouse grounds are beautiful, and there are more scenic look-offs, good beaches for birdwatching and hiking trails along the way.

MARINE DRIVE

The Eastern Shore, which extends along the Atlantic coast between Halifax and Canso, is rugged and relatively undeveloped. A vast network of wilderness lakes and rivers makes the area a favourite with canoeists and campers, hikers and bird watchers. Coastal kayaking is also popular, especially in the area around Tangier. Outdoor enthusiasts can explore the beaches, harbours and islands or the inland forests, lakes and rivers. Several good museums interpret the fishing, lumbering and gold-mining history of this coast.

But to those who choose the Eastern Shore's Marine Drive as an alternative to the Trans-Canada Highway for the trip from Halifax to Cape Breton, take heed. You will find some spectacular coastal scenery, but the 400-kilometre drive along winding roads is best spread over two days.

Lawrencetown Beach is just east of

SHERBROOKE
VILLAGE

Dartmouth. A provincial park, this steep, sandy beach is supervised and has change and canteen facilities. Lawrencetown is relatively exposed, and large waves make it a favourite with Nova Scotia surfers and windsurfers.

Farther along, to the south of Musquodoboit Harbour, is Martinique Beach (the name is tropical, but the crystal-clear water is not). Because of its distance from Halifax, on some summer days you will have this 5-kilometre-long stretch to yourself. The fine sand hardens at the waterline, making Martinique ideal for long walks. Nearby, the Martinique Beach Game Sanctuary is the northernmost wintering ground of the Canada goose. The Salmon River House Country Inn, at Salmon River Bridge, offers six well-appointed guest rooms in an area where accommodations are scarce. On-site outdoor activities include hiking, boating, hunting and fishing. The Fisherman's Life Museum, in

MARTINIQUE (TOP) FISHERMAN'S LIFE MUSEUM (INSETS)

neighbouring Jeddore Oyster Pond, recalls the lives of a turn-of-the-century inshore fisherman, his wife and their 13 daughters. The museum's costumed interpreters are local people who have some wonderful stories to tell.

At Lake Charlotte, the recently developed Memory Lane Heritage Village recalls the more recent past — rural Nova Scotia in the 40s, with bicycles and a 1949 truck for touring the site.

Clam Harbour Beach comes next. Its fine, white sand is ideal for sandcastles. In mid-August, thousands come here for the Clam Harbour Beach Sandcastle and Sculpture Contest, with group and individual competitions for young and old. Some of the sculptures are extremely intricate. On Route 224 toward Middle Musquodoboit is the Moose River Gold Mines and Area Museum, which describes gold mining history and the famous mine disaster of 1936.

Highway 7 continues east through Tangier on its way towards Sherbrooke Village. Tangier is home to Willy Krauch's Danish Smokehouse. Open year-round, Krauch's wood-smoked salmon, eel and mackerel have won customers from around the world. Tangier is *the* centre for sea kayaking. Sea birds, seals and wrecks can be seen from its many inlets and islands. Lessons, rentals and tours can be arranged here.

Farther along Highway 7, on a peninsula that juts into

the Atlantic, is Taylor Head Provincial Park, where there are a number of boardwalks and trails. Both the beach and the views of the ocean are spectacular.

TAYLOR HEAD PROVINCIAL PARK

Sherbrooke Village has been restored to appear as it was during the last half of the 19th century. Area residents work at the village dressed in period costumes and take pride in its history. The result is a low-key living museum, where the past rubs shoulders comfortably with the present.

This area along the banks of the St. Marys River has attracted many people over the centuries. The Mi'kmaq were drawn by the large runs of salmon in the river, as were New England fishermen. In 1755, the French established a fur trading post here (Fort Sainte Marie), where they traded with the Mi'kmaq, fished and cultivated the soil until they were driven out by an English force in 1769.

Around 1800, about 50 settlers from the Truro and Pictou areas moved cross-country to establish new homes. The new arrivals took advantage of the area's most valuable resource, timber, and sawmills began producing lumber for small shipbuilding operations. Sherbrooke, so named in 1815 after Sir John Coape Sherbrooke, Lieutenant-Governor of Nova Scotia, exported timber to Great Britain in locally built ships. Families like the Cummingers and the MacDonalds were involved in both ends of the operation, and grew quite wealthy. During the 1860s and 70s, their shipyards turned out several barques in excess of 500 tons for the carrying trade, as well as many smaller boats for the fishery.

SHERBROOKE VILLAGE

The contributions of these families feature prominently in the restored village. The general store was operated by the Cumminger brothers, Samuel and John. You need only look at the store's elaborate counters to gain some appreciation of their wealth and the woodworking skills associated with shipbuilding. Superior craftsmanship is also apparent at Greenwood Cottage, built by John and Sarah Cumminger in 1871.

The reconstruction of the MacDonald Brothers' water-powered, up-and-down sawmill is located a few minutes away from the main village, and it is wonderful. You can feel the power of the water wheel and see it in the rise and fall of the huge saw blade. All the workings — great belts and pulleys — are exposed. There is much more. Sherbrooke Village has a blacksmith shop, which has operated continuously since it was built in 1870. The Sherbrooke Drug Store was given most of its stock by the Nova Scotia Pharmaceutical Society and has a wonderful display of turn-of-the-century medicines. Among the many other buildings on-site are a Temperance Hall, a boat-building shop, a village potter, a Presbyterian church and a courthouse. Tea and more substantial meals are served at the What Cheer Tea Room.

SHERBROOKE VILLAGE RECAPTURES LATE-19TH-CENTURY LIFE

There is another smokehouse in St. Marys River near Sherbrooke Village.

The provincially run Liscombe Lodge, at nearby Liscomb Mills (about 20 minutes from Sherbrooke Village), offers first-rate accommodation in the lodge or cottages and chalets in peaceful riverside surroundings with beautiful walking trails.

The lighthouse at Port Bickerton, which protected the region's seafaring folk since the 1920s, has been refurbished to its original decor, and has been re-opened as the Nova Scotia Lighthouse Interpretive Centre. Inside, interpretive panels show the history behind the 166 lights that dot Nova Scotia's coastline. Visitors can also find detailed information on the Sable Island and Sambro lighthouses, along with local history concerning the 16 lights in Guysborough County. Stepping from old to new, there is a CD-ROM in English and German, detailing all of the Guysborough County lights. A new trail leads from the lighthouse to a beautiful sandy beach.

LIGHTHOUSE AT PORT BICKERTON

Country Harbour is crossed by a ferry that makes regular crossings year-round. Along this wild and rugged stretch of coastline from Isaac's Harbour to Canso are several interesting little communities that provide shelter and necessaries. If you want to stop along the way and savour the sea for a while, there are secluded housekeeping bungalows at New Harbour and an inn with all the amenities and fine dining at Charlos Cove.

GRASSY ISLAND

Near the end of a peninsula that juts far out into the Atlantic is the fishing village of Canso, one of Nova Scotia's oldest communities. It was the rugged and beautiful nature of this area that inspired some of the most memorable songs of Stan Rogers. His music and his place in local folklore are celebrated at the Stan Rogers Folk Festival in early July. Offshore, Grassy Island is the site of a once-prosperous community of New England fishermen and merchants until 1744, when the fishing station was sacked by a French force from Louisbourg.

The Canso Islands National Historic Site visitor centre tells the story through a brief audiovisual presentation and a series of life-size exhibits detailing the interiors of three Grassy Island properties — a tavern, a merchant's house and the home of a military officer. Between June and September, a daily boat service takes visitors to the island, where an interpretive trail links eight designated sites.

In Canso, the widow's walk at Whitman House, home of the Canso Museum, offers a splendid view.

Route 16 along the edge of Chedabucto Bay takes you to the old town of Guysborough. Along the way you will pass the Queensport lighthouse. Whales can sometimes be spotted from the road. At Guysborough you will find luxury accommodation at the gracious DesBarres Manor Inn, good food and ale at The Rare Bird, a lively waterfront brew pub, a snug harbour with full-service marina and a delightful gallery, Skipping Stone, showcasing Nova Scotia artists and craft. At Boylston you can either continue on Route 16, a faster inland route to Trans-Canada Highway 104, or complete the Marine Drive on Route 344 that hugs the scenic coast until Auld's Cove and the Canso Causeway to Cape Breton.

CABOT TRAIL

BUCK'S COVE

THE CABOT TRAIL,
ONE OF THE WORLD'S
SPECTACULAR DRIVES

It is a rare thing for a road to become more famous than any of the places it passes through, but that is what has happened with Cape Breton's Cabot Trail. Its hairpin turns and spectacular cliff-side views have been thrilling motorists since the 1930s.

If we take A. S. MacMillan (Minister of Highways during the 1920s) at his word, the decision to undertake the costly and ambitious construction of the Cabot Trail was, quite literally, the result of one man's dream. In August 1924, MacMillan went to Cheticamp to look into the possibility of building a road that would extend northward to the community of Pleasant Bay and beyond. Apparently, the trip along the northwestern shore of Cape Breton left quite an impression on the minister. He recalls, in a 1952

document reproduced in the June 1992 issue of *Cape Breton's Magazine*, what took place upon his return to Baddeck: "Some time near morning I fell asleep and dreamed about a wonderful development that I could see underway, numerous houses, cottages and tourist homes in the many bays and inlets as well as sail boats and all kinds of pleasure craft, apparently everybody enjoying themselves."

MacMillan was inspired and the rest, as he would have wanted it, is history. Today, the 300-kilometre Cabot Trail, named for the famous explorer who reputedly landed on the shores of Aspy Bay in June 1497, is a loop that takes you along most of the coastline of northwestern Cape Breton. Contrary to MacMillan's vision, much of that coastline remains undeveloped. This, however, is a good thing. Cape Breton has been named the most scenic island in North America and fourth in

Meat Cove
Bay St. Lawrence
Dingwall
Cape North
Smelt Brook
New Haven
Pleasant Bay
Neils Harbour

N   0   10   20
km

Cabot Trail
Cheticamp
Ingonish
Wreck Cove

Margaree Harbour
Indian Brook
North East
Margaree   Tarbotvale
Englishtown
Goose Cove
St Anns
North Sydney
Sydney Mines
162
Sydney
Broad Cove
Margaree Forks
Inverness
Baddeck
223
125
255
West Lake Ainslie
Mabou
Nyanza
Shunacadie
327
Port Hood
Whycocomagh
Iona
Eskasoni
Bras d'Or Lake
Big Pond
Ceilidh Trail
19
Orangedale
4
Judique
105
Marble Mountain
Roberta
Craigmore
Dundee
St. Peters
Fourchu
104
Port Hastings
4
104
River Bourgeois
247
Ardoise
Fleur-de-lis Trail
Port Hawkesbury
206
D'Escousse
316
344
Arichat
Petit-de-Gras
Atlantic Ocean

the world. Its unspoiled natural beauty has earned it a rating as the second-best sustainable tourism destination in the world. It is also renowned for the friendliness of its people. The Cabot Trail has become not just a scenic drive but a year-round destination offering the best in adventure tourism: golf, hiking, sea kayaking, sailing, skiing and beaches — not to mention the stunning scenery. Outdoor adventurers will want to take most of their vacation to explore the beautiful wilderness areas in Cape Breton Highlands National Park. For the not-so-adventurous the scenery is stunning, and accommodations and dining are as good as you'll get anywhere.

Baddeck is generally considered to be the beginning and end of the Cabot Trail. However, the village was attracting summer visitors long before it earned this distinction. In 1879, Charles Dudley Warner's *Baddeck, and That Sort of Thing* was published. Though not very popular with Cape Bretoners — they were mockingly portrayed as backward and primitive for their tepees and Gaelic speech — the book's description of Baddeck's splendid isolation struck a chord with many American readers. Among those was the inventor of the telephone, Alexander Graham Bell. Seeking refuge from the hot summers of Washington, DC, Bell and his wife, Mabel, decided to stop in at Baddeck on their way to Newfoundland for a holiday in 1885. They fell in love with the place. Eight years later, they built their estate, Beinn Bhreagh (Beautiful Mountain) on a headland overlooking the Bras d'Or Lakes. There, Alexander and Mabel spent many happy summers, until his death in 1922. Their gravesites can be found on the hillside next to Beinn Bhreagh.

ALEXANDER GRAHAM BELL NATIONAL HISTORIC SITE, BADDECK

Today, the Alexander Graham Bell National Historic Site, Nova Scotia's finest indoor museum, offers visitors to Baddeck a chance to learn a great deal about the inventor's life. The site's collection of Bell's artifacts, written materials and personal mementoes is the most comprehensive in the world. The exhibits give a thorough

HYDROFOIL HALL AT THE BELL MUSEUM

and intimate account of Bell's life.

Bell was a compulsive inventor. He may have left the Washington heat behind, but Bell brought his passion for invention and experimentation to his summer home. Among his lesser-known efforts were attempts to develop a multi-nippled sheep for Cape Breton farmers, and a device that would relieve the plight of Banks fishermen by converting fog into drinking water. During his last years, the hydrofoil was Bell's special interest. Several models were built and tested in Baddeck, and a full-sized hydrofoil is housed in the museum.

Baddeck's status as a resort and tourist centre has grown since the Bell era. The friendly bustle of the village makes it a popular stopping place for visitors. Baddeck has a population of approximately 1,000 and about an equivalent number of guest rooms; even so, it is advisable to book early. The Inverary Inn Resort has 125 rooms in five main buildings along with 7 cottages. This full-service resort offers a conference centre, tennis, an indoor pool, canoes, kayaks, bikes and boat cruises and a host of other activities. MacNeil House, on the grounds of the Silver Dart Lodge, has six luxurious suites with jacuzzis, fireplaces and kitchen facilities. Other amenities include live entertainment in the dining room overlooking the Bras d'Or, bicycles for the use of guests, and a lakeside beach. For those who prefer quieter surroundings, the Duffus House Inn (c. 1830) features antique furnishings and English gardens in a waterside setting. Auberge Gisele's Inn, Broadwater Inn and Lynwood Country Inn also offer fine accommodations, with many rooms overlooking the Bras d'Or Lakes. Just before Baddeck at Bucklaw, Castle Moffatt will treat you like royalty.

Baddeck's shops carry a variety of upscale handcrafts and folk art. Fine wool sweaters are sold at Seawinds Chandlery, on the government wharf. Up from the water, Kidston Landing features a wide selection of Nova Scotian crafts, woolens and country clothing. Blue Heron Gifts offers a wide selection of Nova Scotian and Cape Breton books and CDs. The Outdoor Store sells quality outdoor clothing and camping supplies; it's a worthwhile stop for those who plan to spend time in the wilderness areas of Cape Breton Highlands National Park.

Baddeck is full of summertime activity. Since 1904, Baddeck has held its annual regatta in early August. Throughout the summer months, yachts are berthed at the government wharf or at private anchorages along the shores of Baddeck Bay. You can go for a sail on the *Amoeba* at the government wharf. Spectacular views and great golf are to be enjoyed at the Thomas McBroom–designed Bell Bay Golf Course.

BADDECK

Some distance inland, near Baddeck Bridge, is Uisge Bahn Falls Provincial Park, one of the prettiest spots in all of Cape Breton. A network of maintained hiking trails leads through hardwood forest to a dramatic gorge and waterfalls. This is a great place for a picnic. (All the fixings for a delicious lunch are available at the Highwheeler Café in Baddeck or the Herring Choker Deli & Bakery, a kilometre west of the Cabot Trail entrance at Nyanza.)

When leaving the Baddeck area, you have a choice. You can head for Hunters Mountain and the Margaree Valley, which would take you in a clockwise direction around the Cabot Trail, or you can take the counter-clockwise route along the shores of St. Anns Bay and north to Ingonish.

The clockwise route takes you away from the salt water and through the beautiful Margaree Valley. The Margaree is a Canadian Heritage River. Anglers should not pass it by, especially during August and September. Guides are available for salmon and backwater trout fishing. The Margaree Salmon Museum, near North East Margaree, is one of the best privately-run museums in Nova Scotia. If you plan on fishing the river, you should drop in for sure. Fly fishermen will have heard of John Cosseboom; the Cosseboom fly has fooled many Atlantic salmon. Cosseboom was an ardent disciple of Izaak Walton (*The Compleat Angler*) and spent many summers on the Margaree. His is one of several stories well-told by the museum's wonderful collection of fishing memorabilia.

BEINN BHREAGH, WHERE BELL'S DESCENDANTS SPEND THEIR SUMMERS

Nearby, along the mysteriously named Egypt Road, is the Normaway Inn, which has catered to anglers and others since the 1920s. The main lodge and 19 cabins (7 with jacuzzis) are within easy striking distance of some of Nova

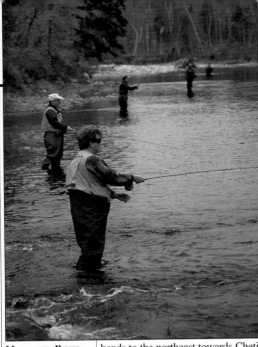

Scotia's best salmon pools. The dining room offers four-course country gourmet dinners.

The trail follows the Margaree until the river spills into the Gulf of St. Lawrence. There is a small sand beach to the south of Margaree Harbour and a larger sand and gravel beach to the north. The larger beach is part of a narrow sandspit that serves as a natural breakwater for the colourful fishing boats of Margaree Harbour. From here, the road

MARGAREE RIVER

bends to the northeast towards Cheticamp. At Cap Le Moine, one of several tiny Acadian villages that dot this shore, Joe's Scarecrow Theatre has been giving visitors the willies for a number of years. The Mask Making Museum (Centre de la Mi-Carême) in nearby St. Joseph du Moine exhibits locally-

made masks and explains the history of the winter festival La Mi-Carême still celebrated in this area.

Cheticamp is the largest and oldest Acadian village along this shore. Cheticantins take special pride in the large co-operatives that dominate the waterfront. They represent the culmination of a long struggle for independence.

NORMAWAY INN IN THE MARGAREE VALLEY

MARGAREE SALMON MUSEUM

When the Treaty of Paris forced the French to abandon the Gulf of St. Lawrence fishery in 1763, merchants from the English Channel Islands were quick to take their place. Charles Robin, a French Huguenot from the Isle of Jersey, set up his operation at Le Chadye (Cheticamp). He encouraged exiled Acadians who had spent time near the French port of St. Malo (just to the south of Jersey) to settle in Cheticamp, where they could work for him. And that's

just what they did for more than a century. The Charles Robin Company ruled Cheticamp. It owned boats and fishing gear. Fishermen were paid in provisions from the company store. Indebtedness to the "Jerseys" was a way of life from the time the Acadians first settled Cheticamp in the 1780s until late in the 19th century. Then Father Pierre Fiset arrived. He devoted himself to the spiritual well-being of the Cheticantins — Cheticamp's beautiful Saint-Pierre

Church was built under his direction — but he also took a special interest in the worldly affairs of his parishioners. Determined to loosen the Jerseys' grip on the community, Father Fiset purchased a store in 1883. He traded in fish and livestock, and in 1888 he built a wharf on the harbour. Five years later, Father Fiset bought Cheticamp Island from the Robins. The extent of his involvement in worldly affairs troubled some clergy, but they did not question his motives.

Fiset died in 1909. Six years later, a group of fishermen founded Cheticamp's first sales co-operative. During the 1930s, they were greatly assisted by another Catholic clergyman, Reverend Moses Coady, a professor at St. Francis Xavier University in Antigonish, who was appointed by the government to help Maritime fishermen organize co-operatives. The so-called Antigonish Movement had its greatest successes in Antigonish County and Cape Breton. Today, there are seven co-operatives in the Cheticamp area — the most in any Acadian region of Nova Scotia. One of the groups to organize a co-operative in Cheticamp during the 1930s was the rug hookers. Rug hooking is an industry with a peculiar connection to the Bells and Baddeck. Cheticamp women had been hooking rugs from old rags for ages when, in 1922, Lillian Burke, an American friend of the Bells, suggested that they would be able to sell their rugs if they switched from rags to wool and began using softer colours. A cottage industry was born. Burke did well selling Cheticamp rugs in New York until 1936, when Alexandre Boudreau, a leader of the local co-op movement, suggested that the women organize themselves.

Now, the Co-opérative Artisanale de Cheticamp Ltée runs the business. Cheticamp rugs are world-famous — especially those of Elizabeth LeFort, whose works can be found at the Vatican, the White House, Buckingham Palace and the Dr. Elizabeth LeFort Gallery & Museum at Les Trois Pignons (The Three Gables) in Cheticamp. Rug hooking is still a cottage industry, but it is no longer quaint. The computerized cash system in the Co-op Artisanale attests to that. Some rugs retail for two thousand dollars. At Le Motif, a local shop featuring needlework and folk art, there are some original rag-style rugs for sale. Asked if they

LE PETIT CERCLE, CHILDREN'S THEATRE, CHETICAMP (TOP) ACADIAN ART (ABOVE)

L'ÉGLISE SAINT-PIERRE, CHETICAMP

151

were coming back, the woman working at the store replied, "We'll see, if people buy them then they're coming back." Cheticantins are not novices when it comes to the business of art. There are plenty more rugs (and a wide selection of Cape Breton and Nova Scotian crafts) at Flora's, one of the province's largest craft shops. But Cheticamp-area artisans do more than hook rugs. Some of Nova Scotia's most interesting folk art is produced here. You'll see colourful whirligigs and gizmos in shops and front yards throughout the Acadian villages along this coast. One of Canada's best folk artists, Bill Roach, works out of the Sunset Art Gallery in Cheticamp. His whimsical, brightly coloured wood carvings — birds, fish and people among them — are prized by collectors worldwide.

RUG HOOKING IS A MAINSTAY OF THE CHETICAMP ECONOMY

Local artists and artisans draw strength from Cheticamp's rich Acadian culture (Acadian flags are everywhere). Locals still speak French with a 17th-century accent. Cheticantins are justifiably proud of Father Fiset's magnificent church. Saint-Pierre, overlooking the village and the bay, anchors the community. Each August, a special mass is held here during the Festival de l'Escaouette, a week-long cultural celebration that brims with Acadian food, song and dance.

The waterfront bustles during summer. Several whale-watching cruises, deep-sea fishing charters and water tours leave from the government wharf and the Quai Mathieu

waterfront boardwalk. Pilot whales and minkes are frequently sighted (fin whales less often) and the landward views of Cheticamp and the Cape Breton Highlands are spectacular.

There are a number of restaurants along the water side of Main Street that feature Acadian cuisine. Savoury meat pies and rich seafood chowders are served with thick slices of homemade bread at the Restaurant Acadien in the Co-op Artisanale. Fruit pies are made the traditional way, with flaky biscuit crusts. Several establishments on the waterfront boardwalk have outdoor patios where you can enjoy a drink and watch the sun set behind Cheticamp Island.

If you plan an overnight stay in Cheticamp, book well in advance. For the most part, the village offers motel-style accommodation along its busy Main Street. Laurie's Motor Inn has many guest amenities, including a whale-watching cruise. Across the harbour, the Cheticamp Island Resort features two-bedroom cottages with housekeeping facilities and ocean swimming. The resort offers weekly rates and is ideal for those who plan an extended stay in the Cheticamp area.

Just to the northeast of Cheticamp is the entrance to Cape Breton Highlands National Park. Established in 1936, the park protects about 950 square kilometres of coastline, wooded valleys and barren plateaus. If you plan to hike, cycle, fish or camp in the park, then stop at the Cheticamp Information Centre for permits and advice. Vehicle permits should be purchased at the centre by anyone intending to use park facilities. Exhibits, including interactive games for children, will introduce you to the park. To get better acquainted, visit the centre's well-stocked bookstore.

PRESQU'ILE

A CHETICAMP CRAFT SHOP (BOTTOM)

Hikers, especially, will find useful resources here. *Walking in the Highlands*, a guide to the park's 26 hiking trails, can be purchased at the centre. So can David Lawley's *Cabot Trail*, an interpretive naturalist's guide to hiking in the area. There are hikes well-suited to a family stroll (like the Lone Shieling Trail near Pleasant Bay) and those with more challenging terrain (the Franey Trail, near Ingonish Beach, ascends 366 metres in only four kilometres). Some offer spectacular coastal scenery (like the Coastal Trail that leaves from Black Brook Beach); others climb to the barren highland plateau (the Lake of Islands Trail, near Ingonish, is a 26-kilometre-long back-country adventure). At the top of the trail, between Cheticamp and Pleasant Bay, is Skyline, the most popular trail (recently upgraded and wheelchair accessible), which affords spectacular ridgeline views. To truly appreciate the grandeur of the Cape Breton Highlands, park the car and go for a walk on any of the 27 maintained trails.

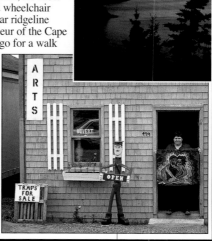

Each September hikers unite at Hike the Highlands Festival, a 10-day festival of guided hikes and special events. Some of these trails are groomed for cross-country skiing in winter.

The 106-kilometre stretch of road between Cheticamp and Ingonish is what made the Cabot Trail famous. Soon after entering the park, the roller coaster ride begins — up French Mountain to a height of 455 metres then down the other side, then another ascent, this time 372 metres to the top of

153

MacKenzie Mountain, and down to Pleasant Bay, with lookoffs along the way. The view from Fishing Cove Lookoff is breathtaking as is the 9-kilometre hike into Fishing Cove. You can camp overnight by the beach and running brook. Check with the Park for a permit. On a crystal clear day you might be able to spy the Magdalene Islands to the northwest, across more than 80 kilometres of water.

Pleasant Bay, following a serpentine descent of MacKenzie Mountain (you can imagine the difficulty of a landward approach to this community before the road was built), is a scenic fishing village with a variety of visitor services. Whale-watching cruises leave from the Pleasant Bay wharf, and the Whale Interpretive Centre provides a wealth of background information with models, exhibits and interactive displays. The coastline north of Pleasant Bay is spectacular and pristine (a community of Tibetan Buddhist monks is located here); pilot whales, grey seals and bald eagles are regularly sighted. You'll find plenty of whales and seabirds among the beautiful folk art creations of Reed Timmons, a local lobsterman and gill-netter. His Pleasant Bay studio is also filled with colourful roosters.

From Pleasant Bay, the trail moves inland towards North Mountain. At the mountain's base is the Lone Shieling, a replica of a Scottish crofter's hut. The hut is the result of an outpouring of Scottish sentiment from a rather unlikely source. Donald MacIntosh, a native of Pleasant Bay, was a geology professor at Dalhousie University in Halifax. When he died in 1934, he left 40.5 hectares at Pleasant Bay to the Crown. His will expressed the desire that the government use the land for a small park where they would construct a cabin modelled after the Lone Shieling on the Isle of Skye. That is how a Skye crofter's cottage came to be tucked among a stand of 350-year-old sugar maples. While the cottage may leave you scratching your head, the massive trees — some are more than 36 metres tall — along the Lone Shieling hiking trail make the stop worthwhile.

From the top of North Mountain (445 metres), the Cabot Trail descends into the Aspy River valley, passing some spectacular gorges along the way. At the bottom, a dirt road leads to Beulach Bahn Falls, an ideal spot for a picnic. Nearby, Arts North is a fine craft store that features the functional and decorative pottery of Linda and Dennis Doyon, and the deceptively simple designs of jeweller Johanna Padelt. The work of other local artisans is on display in the loft.

If you have time to explore this remote and awesome part of the Island, there are some very good accommodations in the area, notably Oakwood Manor, a 81-hectare estate at Cape North. Leave the trail here and head still farther north to Cabot's Landing (site of a picnic park and an 11-kilometre-long sandy beach) and Bay St. Lawrence. To boldly go where few tourists have gone, continue along the shores of Bay St. Lawrence to Capstick and follow the winding dirt road to Meat Cove, a drive you'll not soon forget! Watch out for

THERE ARE PLENTY OF CLIFF-SIDE VIEWS ALONG THE CABOT TRAIL

PLEASANT BAY

CABOT'S LANDING, NEAR CAPE NORTH

moose along the road. For a landward view of the wild beauty of Cape Breton's northern tip, take a bird- and whale-watching boat tour from either Bay St. Lawrence or Dingwall, on Aspy Bay. At Dingwall, Markland Coastal Resort is a luxurious base from which to hike, bike, canoe, kayak, or go whalewatching. The Octagon, an on-site concert hall, has a full schedule of chamber and Celtic music throughout the summer.

Back in the village of Cape North, the Cabot Trail bends to the southeast, towards Ingonish. Not far from Cape North, turn down Shore Road to reach Eagle North for kayaking excursions in South Harbour. Many prefer the alternative coastal route, which takes you through the fishing villages of Smelt Brook, White Point, New Haven and Neils Harbour. At the end of the village of White Point, there is a hiking trail that gives spectacular views of the Aspy Ridge. At Neils Harbour, the Chowder House restaurant makes good use of the village's active fishery in its thick seafood chowders. You

can see the fishing fleet from the restaurant, and walk down to the edge of the Atlantic after your meal.

From Neils Harbour, the trail heads south towards Ingonish. On a hot day, stop at Black Brook Beach along the way. The water is reasonably warm and there are usually great waves for body surfing and boogie boarding (the left side of the beach is less rocky). There is a waterfall next to the beach.

ASPY RIVER

The Ingonish area is the resort centre on the Cabot Trail's eastern shore. The beaches are wonderful. The challenging Highlands Links Golf Course was recently rated by *SCOREGolf* Magazine as the best public course in Canada, and the 71st worldwide by *Golf* magazine. The Middle Head hiking trail runs the length of the narrow peninsula that separates South Bay Ingonish from North Bay Ingonish. Cliff-side views, including an offshore colony of nesting terns at the trail's end, are ample reward for a relatively easy hike.

This same promontory is also the site of the provincially owned Keltic Lodge. Other accommodations in the Ingonish area are more

modestly priced, but some visitors are willing to pay a premium for the lodge's commanding view of Ingonish Beach and South Bay. There is a fine dining room at the Keltic, which features fresh seafood and local produce, elegantly presented. The lodge also offers the weary traveller luxury pampering at their Aveda Spa overlooking Ingonish Beach. Sit in the outdoor hot tub and take in the magnificent scenery. There is ample opportunity to survey the waters of South Bay Ingonish. Whale-watching cruises leave from the ports of Ingonish Beach, North Ingonish and Ingonish Ferry. Minke and pilot whales are frequently sighted and the coastline is pocked with sea caves and unusual rock formations. While most whale cruises use converted fishing vessels, Sea Visions, which runs out of Ingonish Ferry, allows you to hear as well as see the Atlantic from the 11-metre sailing vessel *Avon Spirit*.

After Ingonish, the Cabot Trail snakes its way up and down Cape Smokey — steel yourself for yet another spectacular view before heading south on the home stretch. Unique gifts and clothing (including period costume) are displayed at Sew Inclined in Wreck Cove. There are numerous arts and crafts shops worth a stop along the North Shore including glass artisans and woodsmiths. In Indian Brook, you can see the creations of one of Cape Breton's best artisans at Leather Works. John Roberts got his start doing historic leather-work when someone from Louisbourg approached him to do reproductions for the fortress. Leather buckets and less antiquated leather goods — belts, wallets, work aprons and bags — are handmade on the premises.

Several lovely accommodations have sprung up in the St. Anns Bay region in the past few years, including Cabot Shores Adventure and Retreat Centre and Chanterelle Country Inn. Some are luxury accommodations, with outdoor hot tubs and oceanside swimming.

GAELIC COLLEGE OF CELTIC ARTS AND CRAFTS, SOUTH GUT ST. ANNS

At the Barachois River Bridge, the road forks. Route 312 takes you to Englishtown via a short ferry ride across St. Anns Harbour. (While waiting for the ferry, you can visit Sea Shanty Antique and Crafts, where the quilts — old and new — are of special interest.) Englishtown was home to Angus MacAskill, Cape Breton's famous 2.4-metre, 193-kilogram giant.

From the Barachois River Bridge, the Cabot Trail twists its way toward South Gut St. Anns. Beginning at Tarbotvale, the road passes by several interesting craft shops. Iron Art & Photography is owned by Gordon and Carol Kennedy. Shape Shift Pottery at North River sells beautiful stoneware and porcelain pottery.

The Gaelic College of Celtic Arts and Crafts, the only Gaelic College in North America, teaches traditional Highland music, dance and craft on the shores of South Haven, St. Anns. The Gaelic language is also taught during the six-week summer session. The Gaelic Mod, a festival of Celtic culture, and a festival of Cape Breton fiddling are held here each August.

The Bras d'Or Lakes form Cape Breton's 1,165-square-kilometre inland sea. Two narrow channels — Great Bras d'Or and St. Andrews — and a canal at St. Peter's link this sailors' mecca to the North Atlantic. Numerous islands, harbours, coves and saltwater ponds provide shelter from ocean storms, and the region is virtually fog-free.

At the Atlantic entrance to the Great Bras d'Or Channel there are two islands, Ciboux and Hertford. Each summer the "Bird Islands" host Nova Scotia's largest colony of breeding sea birds — razorbills, guillemots, gulls, kittiwakes, cormorants and the feature attraction, Atlantic puffins. Bird Island Boat Tours operates out of Big Bras d'Or, on Boularderie Island. The two-and-a-half hour boat trip trims the shores of both islands, and the Van Schaiks, long-time operators of the tour, provide a lively and informative narrative.

Its favourable climate, abundant wildlife and outstanding natural beauty have long drawn people to the shores of the Bras d'Or. The Mi'kmaq have been here for centuries. Today, there are four reserves in the area, including Eskasoni, the largest in the province.

The Bras d'Or Lakes Scenic Drive is a signed series of roads skirting almost the entire coastline of the Bras d'Or. It can be accessed at a number of different points. Setting out from Baddeck, head south on the Trans-Canada Highway. Wagmatcook Reserve, just past Nyanza, has a Culture and Heritage Centre that demonstrates and interprets Mi'kmaq culture and history from early times to the present. It also has a unique native crafts shop. Further along at Whycocomagh, the Googoo family has been running the Negemow basket shop for more than 30 years.

DUNDEE RESORT

(Before that, baskets were sold door-to-door.) The craftsmanship is exceptional; so is the smell of sweet grass. Follow the signs with the eagle along the south coast, passing through Orangedale, where the railway station immortalized in the song "Orangedale Station" is now a museum. Continue on the Marble Mountain Road through coves and inlets that are the habitat of many shorebirds and bald eagles.

Perhaps the best view of the Bras d'Or is from Marble Mountain, overlooking West Bay. A steep trail to the abandoned quarry (750 men once mined this hillside) starts from the main road, directly across from a small lookoff and picnic area. Interesting old workings provide a good excuse to stop and catch your breath on the way up. The view from the top — islet-studded West Bay and the wide open waters of the Bras d'Or — will stay with you long after you descend the mountain. Back at the look-off on the main road, a steep path leads downhill to a beach of crushed marble sand. The turquoise water is ice-cold (several spring-fed brooks flow down the hillside) and crystal-clear.

The Dundee Resort is at the head of West Bay. The resort's 60 hotel rooms and 39 cottages are spread out over 223 hectares. Dundee has all the amenities, including an 18-hole championship golf course. The course was built on a steep slope overlooking the bay, making for great views and challenging golf. The resort also has a large marina where you can arrange a cruise on the Bras d'Or.

At Roberta, not far from Dundee, Kayak Cape Breton offers guided sea-kayaking trips on the Bras d'Or and along the Atlantic Coast. The sheltered waters of the Bras d'Or are ideal for beginners

Continuing along the scenic south shore of the lake brings you to St. Peter's. You can picnic beside St. Peter's Canal, a National Historic Site, while watching ships and pleasure craft pass through the old locks from the Atlantic to the Bras d'Or Lakes. At MacIsaac Kiltmakers, you can order a custom kilt or see how one is made. Next door is the home (now a museum) of renowned photographer Wallace MacAskill. The *Bluenose* on the Canadian dime is from one of MacAskill's prints.

At Chapel Island Reserve, one of the oldest Mi'kmaq settlements in the province, daily re-enactments of a 16th-century encampment feature traditional dancing, drumming and storytelling.

Big Pond is the home of Cape Breton singer Rita MacNeil. Many of her awards and records are on display at Rita's Tea Room, in a converted one-room schoolhouse. You

PASTORAL LANDSCAPE ALONG THE CEILIDH TRAIL

may well see Rita here or at the Big Pond Festival, a week-long celebration of folk music held each July.

Continue through the charming village of East Bay and the Eskasoni First Nations Reserve to the Grand Narrows Bridge. Across the bridge is Iona, site of the Nova Scotia Museum's Highland Village. Bras d'Or also attracted European settlers — mostly Scots, like the MacNeils from the Hebridean Island of Barra, who came to Iona towards the end of the 18th century. In 1956, Iona was chosen by the Association of Scottish Societies as the site for a proposed village that would depict the evolution of Scottish settlement in this part of Nova Scotia. Overlooking the Barra Strait, the Nova Scotia Highland Village tells its story through a series of 10 structures, beginning with a Hebridean Black House and ending with an early 20th-century home. Also included in the tour are a blacksmith forge, carding mill, and a 19th-century church, recently relocated to the site after being floated down the lake from the community of Malagawatch.

From Iona you have two choices. You can take a car ferry at Little Narrows back to Highway 105, on which you can return to Baddeck or go to the Canso Causeway. Or, if you want to complete the drive around the northern loop of the Bras d'Or, recross the Grand Narrows bridge and follow Route 223.

Those who have travelled from the Canso Causeway to Baddeck via the Trans-Canada Highway, and driven the Cabot Trail in a counter-clockwise direction, might carry on through the Margaree Valley towards Margaree Forks and back to the 105. Or, if you are returning to the Canso Causeway, you might consider taking the alternative Route 19 (the Ceilidh Trail) at Margaree Forks. The Ceilidh Trail, as its name suggests, is the musical heartland of Cape Breton. It passes through villages like Judique and Mabou that have produced Celtic music luminaries John Allan Cameron, Natalie MacMaster, the Rankins, Celtic "bad boy" Ashley MacIsaac and many others. The western shore's strong Scottish identity is preserved in its music, schools and institutions. Mabou and Port Hood offer Gaelic in their schools — but not to attract tourists. The series of summer ceilidhs and square dances, held between Margaree Valley and Judique draw great crowds from the local population as well as visitors.

ATLANTIC PUFFINS ARE AMONG THE THOUSANDS OF SEA BIRDS THAT COLONIZE THE "BIRD ISLANDS"

The Ceilidh Trail rivals the Cabot Trail for beautiful (if more pastoral) views — especially between Inverness and Mabou, and along the Colindale Road, between Mabou and Port Hood. And there is great saltwater swimming at Inverness, Mabou and Port Hood beaches as well as the shore road between Port Hood and Judique. (The water of the Northumberland Strait is comfortably warm during summer.) Inverness is the largest community on the Ceilidh Trail and provides all services. The Inverness Miners'

Museum presents the coal mining history of the area. Local arts and crafts are available here and at the Inverness County Centre for the Arts. Just 5 km from Inverness is Broad Cove, site of one of the biggest Scottish music events of the year. The Broad Cove Concert has been held the last Sunday in July since 1957. The MacLeod Inn, with six spacious rooms is just up the road. Other accommodations in the area include motels, cottages and bed and breakfasts. Cape Mabou/Sight Point hiking trails provide panoramic views of the highlands and seascapes.

The Glenora Inn & Distillery Resort offers nine comfortable rooms as well as six hillside chalets in a unique complex. Glenora is North America's only distiller of single malt whisky. Tours are provided and the single malt, Kenloch, is on sale in the gift shop. Inland from Glenville, amidst the rolling hills of the Mabou Highlands, is Lake Ainslie. The 53-kilometre, fairly level, route around the lake is a popular cycling trail. In West Lake Ainslie, Tulloch Inn, with six bright, airy rooms, licensed dining room and gift shop caters to environmental sensitivities.

The Duncreigan Country Inn, overlooking Mabou Harbour, has eight spacious guest rooms with bay windows. The menu at the inn's excellent dining room includes seafood and local lamb seasoned with garden-fresh herbs. An on-site gift shop features the work of Maritime artists and artisans. The Mull Café and Deli, operated by the Mullendores of The Duncreigan, offers informal, family-oriented dining with the same quality you'd find at the inn. The Red Shoe Pub, housed in an extensively renovated, 130-year-old Mabou storefront, features traditional music every evening and offers a full menu of Nova Scotia home cooking until closing seven days a week. The An Drochaid (The Bridge) Museum in Mabou presents the Gaelic culture of the area.

Port Hood marks the end of the Mabou Highlands, which stretch from Inverness and Lake Ainslie. Port Hood is a full-service community with some fine accommodation and dining. Hillcrest Hall Country Inn is a nicely restored and well-appointed old mansion with a fascinating history, great views and a licensed dining room. Haus Treuburg Inn & Cottages is a heritage house with European-style cottages. Their licensed gourmet restaurant features a unique "German Sunday morning breakfast" available daily. There are a number of warm-water beaches around Port Hood.

Judique is another staunchly Scottish community whose musical traditions are preserved and promoted at the Celtic Music Interpretive Centre. Find out about performances and ceilidhs by visiting the centre's website (www.celticmusicsite.com).

If the Cabot Trail is your destination, it may be well worth your while to plan on making the journey one way, either up or back, along the richly scenic and cultural Ceilidh Trail.

FLEUR-DE-LIS AND MARCONI TRAILS

KING'S BASTION BARRACKS, FORTRESS OF LOUISBOURG NATIONAL HISTORIC SITE

The eastern edge of Cape Breton Island has a French flavour. Starting at Port Hawkesbury, near the Canso Causeway, the Fleur-de-Lis Trail follows the rugged coastline through picturesque Acadian villages. Fishing has been a way of life along this coast since Basque and Portuguese fishermen sought shelter here in the early 1500s. In little coves and harbours you will see colourful houses, lovely wooden churches and wharves stacked with nets and traps dotting the shoreline. You will hear French spoken and taste Acadian cuisine along the way. At the magnificent Fortress of Louisbourg National Historic Site, the Fleur-de-Lis Trail meets the Marconi Trail, which carries on to Glace Bay, linking three sites of Guglielmo Marconi's historic wireless transmissions.

At Louisdale, cross the Lennox Passage Bridge to the cluster of islands that make up lovely Isle Madame, where there are picturesque old fishing villages. Arichat was a busy seaport in the mid-18th century and throughout the time of tall ships. Le Noir Forge museum, on the waterfront, is a restored French stone blacksmith shop. There are several accommodations in Arichat. L'Auberge Acadienne has eight rooms in the inn, nine motel units and a dining room. Vollmer's Island Paradise on nearby Janvrin Island offers seven fully equipped cottages and a small but very good dining room. Bookings must be made a day or two in advance, as all the meals are made from scratch. Petit-de-Grat is the oldest fishing settlement in the area. Nearby, Little Anse is a picturesque spot favoured by photographers. A hiking trail leads to a view of the lighthouse that guards the entrance to the Strait of Canso. With its many little coves, bays and inlets, this area is well-suited to exploring by sea kayak. Cycling is also a good way to see Isle Madame. D'Escousse, settled in the 1700s, is another pretty fishing village. Rejoining Route 4 on the mainland, you will pass through scenic River Bourgeois to historic St. Peter's. The trail follows Route 247 to L'Ardoise. The excellent sandy beach at nearby Point Michaud is a good place to stop for a picnic. Continuing on Route 327 leads to Marion Bridge, "down on the Mira," the river of the famous song, which is also famous for fishing. Nearby, Two Rivers Wildlife Park displays many native Nova Scotian animals in a natural setting overlooking the Mira and Salmon rivers.

A trip to Louisbourg, where the reconstructed Fortress of Louisbourg National Historic Site brings history to life, provides one of the province's most rewarding experiences.

LOOKING ACROSS LOUISBOURG HARBOUR FROM THE FORTRESS

Tourism has replaced the fishery as the economic mainstay of the modern town, which is situated at the sheltered northern end of the harbour. The Louisbourg lighthouse is adjacent to the ruins of Canada's first lighthouse, which dates back to 1734. Visitors can enjoy a stroll along the harbourfront boardwalk, and nearby are Louisbourg Market Square, shops, museums, a ship chandlery, accommodations and a post office.

Visitors can take in live theatre and concerts at the 17th-century–style Louisbourg Playhouse during the summer and fall, and in August, the Louisbourg CrabFest celebrates the bounty of the sea. The S&L Railway Museum houses the visitor information centre, along with exhibits that tell the story of the Sydney and Louisburg Railway and railway technology.

FRÉDÉRIC GATE

**THE QUAY,
FORTRESS OF
LOUISBOURG
NATIONAL
HISTORIC SITE**

A few minutes' drive from the town, you will find the entrance to the 18th-century fortress and the gateway to a living museum.

By the Treaty of Utrecht in 1713, the French agreed to leave their fishing station at Placentia, in Newfoundland, and give up Acadia (which included present-day mainland Nova Scotia) to the British. In exchange, France was allowed to hold on to the islands in the Gulf of St. Lawrence. Ile-Royale (Cape Breton) would emerge as the most important of these, and within a short time, the French had established the Fortress of Louisbourg on its southeastern shore. There, they were soon landing 13,600,000 kilograms of cod a year, worth two to three times the value of the fur trade at Quebec and Montreal. They also had an imposing fortress that lay between the British colonies of Newfoundland and Nova Scotia and, in the fishery, a ready-made training ground for their navy. It is no wonder that the French said of the bargain that they had received an ingot of gold for a bar of silver.

As an entrepôt — a clearinghouse for commodities from France, New France, New England and the West Indies — Louisbourg flourished. Outbound ships, their holds brimming with cod, would return to Louisbourg laden with West Indian rum and sugar, cloths from Carcassonne and the wines of Provence. Enticed by such rich cargoes, wealthy New England merchants supplied wood products and foodstuffs in exchange for them. To a lesser extent, traders from Nova Scotia and Quebec did the same. Atlantic trade filled Louisbourg's harbour and quickened its waterfront.

The quay was a lively place. Scores of shallops (small boats) manoeuvred between large traders so that fishermen could bring their codfish to shore, where they would soon be drying on flakes. Sailors on leave crowded into the inns and taverns that lined the south side of the quay — and Louisbourg fathers made sure their daughters were accounted for. Commercial necessity overcame the difficulty of haggling with someone who spoke a different language.

Goods flowed back and forth between ship and shore.

By 1760 it was over — the town deserted, the fortress destroyed. Louisbourg's commercial promise had been fulfilled, but its military promise had not.

Twice in its short history, Louisbourg fell. When France declared war on Britain in 1744, Louisbourg's commander went on the offensive in the New World, and the British outpost at Canso was captured. A campaign against Annapolis Royal was less successful, but reprisals seemed unlikely. Louisbourg was too well defended and the British seemed unwilling to expend much effort against it.

An attack did come in 1745 — from an unexpected quarter. William Shirley, Governor of Massachusetts, succeeded in raising a force of 4,000 New England militiamen for the purpose. Shirley was strongly supported by wealthy merchants, and the proposed campaign was, in part, a reflection of their desire to take over control of the rich Louisbourg fishery. The militia, under the leadership of General Pepperell, and with the help of a British naval squadron from the West Indies, succeeded in taking the fortress after a 46-day siege.

During the intense negotiations that followed the end of the war in 1748, the British sacrificed Louisbourg in order to hold on to some of their European gains. The following year, Louisbourg was returned to the French. New Englanders were outraged.

In 1756, when war broke out again, the British strategy was to attack France through its colonies and foreign trade. Louisbourg was an obvious target. The town endured several blockades until 1758, when an irresistible combination of British land and sea power overwhelmed the fortress. The French surrendered Louisbourg in July. Two years later, rather than run the risk that Louisbourg would be returned to the French in future negotiations, British engineers were ordered to blow up the fortifications.

The town barely survived. A few people settled in the

SUNRISE AT LOUISBOURG

FORTRESS LOUISBOURG (ABOVE AND BELOW)

sheltered northern end of the harbour. Daily, fishermen made the melancholy trip out of the harbour, past the Royal Battery, around Careening Point, to gaze upon the desolation of the fortress on their way to the fishing grounds.

The reconstruction of Fortress Louisbourg began in 1963 as a creative response to severe unemployment in Cape Breton's coal mines. More than 150 out-of-work coal miners were employed in the project as stonemasons, labourers and carpenters. Researchers had found the original drawings for the military buildings in Paris. Archaeological and graphic evidence was used to reconstruct civilian buildings. The entire effort was characterized by a meticulous devotion to Louisbourg's past.

Proof of this devotion abounds. Buildings sit on their original foundations. Dormer windows jut from gabled roofs, as they did in Poitou, Saintonge and Brittany in the 18th century. Plank siding and a clutter of chimneys speak to an ongoing struggle with cold and damp. Everywhere, timber, sod, stone, mortar and mud have been used to resurrect one-quarter of the original town — over 50 buildings in all.

Details help convince. The sculptured trophies atop the Dauphin Gate were quarried from the same French limestone as the originals. In the Carrerot property, mortar laced with glass in the south cellar was used to keep out rats.

Louisbourg's authenticity goes beyond architecture. Bread is baked in the Royal Bakery; savoury dishes simmer in the Engineer's House. The Governor's Apartments are appointed according to Governor Jean-Baptiste-Louis Le Prevost Duquesnel's inventory. They are comfortable and luxurious, well suited to sipping fine Bordeaux. This is a marked contrast to the Hotel de la Marine — a sturdy tavern run by a fisherman where rum

and sapinette (spruce beer) flowed freely. Finally, there are the people. Parks Canada has endeavoured to recreate a moment in the summer of 1744, and the players know their roles. And, whether by design or not, they seem to fit them. The woman who plays the 18th-century harpsichord in the Ordonnateur's Property does not look out of place. Neither do the soldiers who bear precise reproductions of 1734 French-made flintlock muskets. The man carting firewood to houses along the quay looks just right. Children roll hoops through the streets.

COASTLINE NEAR LOUISBOURG LIGHTHOUSE

Plan on taking an entire day to fully appreciate Fortress Louisbourg. Ask questions of those who work there. Their answers do more than just inform — they lend flavour to this 18th-century French garrison town.

Should you choose to stay overnight in the town of Louisbourg, there are many good accommodations available. The Louisbourg Harbour Inn is a century-old sea captain's house with balconies overlooking the fortress and the harbour. Five of the inn's eight rooms have jacuzzis. Louisbourg Heritage House B&B is a beautifully restored Victorian (c. 1886) rectory with six beautifully-furnished rooms. Close to the fortress entrance, the Cranberry Cove Inn is another restored turn-of-the-century home. It, too, combines antique furnishings and other traditional touches with modern conveniences like gas fireplaces and jacuzzis. Point of View Suites, at the Louisbourg gates, offers views of the fortress and the ocean from its 16 luxury suites as well as nightly lobster and crab dinners. There is also an RV park near the fortress.

The former city of Sydney, now the hub of Cape Breton Regional Municipality, has long prided itself on being the "industrial heart of Cape Breton." Founded in 1785 by Col. J. F. W. DesBarres, Sydney was first settled by Loyalists from New York State, who were followed by immigrants from the Scottish Highlands. The construction early in this century of the Dominion Steel and Coal Company steel plant (now Sydney Steel) took full advantage of the large protected harbour and provided the mainstay of the city's economy for nearly 100 years.

Wentworth Park, a narrow green area near the city centre, has duck ponds, walking paths, picnic areas and a bandstand. A 3-kilometre boardwalk along the harbourfront is a focal point of summer activity. Cossit House, built in 1787 on Charlotte Street, is the city's oldest, and now is a provincial museum. Nearby are Jost Heritage House and the Cape Breton Centre for Heritage and Science. Tiny St. Patrick's Church, the oldest Catholic Church in Cape Breton has been restored as a museum depicting Sydney's past. Centre 200 is the venue for sports and culture events throughout the year.

LOUISBOURG HERITAGE HOUSE B&B

In other parts of this area there are still places that reveal the pride and prosperity that were such a part of the

167

GOWRIE HOUSE, SYDNEY MINES

island's past. The Gowrie House in Sydney Mines was built in 1830 for Samuel Archibald, agent-general of the General Mining Association, which ran the coal mines. It remained in the Archibald family until 1975, when the present owner purchased it. For an overnight stay in metropolitan Cape Breton, there is no better spot. Guest rooms and common areas have since been furnished with beautiful Staffordshire figurines, Chippendale chairs and more. A four-course dinner is served each evening; reservations are a must. Visitors to and from Newfoundland find the Gowrie House especially convenient, as it is only minutes away from the ferry terminal in North Sydney.

In Glace Bay, the Savoy Theatre on Union Street is another reminder of a time when Cape Breton industry boomed and the population of coal-mining towns exploded. Built in 1901, the theatre quickly became the venue for a host of cultural activities that Glace Bay residents demanded and could easily support. When the entire Union Street block burned to the ground in 1927, Glace Bay's prosperity was on the wane, but still sufficient enough to quickly rebuild the Savoy — this time with ornamental touches that include the iron rococo chandeliers that hang from the ceiling today. The 761-seat theatre stages theatrical and musical productions throughout the year and is considered one of the finest performance venues in the Atlantic region.

MINERS' MUSEUM, GLACE BAY

At the edge of town, a national historic site commemorates Guglielmo Marconi's experiments with wireless communication. After he received the first trans-Atlantic signal at St. John's, Newfoundland, in 1901, several Canadian communities courted Marconi. He chose to conduct his experiments in Glace Bay. In December 1902, Marconi successfully transmitted signals from here to Poldhu, Cornwall. His story is well told at the museum.

Visitors to Glace Bay should also take an underground tour at the Miners' Museum. Retired coal miners tell of the dangerous and gritty life below the surface, and of the

men who died in explosions, cave-ins, floods and even in union clashes with company police. The Men of the Deeps, a choir of Cape Breton coal miners, which has gained worldwide recognition, performs several concerts at the museum during the summer.

CONTENTS

★ denotes a location recognized by
the publisher for its high quality.

GETTING THERE

BY LAND

The Trans-Canada Highway enters Nova Scotia from New Brunswick. Visitors from the United States must pass through Canada Customs checkpoints before entering the country.

Greyhound from New York (800 231-2222) connects with Acadian Lines (800 567-5151) in Bangor, Maine, and Voyageur from Montreal (613 238-5900) connects with SMT bus lines in New Brunswick (506 458-6000). SMT connects with Acadian Lines (902 454-9321), which offers bus service to most Nova Scotia destinations from Amherst.

VIA Rail Canada (888 842-7245) provides train service to Halifax via Montreal.

The 12.9-kilometre Confederation Bridge joins Borden-Carleton, Prince Edward Island, and Cape Jourimain, New Brunswick, near the Nova Scotia border.

BY SEA

There are several options for car-ferry trips to Nova Scotia.

Bar Harbor, Maine, or Portland, Maine, to Yarmouth, Nova Scotia

Daily service from May to October aboard the *Cat*. Contact: Bay Ferries Ltd, PO Box 634, Charlottetown, PE, C1A 7L3; 877 359-3760; www.catferry.com.

Saint John, New Brunswick, to Digby, Nova Scotia

Ferry service across the Bay of Fundy. Please contact Bay Ferries Ltd, 888 249-7245; www.nfl-bay.com for up-to-date information.

Prince Edward Island to Nova Scotia

Daily service between May 1 and December 20 from Wood Islands, PEI, to Caribou, NS. Northumberland Ferries, PO Box 634, Charlottetown, PE, C1A 7L3; 800 565-0201 in NS or PEI; elsewhere 902 566-3838. No reservations.

Newfoundland to North Sydney, Nova Scotia

Daily service from Port-aux-Basques to North Sydney; additional service during peak. Monday, Wednesday and Friday service from Argentia to North Sydney, mid-June through mid-September only. Marine Atlantic/Reservations, 355 Purves St, North Sydney, NS, B2A 3V2. In the USA and Canada, 800 341-7981; www.marine-atlantic.ca.

BY AIR

Air Canada (888 247-2262; www.aircanada.ca) provides daily flights to Nova Scotia from most Canadian cities. Air Canada Jazz (www.flyjazz.ca), a subsidiary of Air Canada, is a regional carrier providing short-haul and connector flights between many cities in Canada and the US.

WestJet (800 538-5696, www.westjet.com) is a discount airline offering economy flights to Halifax from many Canadian and US cities.

Air Canada, in partnership with United Airlines, services destinations in the United States and worldwide through all major US airports.

Several airlines offer regularly scheduled flights between Halifax and a number of European destinations (ask about charters as well).

Most air traffic to Nova Scotia touches down at the Halifax International Airport, with connecting flights to Yarmouth and Sydney. Car rentals may be arranged at all three airports.

Airporter Inc. offers a shuttle service approximately every hour to major downtown hotels. One-way fare is $16, round trip is $28. The Halifax airport is located about 40 kilometres northeast of the city, and the 30- to 40-minute cab or limousine ride to downtown Halifax costs about $53.

TRAVEL ESSENTIALS

MONEY

American currency can be exchanged at any bank in Nova

Scotia at the prevailing rate. There are also currency exchange booths at the visitor information centre in Yarmouth and at the Halifax International Airport. Units of currency are similar to those of the United States, except for Canadian two-dollar and one-dollar coins.

Traveller's cheques, major US credit cards and debit cards are accepted throughout Nova Scotia, although you may require cash in some rural areas. Traveller's cheques in Canadian funds can be purchased in the US. Cheques issued by Visa, American Express and Thomas Cook are widely recognized.

American visitors may also use bank or credit cards to make cash withdrawals from automated teller machines that are tied into international networks such as Cirrus, Interac and Plus. These can be found in most towns throughout the province.

PASSPORTS
Passports and visas are not required for American visitors, although some proof of citizenship or residency might be (a birth certificate or Alien Registration Card will serve). At the border, expect to be asked where you live, why you are coming to Canada, and for how long. Before travelling it would be wise to check with Citizenship and Immigration (800 461-9999; www.cbsa.gc.ca) for the latest information. Citizens of other countries should check with the nearest Canadian embassy or High Commission regarding entry requirements (www.cic.gc.ca).

CUSTOMS

Arriving
Visitors to Canada may bring certain duty-free items into the country as part of their personal baggage. These items must be declared to Customs upon arrival and may include up to 200 cigarettes, 50 cigars, 200 grams of manufactured tobacco and 200 tobacco sticks. Visitors are also permitted 1.14 litres (40 oz.) of liquor or 1.5 litres (52 oz.) of wine, or 8.5 litres (24 12-oz. cans or

bottles) of beer.

Gift items — excluding tobacco and alcohol products — for Canadian residents that do not exceed $60 are also duty-free. Packages should be marked "Gift" and the value indicated.

Boats, trailers, sporting equipment, cameras and similar big-ticket items may enter Canada free of duty. However, Canada Customs may require a refundable deposit to ensure that these goods are not sold for profit. It might be better to register such items with customs officials in your own country, so that when you re-enter you have evidence that they were not bought in Canada.

Some items are strictly controlled in Canada. Weapons and firearms are prohibited, with the exception of rifles and shotguns for hunting purposes which must be declared. Regulations for temporarily importing firearms or for borrowing firearms while in Canada have changed within the past couple of years. For detailed current information contact the Canadian Firearms Centre (800 731-4000; www.cfc.gc.ca).

Plant material will be examined at the border (www.inspection.gc.ca). Veterinarian's certificates are required for all pets.

For further information on Canadian customs regulations, contact Canada Customs and Revenue Agency (in Canada, 800 461-9999; www.ccra-adrc.gc.ca).

Departing
To find out about US customs regulations and what other restrictions and exemptions apply, contact your local customs office or the US Customs Service, Box 7407, Washington, DC, 20044; 202 927-2095; www.customs.gov/travel/travel.htm. Ask for a copy of *Know Before You Go*.

Travellers from other countries should also check on customs regulations before leaving home.

TAXES

Harmonized Sales Tax (HST)
Most goods and services sold in Nova Scotia are subject to the Harmonized Sales Tax, a 14-percent federal/provincial tax that may be either included in or added to the price.

Out-of-country visitors are eligible for rebates of the HST paid on short-term accommodations, and also on goods purchased for use outside Canada if removed from Canada within 60 days of purchase. Rebate forms are available from visitor information centres, Revenue Canada offices, Canada Customs ports and many hotels and inns.

GUIDES

The *Nova Scotia Doers' and Dreamers' Guide* is an indispensable aid to visitors. To obtain a copy call toll-free 800 565-0000 or see www.novascotia.com. The guide is also available at visitor information centres throughout Nova Scotia.

GETTING ACQUAINTED

TIME ZONE

Nova Scotia falls within the Atlantic Time Zone, which is one hour later than the Eastern Time Zone. Daylight Saving Time, when the clocks are advanced one hour, is in effect from early April until late October.

CLIMATE

Nova Scotia's climate is influenced by the sea. Summers are cooler and winters milder than in central Canada. Average daily maximum temperatures for Halifax:

Jan.	1°C	33°F
Feb.	1°C	33°F
Mar.	4°C	39°F
Apr.	9°C	48°F
May	14°C	58°F
June	19°C	67°F
July	23°C	73°F
Aug.	24°C	74°F
Sept.	19°C	67°F
Oct.	14°C	58°F
Nov.	9°C	48°F
Dec.	3°C	37°F

GETTING AROUND

BUS TOURS

Seasonal bus tours of the province are available through a number of tour operators, including Ambassatours (800 565-7173), Atlantic Tours (902 423-6242), and Aberdeen Tours (866 831-2277). Several tour operators will arrange customized itineraries for groups.

BY CAR

Nova Scotia highway maps are available at visitor information centres throughout the province. Highways are generally well maintained. Speed limits vary depending on the type of highway, with the 100-level controlled access highways having the highest limit, 110 km/hr (65 mph). The speed limit is 50 km/hr (30 mph) in cities and towns. In Nova Scotia, seat belt use is compulsory for driver and passengers.

A valid United States driver's license is also valid in Nova Scotia. Evidence of the car's registration is required (a car rental contract will also serve). US motorists may obtain a Non-Resident Inter-Province Motor Vehicle Liability Insurance Card through their own insurance companies as evidence of financial responsibility within Canada.

Car Rentals
All major car rental agencies are represented in Nova Scotia. Representatives at the Halifax International Airport are listed below:
Avis: 800 437-0358
Budget: 800 268-8900
Hertz: 800 263-0600
Thrifty: 800 847-4389
National Car and Truck Rental: 800 227-7368
Consult the Yellow Pages of local telephone directories for local agencies that may offer lower rates.

LODGING

For a complete listing of accommodations in the province, including campgrounds, consult the *Nova Scotia Doers' and Dreamers' Guide* (see Travel Essentials). Hostellers should contact Hostelling International — Nova Scotia, 1253 Barrington St, Halifax, Nova Scotia, B3J 1Y3; 902 422-3863; www.hihostels.ca. Other resources available at local bookstores include an illustrated guide to some of Nova Scotia's most distinctive inns — Elaine Elliot and Virginia Lee's *Maritime Flavours*.

Many establishments are members of Nova Scotia's Check In Reservation and Information Service (see Travel Essentials). Membership is indicated by a check mark in the *Nova Scotia Doers' and Dreamers' Guide*. In general, the accommodations listed below are the best of their kind in Nova Scotia. Most have distinguishing features that will enhance your stay. Approximate prices are indicated, based on the average cost, at time of publication, for two persons staying in a double room (excluding taxes): $ = under $100; $$ = $100–$150; $$$ = more than $150.

The area code for all of Nova Scotia is 902.

HALIFAX

- Casino Nova Scotia Hotel, 1919 Upper Water St, Halifax; 866 425-4329; www.casinonovascotiahotel.com. Luxury accommodation on the Halifax waterfront (ask for a room on the harbour side) with an informal touch. Indoor pool, sauna, whirlpool. Near casino with slot machines and table games. Adjacent to the Historic Properties. Open year-round. $$$
- Delta Barrington, 1875 Barrington St, Halifax; 800 268-1133; www.deltabarrington.com. Close to the Historic Properties and most attractions. Adjoins Barrington Place Mall, restaurants and pubs. Open year-round. $$$

- Delta Halifax, 1990 Barrington St, Halifax; 800 268-1133; www.deltahalifax.com. Top-floor restaurant with sweeping view of the city and harbour. All amenities. Adjoins Scotia Square shopping mall. Open year-round. $$$
- Four Points by Sheraton, 1496 Hollis St, Halifax; 866 444-9494. Central to downtown. All amenities. Indoor parking. Open year-round. $$$
- ★The Halliburton, 5184 Morris St, Halifax; 420-0658; www.thehalliburton.com. Small, elegant hotel near downtown. Registered Heritage Property incorporating three 19th-century townhouses in downtown Halifax. Open year-round. $$$
- Inn on the Lake, Fall River; 800 463-6465; www.innonthelake.com. Two hectares of parkland with private freshwater beach and outdoor pool, courtesy shuttle to airport (10 minutes away). Open year-round. $$$
- Lord Nelson Hotel and Suites, 1515 South Park St, Halifax; 800 565-2020; www.lordnelsonhotel.com. Renovated historic hotel adjacent to Public Gardens and shopping. Dining room, fitness centre, business services. Open year-round. $$$
- ★Pepperberry Bed & Breakfast, 2688 Joseph Howe Dr, Halifax; 877 246-3244; www.pepperberryinn.com. Park-like setting near Armdale Rotary. Heritage property decorated with artistic panache. Full breakfast. Open year-round. $$$
- Prince George Hotel, 1725 Market St, Halifax; 800 565-1567; www.princegeorgehotel.com. Central downtown location with all the amenities. Underground parking. Open year-round. $$$
- Radisson Suite Hotel Halifax, 1649 Hollis St, Halifax; 800 333-3333; www.radissonhalifax.com. Two-room suites, most overlooking harbour. All amenities. Pool, fitness centre, club room, complimentary

continental breakfast. Open year-round. $$$

- Sterns Mansion B&B, 17 Tulip St, Dartmouth; 800 565-3885; www.sternsmansion.com. Four guest rooms with four-poster beds, two with jacuzzis. Full breakfast. Close to downtown and ferry. Open year-round. $$$

- Westin Nova Scotian Hotel, 1181 Hollis St, Halifax; 888 679-3784; 877 993-7846; www.westin.ns.ca. Comfortable rooms, historic hotel, a short walk south of downtown at old train station. Indoor pool, sauna, spa, tennis court. Open year-round. $$$

LIGHTHOUSE ROUTE

Peggys Cove to Hubbards

- Oceanstone Inn and Cottages, 8650 Peggys Cove Rd, Indian Harbour; 866 823-2160; www.oceanstone.ns.ca. Secluded 20-acre oceanfront getaway. Housekeeping cottages with fireplace; rooms or suites in inn. Beach, spa, fine dining. Open year-round. $$$

- Rosewood Cottages, 187 Shore Club Rd, Hubbards; 888 265-9950; www.rosewoodonthecove.com. Nine well-furnished seaside cottages with full kitchen, fireplace, gas BBQ, deck. Heated outdoor pool. Open year-round. $$$

- Surfside Inn, 9609 Hwy 3, Queensland; 800 373-2417; www.thesurfsideinn.com. Victorian elegance with modern amenities. Rooms or suite. Ocean views. Breakfast included. Casual fine dining. Open year-round. $$

Chester and Mahone Bay

- Bayview Pines Country Inn, 678 Oakland Rd, Indian Point, Mahone Bay; 866 624-9970; www.bayviewpines.com. A 14-acre property with hilltop view of Mahone Bay; century-old farmhouse and converted barn with stylish furnishings. Open year-round. $$

- Mahone Bay Bed & Breakfast, 558 Main St, Mahone Bay; 866 239-6252; www.bbcanada.com/4078.html.

Restored 1860 stately home; antiques, art, wraparound porch, all amenities. $

- Oak Island Resort and Spa, PO Box 6, Western Shore; 800 565-5075; www.oakislandresortandspa.com. Recently renovated oceanfront resort and chalets. All-inclusive packages include golfing, sailing and whale-watching. Open year-round. $$/$$$

- Red Barn Cottages, Clearland, Mahone Bay; 624-0800; www.redbarncottages.com. Fully equipped family-oriented housekeeping cottages on old farm property 1.5 km from Mahone Bay. Air conditioning, screened porches, pool, large barn with pool table, games, videos. Open May–Oct. $$

- Sword and Anchor B&B, 5306 Hwy 3, Chester Basin; 877 639-3966; www.swordandanchor.com. Eight rooms in 1882 waterfront property; one oceanfront cottage. Full breakfast. Open year-round. $

Lunenburg

- Addington Arms, 27 Cornwallis St, Lunenburg; 877 979-2727; www.addingtonarms.com. Steam room, aroma and sound therapy. Full breakfast. Downtown, waterviews. Open year-round. $$$

- Boscawen Inn & McLachlan House, 150 Cumberland St, Lunenburg; 800 354-5009; www.boscawen.ca. Two heritage properties in the heart of old Lunenburg. One-of-a-kind rooms; upscale and casual dining rooms. Open May–Dec. $$/$$$

- 1860 Kaulbach House Historic Inn, 75 Pelham St, Lunenburg; 800 568-8818; www.kaulbachhouse.com. Award-winning restoration in old Lunenburg, this gracious B&B with seven air-conditioned rooms offers gourmet breakfast, harbour views. Walk to town attractions Open May–Dec. $$

- Lunenburg Arms, 94 Pelham St, Lunenburg; 800 679-4950; www.lunenburgarms.com. A 26-room hotel in Old Town with harbour views and all amenities. Open year-round. $$$

- Lunenburg Inn, 26 Dufferin St, Lunenburg; 800 565-3963; www.lunenburginn.com. An 1893 heritage inn with sun deck and covered verandah, complimentary full breakfast. Open Apr–Oct. $$
- Salty Rose Beach Houses, Rose Bay; 877 766-4923; www.saltyrose.com. Six secluded oceanfront housekeeping cottages, fully-equipped, tastefully appointed; wood stoves, screened decks, gas BBQs. Open year-round. $$$

Liverpool and Shelburne
- Cooper's Inn, 36 Dock St, Shelburne; 800 688-2011; www.thecoopersinn.com. Loyalist home built around 1785. Six guest rooms and one luxury suite in main building and adjoining cooperage, with views of Shelburne Harbour. Open Apr–Oct. $$
- Lane's Privateer Inn, 27 Bristol Ave (Rte 3), Liverpool; 800 794-3332; www.lanesprivateerinn.com. Twenty-seven rooms in restored heritage property overlooking Mersey River. Dining room and pub. Open year-round. $$
- Quarterdeck Beachside Villas & Grill, Summerville Beach; 800 565-1119; www.quarterdeck.ns.ca. Beachside resort with all the amenities including jacuzzis, fireplaces and kitchen facilities. Dining room. Open year-round. $$$
- White Point Beach Resort, White Point Beach; 800 565-5068; www.whitepoint.com. 74-room resort with extensive recreational facilities, including golf, tennis, boating, swimming pools and kilometre-long white sand beach. Also 44 cottages. Open year-round. $$$
- Whitman Inn, 12389 Hwy 8, Kempt; 800 830-3855; www.whitmaninn.com. Close to Kejimkujik National Park. Turn-of-the-century homestead with indoor pool and sauna. Park-related recreational packages for canoeing, bicycling and cross-country skiing. Open Feb–Oct. $

Yarmouth
- Charles C. Richards House B&B, 17 Collins St, Yarmouth; 866 798-0929; www. charlesrichardshouse.ns.ca. Three guest rooms in Queen Anne mansion in historic district. Full breakfast, high tea. Open year-round. $$$
- Guest Lovitt House B&B, 12 Parade St, Yarmouth; 866 742-0372; www.guestlovitt.ca. Open year-round. $$$
- Harbour's Edge Bed and Breakfast, 12 Vancouver St, Yarmouth; 742-2387; www.harboursedge.ns.ca. Open year-round. $$
- Manor Inn Lakeside, Route 1, Hebron; 888 626-6746; www.manorinn.com. Inn, coach house and adjacent motel set on 9 acres of landscaped grounds on Doctors Lake. Breakfast included; evening dining available every night. Open year-round. $$/$$$
- Rodd Grand Yarmouth, 417 Main St, Yarmouth; 800 565-RODD; www.rodd-hotels.ca. Modern full-service hotel with indoor pool. Open year-round. $$$
- Trout Point Lodge, East Kemptville Rd, off Hwy 203; 482-8360; www.troutpoint.com. Granite and log lodge, rustic furniture. Seafood restaurant. Two hundred acres on lake and river. Fishing, kayaking, canoeing, nature trails. Open May–Nov. $$$

EVANGELINE TRAIL

Wolfville to Middleton
- Blomidon Inn, 195 Main St, Wolfville; 800 565-2291; www.theblomidon.net. Sea captain's mansion from the grand shipbuilding era of the 1880s. Evening dining. Open year-round. $$/$$$
- By the Dock of the Bay Cottages, Haddock Alley, Margaretsville; 800 407-2856; www.cottagesnovascotia.com. Two- and three-bedroom housekeeping beach houses on the Bay of Fundy, very near

water's edge amidst gorgeous gardens. Open May–mid-Oct. $$

- Century Farm Inn, 10 Main St, Middleton; 800 237-9896; www.centuryfarminn.com. Victorian farmhouse on working fruit and vegetable farm. Complimentary full breakfast. Open June–Sept. $
- Falcourt Inn, 8979 Hwy 201 Nictaux; 800 464-8979; www.falcourtinn.ns.ca. Restored 1920s lodge on Nictaux river. Seven guest rooms (one wheelchair-accessible) and two-bedroom guest house. Complimentary breakfast; evening dining. Open year-round. $$
- Olde Lantern Inn, 11575 Hwy 1, Grand Pré; 877 965-3845; www.oldlanterninn.com. Replica of 1700s Cape situated in vineyard next to winery and restaurant. Open year-round. $$
- Tattingstone Inn, 620 Main St, Wolfville; 800 565-7696; www.tattingstone.ns.ca. Tastefully decorated B&B inn and carriage house with tennis court, outdoor pool, library and music room. Open year-round. $$
- Victoria's Historic Inn and Carriage House B&B, 600 Main St, Wolfville; 800 556-5744; www.victoriashistoricinn.com. Picturesque 1893 Registered Heritage Property. Luxury suites with jacuzzi whirlpool bath; full breakfast, afternoon tea. Open year-round. $$$

Annapolis Royal and Digby
- Bread and Roses Inn, 82 Victoria St, Annapolis Royal; 888 899-0551; www.breadandroses.ns.ca. Restored Queen Anne Revival mansion with many unique architectural details, antique furnishings. Full breakfast included. Open year-round. $$
- Brier Island Lodge & Restaurant, Westport, Brier Island; 800 662-8355; www.brierisland.com. Modern rooms with ocean view, dining room. Excellent opportunities for whale- and bird-watching. Open May–Oct. $/$$
- ★The Digby Pines Resort, Shore Rd, Digby; 800 667-4637; www.signatureresorts.com. Full-scale luxury resort with championship golf course and all other amenities. Hotel rooms and suites plus 30 cottages with stone fireplaces. Open May–mid-Oct. $$$
- Dockside Suites, 34 Water St, Digby; 866 445-4950; www.fundyrestaurant.com. Six air-conditioned housekeeping suites overlooking the Digby scallop fleet. Open year-round. $$
- Garrison House Inn, 350 Saint George St, Annapolis Royal; 866 532-5750; www.garrisonhouse.ca. Small inn, overlooking Fort Anne, built in 1854; fine dining. Open Apr–Dec. $$/$$$
- Milford House, Route 8, South Milford; 877 532-5751; www.milfordhouse.ca. Secluded historic lodge amidst large wooded acreage between Annapolis Royal and Kejimkujik National Park. Twenty-seven rustic lakeshore cabins with fireplaces. Country breakfasts and dinners in the main lodge (MAP). Open July–mid-Oct. Two winterized cabins available year-round. $$
- Queen Anne Inn, 494 Upper Saint George St, Annapolis Royal; 877 536-0403; www.queenanneinn.ns.ca. Registered Heritage Property. Breakfast in elegant dining room. Open Apr 15–Oct 31. $$/$$$
- Thistle Down Country Inn, 98 Montague Row, Digby; 800 565-8081; www.thistledown.ns.ca/theinn. Edwardian inn on the water's edge. Twelve comfortable rooms (six modern harbourside units), dinner for guests. Open May 1–Nov 30. $$

GLOOSCAP TRAIL

Truro and Maitland
- Cresthaven by the Sea Country Inn, 19 Ferry Lane, Maitland; 866 870-2001; www.cresthavenbythesea.com. Greek revival shipbuilders home with view of Tidal Bore. Open

year-round. $$
- Irwin Lake Chalets, Old Barns (near Truro), Route 236, off Hwy 102, Exit 14; 866 554-7946; www.irwinlakechalets.com. Six comfy lakeside log chalets in 500-acre unspoiled wilderness setting; one- and two-bedroom, heated, wood stoves, covered decks, BBQs. Fishing, hiking, canoeing. Open year-round. $$
- Regent Bed and Breakfast, 175 East Victoria St, Amherst; 866 661-2861; www.theregent.ca. One of Amherst's fine old homes, now a fine B&B. Open year-round (off season by reservation). $$
- The John Stanfield Inn, 437 Prince St, Truro; 800 561-7666; www.johnstanfieldinn.com. Impressive Queen Anne-style mansion, beautiful woodwork, period furnishings, modern amenities; fine dining. Open year-round. $$$

Economy and Parrsboro
- Four Seasons Retreat, 320 Cove Rd, Economy; 888 373-0339; www.fourseasonsretreat.ns.ca. Eleven beautiful housekeeping cottages on the cliffs overlooking Minas Basin. Swimming, skiing, hiking trails. Open year-round. $$
- Gillespie House Inn, 358 Main St, Parrsboro; 877 901-3196; www.gillespiehouseinn.com. An 1890 Victorian farmhouse with antiques, fireplaces, down duvets. Lovely gardens and lawns. Near Fundy hiking, rockhounding. Open year-round. $$

SUNRISE TRAIL

Lorneville to Tatamagouche
- ★Amherst Shore Country Inn, Route 366, Lorneville; 800 661-2724; www.ascinn.ns.ca. Small inn with lovely ocean view, private beach and renowned dining room. Open May–Oct, weekends Dec–Apr. $$
- The Cottages at Cambra Sands, 643 North Shore Rd, Malagash; 866 559-0705; www.cambrasands.com. Well-appointed new housekeeping cottages (one-, two- and three-

bedroom) with all amenities; private beach. Open year-round. $$$
- Train Station Inn, 21 Station Rd, Tatamagouche; 888 724-5233; www.trainstation.ns.ca. Three guest rooms in restored century-old train station plus seven guest cabooses reflect railways' past. All modern amenities. Dining car. Open Apr–Oct. $$

Pictou and Antigonish
- Antigonish Victorian Inn, 149 Main St, Antigonish; 863-1103; www.bbcanada.com/5491.html. Magnificent turreted Victorian mansion-cum B&B; sumptuously decorated rooms with mod cons. Open year-round. $$
- Braeside Inn, 126 Front St, Pictou; 800 613-7701; www.braesideinn.com. Eighteen air-conditioned rooms, dining with harbour view. Open year-round. $$
- Consulate Inn, 157 Water St, Pictou; 800 424-8283; www.consulateinn.com. Bed-and-breakfast accommodation in a restored c. 1810 property overlooking Pictou harbour. Open year-round. $$
- ★Pictou Lodge Resort, Braeshore Road, Pictou; 888 662-7484; www.maritimeinns.com. Rustic 1920s resort with modern amenities. Standard hotel accommodation or multiple-bedroom log cottages with huge stone fireplaces and screened-in sunporches. Open mid-May–mid-Oct. $$$

MARINE DRIVE
- DesBarres Manor Inn, 90 Church St, Guysborough; 533-2099; www.desbarresmanor.com. Ten large, well-appointed rooms in elegant mansion. Fine dining. Open mid-May–mid-Oct. $$$
- ★Liscombe Lodge, Liscomb Mills; 800 665-6343; www.signatureresorts.com. Full-service resort featuring sport fishing packages (guides available), boat rentals and marina. Hotel and cottage-style accommodations, some

overlooking the beautiful Liscomb River. Enclosed pool and fitness centre. Fine dining. Open mid-May–Oct. $$$

- Lonely Rock Seaside Bungalows, 150 New Harbour Rd, New Harbour; 866 248-1877; www.lonelyrock.com. Fully equipped family housekeeping cottages with ocean views and sand beach. Open year-round. $$$

- Salmon River House Country Inn, 9931 Hwy 7, Salmon River Bridge; 800 565-3353; www.salmonriverhouse.com. Seven well-appointed guest rooms. On-site hiking, boating, hunting and fishing. Licensed dining. Open May–Oct. $$

CABOT TRAIL AND CEILIDH TRAIL

Cabot Trail

- Auberge Giselle's Inn, 387 Shore Rd, Baddeck; 800 304-0466; www.giseles.com. 75 rooms overlooking gardens and Bras d'Or Lakes. All amenities; dining room. Open May–Oct. $$$

- Broadwater Inn and Cottages, Bay Rd, Baddeck; 877 818-3474; www.broadwater.baddeck.com. Historic property with charming B&B and nine housekeeping log cottages overlooking Bras d'Or. Cottages open year-round; B&B Apr–Nov. $$

- Cabot Shores Adventure and Retreat Centre, 30 Buchana Dr, Indian Brook; 866 929-2585; www.cabotshores.com. Rustic comfort in environmentally responsible lodge and cabins. Outdoor activities for the whole family. Open year-round. $$$

- Castle Moffett, 11980 Hwy 105, Bucklaw, Baddeck; 888 756-9070; www.castlemoffett.com. Luxury suites with king or queen canopy or four-poster beds, fireplaces, views of Bras d'Or Lakes, fine dining. Open May–Oct. $$$

- Chanterelle Country Inn and Cottages, 48678 Cabot Trail, North River; 866 277-0577; www.chanterelleinn.com. Environmentally friendly

property in tranquil setting overlooking St Ann's Bay. Open May–Oct. $$

- Cheticamp Island Resort, Cheticamp Island; 849-6444; www.cheticampislandresort.com. Two-bedroom housekeeping cottages. Ocean swimming. Daily and weekly rates. Open mid-June–mid-Oct. $$

- Crown Jewel Resort Ranch, 992 Westside Baddeck Rd, 8 km north of Baddeck; 295-1096; www.crownjewelresort.com. Fly-in adventure vacation on 800-acre ranch with working animals, eco-adventures, fine dining. Open year-round. $$$

- Duffus House Inn, 108 Water St, Baddeck; 295-2172; www.baddeck.com/duffushouse. Seven rooms (4 with sitting rooms) in gracious 1830s home with antique furnishings, verandah, patio, gardens. Private wharf. Open June–mid-Oct. No pets. $$

- Dundee Resort & Golf Club, West Bay; 800 565-1774; www.dundeeresort.com. Golf with outstanding views of the Bras d'Or; marina and boat rentals, indoor and outdoor pools; lighted tennis. Sixty hotel rooms, 38 one- and two-bedroom cottages. Open mid-May–Oct. $$$

- Inverary Resort, Shore Rd, Baddeck; 800 565-5660; www.inveraryresort.com. Seven cottages, 125 rooms and 52 motel units. Licensed dining room and pub, indoor and outdoor pools, complimentary boat tours and other resort facilities. Open year-round. $$$

- ★Keltic Lodge, Middle Head Peninsula, Ingonish Beach; 800 565-0444; www.signatureresorts.com. Full-scale luxury resort with championship golf course (many say the best in Nova Scotia). Choose from the main lodge, White Birch Inn or cottages. Outdoor heated pool, hiking trails. Open mid-May–mid-Oct. $$$

- Laurie's Motor Inn, 15456 Laurie Rd, Cheticamp; 800 959-4253; www.lauries.com. Fifty-four motel units, six suites;

dining room. Whale cruises arranged. Open Apr–Oct. $$
- MacNeil House, 257 Shore Rd, Baddeck; 888 662-7484; www.maritimeinns.com. Luxury suites with all the amenities. Swimming pool or saltwater swimming in the Bras d'Or. Open mid-May–mid-Oct. $$$
- ★Markland Coastal Resort, Dingwall; 800 872-6084; www.marklandresort.com. Secluded coastal resort with log cabins, heated outdoor pool, ocean beach and fine dining. Concert hall; outdoor adventure tours. Open mid-June–mid-Oct. $$$
- Normaway Inn, 691 Egypt Rd, Margaree Valley; 800 565-9463; www.normaway.com. Relaxing old-style resort, nine rooms in lodge, 17 cabins with woodstoves and screened porches (7 have jacuzzis). Excellent salmon and trout fishing nearby. Open mid-June–mid-Oct. $$$

Ceilidh Trail
- Duncreigan Country Inn, Mabou; 800 840-2207; www.duncreigan.ca. Four spacious guest rooms with antique furnishings in Main Inn and four large rooms in adjacent Spring House. Fine dining. Open year-round. $$
- Glenora Inn and Distillery Resort, Hwy 19, Glenville; 800 839-0491; www.glenoradistillery.com. Nine rooms and six housekeeping chalets. Tours of Canada's only single-malt distillery. Open mid-May–mid-Oct. $$/$$$
- Haus Treuburg, 175 Main St, Port Hood; 787-2116; www.haustreuburg.com. Guest house and cottages close to warm saltwater swimming. Complimentary German-style breakfast at guest house. Licensed restaurant. Open May–Dec. $$
- Hillcrest Hall Country Inn, 24 Main St, Port Hood; 888 434-4255; www.hillcresthall.com. Restored Queen Anne Revival inn with views of harbour. One of 11 units is wheelchair accessible.

Licensed dining room. Open mid-June–mid-Oct. $
- MacLeod Inn, Broad Cove Rd, Broad Cove; 258-3360; www.macleods.com. Comfortable B&B with views of Mabou Highlands and Gulf of St Lawrence. Open June–Oct. $
- Tulloch Inn, West Lake Ainslie; 866 707-4300; www.tulloch-inn.ca. One wheelchair-accessible room and one environmentally friendly room in family-friendly inn. Breakfast; licensed dining room. Open year-round. $$

FLEUR-DE-LIS AND MARCONI TRAILS AND METRO CAPE BRETON
- Cambridge Suites Hotel, 380 Esplanade, Sydney; 800 565-9466; www.centennialhotels.com/cambridge. On Sydney waterfront. Suite accommodation with housekeeping facilities. Rooftop spa pool and exercise facilities. Complimentary breakfast. Open year-round. $$$
- Cranberry Cove Inn, 12 Wolfe St, Louisbourg; 800 929-0222; www.louisbourg.com/cranberry cove. Seven guest rooms (some with jacuzzis) in a fully renovated turn-of-the-century home near Fortress; full breakfast. Open May–Oct. $$
- Delta Sydney, 300 Esplanade, Sydney; 800 268-1133; www.deltahotels.com/prov/p_novascotia.html. Harbour view with 152 rooms, all amenities, pool, water slide. Open year-round. $$/$$$
- ★Gowrie House Country Inn, 840 Shore Rd, Sydney Mines; 800 372-1115; www.gowriehouse.com. Beautifully furnished 1830 home with elegant antique-filled guest rooms. Renovated caretaker's cottage with fireplace. Exceptional dining. Open May–Oct. $$$
- L'Auberge Acadienne, 2375 High St, Arichat; 877 787-2200; www.acadienne.com. 19th century Acadian-style country inn on Isle Madame. Open year-round. $
- Louisbourg Harbour Inn, 9 Lower Warren St, Louisbourg; 888 888-8466;

www.louisbourg.com/louisbourg
harbourinn. Eight well-appointed
guest rooms in a century-old
captain's house overlooking
Louisbourg Harbour. Full
breakfast. Open mid-June–mid-
Oct. $$
• Louisbourg Heritage House B&B,
7544 Main St, Louisbourg; 888
888-8466; www.louisbourg.com
/louisbourgheritagehouse. Open
July–Sept. $$
• Point of View Suites, 15
Commercial St Ext, Louisbourg;
888 374-8439;
www.louisbourgpointofview.com.
Sixteen oceanfront suites near
the gates of Fortress Louisbourg;
balconies and decks overlooking
Fortress and ocean. Open mid-
May–mid-Oct. $$/$$$

DINING

Nova Scotia cuisine is a delight.
Tastefully and imaginatively
prepared seafood, fresh Annapolis
Valley produce and Pictou County
lamb are among the many
specialties of Nova Scotia
restaurants. Local wines are
inexpensive and surprisingly good.
   Where to Eat in Canada
(Oberon Press) is updated annually
and includes many of the
province's finer restaurants.
Maritime Flavours is an illustrated
guide to the best and most
distinctive dining establishments in
the Maritime provinces,
accompanied by a selection of their
favourite recipes. See Dining p. 34.
   Approximate prices are
indicated, based on the average
cost, at time of publication, of
dinner for two including wine
(where available), taxes and
gratuity: $ = under $50; $$ =
$50–90; $$$ = over $90.
   The area code for all of Nova
Scotia is 902.

HALIFAX
• Baan Thai, 1569 Dresden Row,
Halifax; 446-4301. Very good,
reasonably priced Vietnamese
food. Open daily for dinner;
closed Mon. $$
• Bish World Cuisine, Bishop's
Landing, 1475 Lower Water St,

Halifax; 425-7993. Wonderful
waterfront location with outdoor
patio in summer; imaginative
appetizers; local seafood and
rack of lamb; good wine list.
Open Mon–Sat 5:30–10 pm. $$$
★The Chickenburger, 1531
Bedford Highway, Bedford. A
landmark since the 1940s. Still
has a juke box (although now it
plays compact discs). Chicken
burgers and real, old-fashioned
milkshakes are the staples. Open
9 am–1 am daily. $
• Cheelin, Brewery Market, 1496
Lower Water St, Halifax; 422-
2252. The best Chinese food in
Halifax. Open for dinner
Tues–Sun 5–10 pm, lunch
Mon–Sat 11:30 am–2:30 pm. $$
★Chives Canadian Bistro, 1537
Barrington St, Halifax; 420-
9626; www.chives.ca. Changing
menu of traditional Nova Scotian
fare with local seasonal
ingredients. Open daily 5–9:30
pm. $$$
★Da Maurizio, 1496 Lower Water
St, Halifax; 423-0859. Elegant
Italian dining in the restored
Brewery Market complex. One
of Nova Scotia's best restaurants.
Open Mon-Sat 5:30–10 pm;
closed Sun. $$$
• Deco, 5518 Spring Garden Rd,
Halifax; 423-9795. Casual fine
dining in an elegant 20s style
room. Open daily: lunch
Mon–Fri 11:30 am–5 pm; dinner
Sun–Thurs 5–10 pm, Fri and Sat
5–11pm, Sat and Sun brunch 9
am–3 pm. $$
★Fid, 1569 Dresden Row, Halifax;
422-9162; www.fidcuisine.ca.
Small, creative, fusion menu
featuring seasonal and local
ingredients. Open daily for
dinner 5–10 pm, lunch Wed–Fri
11:30 am–2 pm, closed Mon.
$$$
• Hamachi House, 5190 Morris St,
Halifax; 425-7711. Japanese
menu and floating sushi bar.
Open Mon–Sat 11:30 am–11 pm,
Sun 4–10 pm. $$
• Hamachi Steakhouse, Bishop's
Landing, 1477 Lower Water St,

Halifax; 422-1600. Japanese-style steakhouse with interesting seafood dishes as well. Open Mon–Sat 11:30 am–2:30 pm, dinner 5–10 pm, Fri and Sat till 11 pm, Sun 4–10 pm. $$

- Il Mercato, 5650 Spring Garden Rd, Halifax; 422-2866. Casual northern Italian dining with great desserts. Busy and friendly. Open Mon–Sat, 11 am–11 pm. $$

- Inn-on-the-Lake, Fall River; 861-3480; www.innonthelake.com. Located on beautiful Lake Thomas, meals are served in the dining room, on the terrace or in Oliver's pub. Open daily 7 am – 10 pm. $$$

★Jane's on the Common, 2394 Robie St, Halifax; 431-5683; www.janesonthecommon.ca. Imaginative, inexpensive dining in a diner format. Short wine list. Open for lunch Tues–Fri, dinner Tues–Sun, brunch Sat and Sun. $$

★La Perla, 73 Alderney Dr, Dartmouth; 469-3241. Distinctive northern Italian cuisine, a minute's walk from the ferry terminal. Open Mon–Fri, 11 am–9:30 pm, weekends, dinner only. $$$

- McKelvie's, 1680 Lower Water St, Halifax; 421-6161; www.mckelvies.ca. Fresh seafood, also an on-site bakery. Open daily June–Sept, 11:30 am–10 pm. $$$

- Opa! 1565 Argyle St, Halifax; 492-7999. Atmospheric taverna featuring grilled seafood and traditional Greek favourites. Open Mon–Sat, 11 am–11 pm. $$

- Press Gang, 5218 Prince St, Halifax; 423-8816; www.thepressgang.ca. Fine dining in an intimate and historic setting. Popular both with locals and visiting celebrities. Open daily for dinner. Reservations recommended. $$$

- Ryan Duffy's Steak and Seafood, 5640 Spring Garden Rd, Halifax; 421-1116. Classic steak house with the city's best steaks, cut to the size you want, and Caesar salads made at your table. Open daily 5–10 pm, Sat to 11 pm; lunch Mon–Fri 11:30 am–2 pm. $$$

- Saege, 5883 Spring Garden Rd, Halifax; 429-1882; www.saege.ca. Stylish, creative and delicious dishes in a cozy bistro atmosphere. Excellent wines. Open Tues–Sun, 7 am–10 pm. Open daily for breakfast, lunch and dinner; closed Mon. $$$

- Satisfaction Feast Vegetarian Restaurant, 1581 Grafton St, Halifax; 422-3540. Delicious and inexpensive vegetarian fare, especially the soups and breads. There is a bakery on-site. Open daily, 11:30 am–9:30 pm; closed Sun; shorter hours off-season. No liquor. $

- Stories at The Halliburton, 5184 Morris St, Halifax; 444-4400; www.thehalliburton.com. Specialties include fresh Atlantic seafood and wild game entrées. Light fare and cocktails in the outdoor garden café. Open daily 5:30–9 pm. $$$

★Sweet Basil Bistro, 1866 Upper Water St, Halifax; 425-2133. Fine presentation and service. Good for fresh seafood. Open daily 11:30 am–10 pm (Sat and Sun from 10 am). $$

LIGHTHOUSE ROUTE

Peggys Cove and Hubbards

★Rhubarb Grill at Oceanstone Inn, 8650 Peggys Cove Rd, Indian Harbour; 823-2160; www.oceanstone.ns.ca. Casual fine dining in a unique seaside setting. Open June–Dec. $$$

- Shore Club Lobster Supper, Hubbards; 857-9555; www.lobstersupper.com. Boiled lobster, mussels and salad bar; children's menu. Open Wed–Sun, June–early Oct. $$

- Sou'wester, Peggys Cove; 823-2561. Excellent chowders, tasty lobster and traditional Nova Scotia desserts like gingerbread and apple crisp. Open daily 8 am–9 pm (Nov–Apr, 10 am–6 pm). $$

Chester and Mahone Bay

- The Biscuit Eater, 16 Orchard St, Mahone Bay; 624-2665. A delightful café with excellent teas and coffees, unusual sandwiches, soups and sweets amidst stacks of books in a warm, eclectic atmosphere. Open daily, 9 am–5 pm; closed Tues.

- Cheesecake Gallery, South Main St, Mahone Bay; 624-0579. Fine casual dining. Open daily in summer. $$
- Innlet Cafe, Kedy's Landing, Mahone Bay; 624-6363. Refreshing seafood-garnished salads or more substantial dishes for dinner; lots of seafood. Try the front terrace on a warm evening, with a view of the water and Mahone Bay's three churches. Open daily 11:30 am–9 pm. $$
- ★Julien's Pastry Shop, 43 Queen St, Chester; 275-2324. A French pâtisserie and bakery featuring croissants, European breads, light lunches (famous lobster sandwiches) and deli. Open daily 8 am–6 pm. Shorter hours and closed Monday during off-season. $
- Nicki's Inn, Chester. 275-4342; www.aco.ca/nickis.html. Open Wed–Sat 5–9 pm; Sun 4–8 pm (carvery). Fine dining. Good wine list. $$$
- Saltspray Café, 621 South Main St, Mahone Bay; 624-0457. Home-style cooking and to-die-for pies. Try the seafood chowder and half lobster sandwich. Save room for peanut butter chocolate pie. Deck overlooking water. Open year-round, daily 8 am–8 pm (9 pm in summer). $$
- Seaside Shanty, Hwy 3, Chester Basin; 275-2246. Big helpings of fresh seafood. Great chowder. Open daily 11:30 am–10 pm. Shorter hours during off-season. $$

Lunenburg

- Black Forest, Hwy 3, Martin's Brook; 634-3600. German and Canadian fare. Specialities are schnitzel and spatzle. Open mid-Apr–mid-Dec, 11:30 am–9 pm. $$
- Boscawen Inn, 150 Cumberland St, Lunenburg; 634-3325. A restored Victorian mansion specializing in fresh local seafood. Afternoon tea in the drawing rooms. Open for breakfast and dinner daily, Easter–Dec. $$$
- ★Fleur de Sel, 53 Montague St, Lunenburg; 640-2121. Fine dining with European flair; changing menu features local seafood and organic vegetables. Open daily in summer for dinner, 5–10 pm; Thurs–Sat for lunch, 11:30–2. Shorter hours off-season.
- LaHave Bakery, LaHave; 688-2908. Home baking using clear spring water and locally grown, fresh-milled grains. Sandwiches made to order. Open Mon–Fri, 9 am–5:30 pm, weekends 9 am–7 pm. Longer hours during season. No liquor. $
- Magnolia's Grill, 128 Montague St, Lunenburg; 634-3287. Bustling atmosphere, tasty and innovative dishes, and lots to look at on the walls while you wait. Key lime pie for dessert. Open Mon–Sat for lunch and dinner, Apr–late Oct. $$
- The Old Fish Factory Restaurant, at the Fisheries Museum, Lunenburg; 800 533-9336; www.oldfishfactory.com. Good selection of seafood. Watch the sunset over the harbour as you dine. $$

Liverpool and Shelburne

- Charlotte Lane Café, 13 Charlotte Lane, Shelburne; 875-3314; www.charlottelane.ca. Relaxed dining, meals prepared by award-winning chef in a heritage property. Open May–Dec, Tues–Sat, lunch 11:30 am–2 pm, dinner 5–8 pm (evening reservation recommended). $$
- Lane's Privateer Inn, 27 Bristol Ave, Liverpool; 800 794-3332; www.lanesprivateerinn.com. Dining room and pub. Good pasta and seafood. Open daily 7 am–10 pm (9 pm in winter). $$
- Quarterdeck Beachside Villas and Grill, Summerville Centre; 683-2998; www.quarterdeck.ns.ca. Bright restaurant with view of white sand beaches, serving good food. Open daily 11:30 am–late, mid-May–mid-Oct. $$
- Seawatch Restaurant, White

Point Beach Resort, White Point; 354-2711; www.whitepoint.com. Informal dining room, suitable for children, serves steak and seafood. Open daily for breakfast, lunch and dinner. $$

Yarmouth

- Chez Bruno, 278 Main St, Yarmouth; 742-0031. Organic vegetables, fresh fish, free-range chicken all impeccably prepared. Open Mon, Tues 10 am–4 pm; Wed–Sat until 8 pm, Sun noon–7. $$
- Rudders, 96 Water St, Yarmouth; 742-7311. A seafood restaurant and microbrewery in an historic building overlooking the water. Open year-round, 11 am until late. $$

EVANGELINE TRAIL

Wolfville to Kentville

★Acton's Grill and Café, 406 Main St, Wolfville; 542-7525. Elegant summer lunches, chilled soups, an interesting buffet and open-air patio. One of Nova Scotia's very best restaurants. Open daily for lunch and dinner. $$$
- Between the Bushes, 1225 Middle Dyke Rd, Sheffield Mills; 582-3648. Fine dining in the middle of a big blueberry field; notable fresh scallops and haddock and, of course, blueberry desserts. Open Wed–Sun for lunch and dinner; Tues for lunch; shorter hours off-season. $$$
- Blomidon Inn, 195 Main St, Wolfville; 542-2291; www.blomidon.ns.ca. Dine in an elegant restored sea captain's mansion, built in 1877. Open daily for lunch and dinner, 11:30 am–2 pm and 5–9:30 pm, year-round. $$$
- Evangeline Café, Evangeline Motel, 11668 Hwy 1, Grand Pré; 542-2703; www.evangeline.ns.ca. Fabulous Valley fruit pies. Open daily to 7 pm, early May–late Oct. No liquor. $
- Falcourt Inn, 8979 Hwy 201, Nictaux; 825-3399. A restored fishing lodge with an exceptional view, and specializing in seafood, and featuring creative beef and chicken dishes. Open daily 5–8:30 pm, year-round. $$
- Le Caveau at Grand Pré Winery, Hwy 1, Grand Pré; 542-7177; www.grandprewines.ns.ca. Northern European cuisine served in an attractive vineyard setting. Open daily May–Oct for lunch and dinner; Apr, Nov, Dec, dinner only. Reservations recommended. $$$
- Lobster Pound, Halls Harbour; 679-5299. Only lobster, but some of the best to be had anywhere. Take it away to cook yourself, or take it to the boiling shack. Open noon–7 pm, mid-May–Oct; 11:30 am–8:30 pm, July and Aug. $$
- Old Orchard Inn, Greenwich, near Wolfville; 800 561-8090; www.oldorchardinn.com. Something for everyone, good family dining. Open year-round. $$
- Paddy's Brewpub, 42 Aberdeen St, Kentville; 678-3199; www.paddyspub.ca. Open year-round, kitchen 11 am–10 pm. $
★Tempest, 117 Front St, Wolfville; 542-0588. Fine dining, world cuisine, ethnic lunches, fusion dinners and French accents. Open daily, noon–2:30pm, 5:30–9:30 pm; closed Mon in winter. Phone ahead to confirm restaurant has re-opened. $$$

Annapolis Royal to Digby

- Brier Island Lodge, Westport, Brier Island; 839-2300; www.brierisland.com. Acadian dishes and lots of seafood, from fish cakes to Solomon Gundy. Open 7–10 am, 11:30–2 pm and 6–9:30 pm daily, June–Oct. $$
- Chez Christophe, Hwy 1, Grosses Coques; 837-5817. Acadian cooking: chicken fricot, rappie pie, and seafood as well, served in a homey atmosphere. Open Tues–Sun, 6 am–10 pm. $
- Cape View Restaurant, Mavillette Beach; 645-2519. Seafood and Acadian specialties. Open late Mar–end Dec, with limited opening days in fall and winter, 11 am–8 pm. $$
★Digby Pines Resort Hotel, Shore Rd, Digby; 245-2511;

www.signatureresorts.com. Specializing in local fish and seafood, in the luxurious surroundings of the Pines Resort Hotel. One of Nova Scotia's best restaurants. Open daily for breakfast 7–10 am, restaurant lunch noon–2 pm, dinner 6–9 pm, May–Dec. Don't miss Sunday brunch, mid-June–Sept. $$$

- Fundy Restaurant, 34 Water St, Digby; 866 445-4950; www.fundyrestaurant.com. Open year-round, daily, 7 am–10 pm in summer, 11–9 in winter. $$
- Garrison House Inn Restaurant, 350 Saint George St, Annapolis Royal; 532-5750; www.come.to/garrison. Understated entrées with fresh and simple vegetable accompaniments. Save room for dessert — the strawberry rhubarb pie is wonderful! Open for dinner 5:30–9 pm, May–Oct. $$
- Leo's Café, Saint George St, Annapolis Royal; 532-7424. Tasty soups and sandwiches. Don't expect a quick lunch in mid-summer; it's apt to be crowded. Open daily 11:30 am–6 pm, mid-Mar–late Dec. Licensed for beer and wine only. $
- Restaurant Chez Christophe, 2655 Route 2, Grosses Coques; 837-5817. Acadian favourites and more. Open year-round, 11:30 am-2 pm and 4:30-8pm. Reservations recommended. $

GLOOSCAP TRAIL
- Diane's Restaurant, 81 Wharf Rd, Five Islands; 254-3190. A good feed of fried clams right at the source. Open weekends only Apr–May, summer open daily, 11 am–10pm. $
- Lightkeeper's Kitchen, Cape d'Or, Advocate Harbour; 670-0534. Great seafood and organic vegetables served up in a charming old lighthouse. Open mid-May–Oct, 11 am–4 pm; 5:30–9pm. $$
- Macombers at Cresthaven by the Sea Country Inn, 19 Ferry Lane, Maitland; 866 870-2001; www.cresthavenbythesea.com. Casual fine dining. The coquilles St-Jacques is ever popular. Open

daily 5:30–9 pm, mid-May–mid-Oct. $$
- Murphy's Fish & Chips, 88 Esplanade, Truro; 895-1275. One of the best of its kind in Canada. Fried Digby clams and the seafood platter are favourites. Open daily 11 am–7 pm, Fri until 8 pm, Sun noon–7 pm. $
- The Wooden Hog, 627 Prince St, Truro; 895-0779. Simple lunch and traditional dinner fare; wide selection of teas and coffees. Open year-round Mon–Sat, 9 am–10 pm. $

SUNRISE TRAIL
- Amherst Shore Country Inn, Hwy 366, Lorneville; 661-2724; www.ascinn.ns.ca. A different four-course gourmet meal each night. Open daily 7:30 pm, May–Oct. By appointment only. $$$
- Braeside Inn, 126 Front St, Pictou; 485-5046; www.braesideinn.com. Fresh Nova Scotia seafood and prime rib of beef. Hillside view of Pictou Harbour. Open daily 5:30–8:30 pm by reservation. $$
- Gabrieau's Bistro, 350 Main St, Antigonish; 863-1925. Innovative appetizers, light pasta and exceptional desserts. Open year-round Mon–Thurs, 11 am–9:30 pm, Fri and Sat to 10 pm. $$
- Mill Room, Balmoral Hotel, Hwy 6, Tatamagouche; 657-2000. German specialities including sausages, sauerkraut and schnitzel as well as Canadian dishes featuring local seafood. Open daily noon–8 pm. $
- Pictou Lodge Resort, Braeshore Rd, Pictou; 485-4322; www.maritimeinns.com. Fireside and ocean-view dining in this resort since the 1920s. Open mid-May–mid-Oct, hours vary seasonally. $$$

MARINE DRIVE
- Des Barres Manor Inn, 90 Church St, Guysborough; 533-2099; www.desbarresmanor.com. Fresh local produce, seafood and lamb. Open mid-May–Thanksgiving, daily at 7 pm by reservation only. $$
- Liscombe Lodge, Hwy 7,

Liscomb Mills; 800 665-6343; www.signatureresorts.com. A relaxed resort setting and casual dining room with an accomplished kitchen. Planked salmon is a speciality; watch it being cooked on the outdoor open fire. Open daily for breakfast, lunch and dinner, May–Oct. $$$

- Rare Bird Pub, Guysborough; 533-2128. A fine brewpub on the waterfront with good pub food. Open mid-May–mid-Oct, daily 11 am–10 pm; weekends until 1 am. $

- Salmon River House, Hwy 7, Head of Jeddore; 889-3353; www.highway7.com. Fresh boiled lobster and steaks on the verandah overlooking the Salmon River. Open daily for breakfast and dinner (by reservation only from Nov–Apr). $$

- SeaWind Landing Country Inn, 1 Wharf Rd, Charlos Cove; 800 563-4667; www.seawindlanding.com. Picnic lunches available to guests. Open to the public for dinner by reservation only, mid-May–mid-Oct. $$

CABOT TRAIL AND CEILIDH TRAIL

- Acadien, in the Co-opérative Artisanale, 15067 Main St, Cheticamp; 224-3207. Authentic Acadian specialities including tourtière, chowders and fish cakes. Open daily, early May–late Oct. Hours vary seasonally (late June–late Sept, 7 am–9 pm). $$

- Castle Rock Country Inn, Cabot Trail, Ingonish Ferry; 888 884-7625; www.ingonish.com/castlerock. Seasonal cookery featuring local ingredients in a spectacular location overlooking Ingonish Bay. Open daily for breakfast and dinner. $$

- Chanterelle Country Inn, Cabot Trail, North River, St Anns Bay; 866 277-0577; www.chanterelleinn.com. Cuisine based on organically-grown ingredients in an attractively-appointed setting overlooking St Anns Bay. Open for dinner 6–8:30 pm by reservation (closed Mon) from May–Oct. $$

- Chowder House, Cabot Trail, Neil's Harbour; 336-2463. $

- Duncreigan Country Inn, Mabou; 800 840-2207; www.duncreigan.ca. High-quality country dining in a tranquil setting. Open 5:30–8:30 pm by reservation, July–mid-Oct, closed Sun in winter. $$$

- Haus Treuburg, 175 Main St (Hwy 19), Port Hood; 787-2166. German-style breakfast for guests. Try the homemade soup, Atlantic salmon and apple strudel for dinner. Open daily 7 pm, June–Dec by reservation only. $$$

- Herring Choker Deli, on the Trans-Canada Highway between Baddeck and Whycocomagh; 295-2275. Coffee shop and family restaurant. Speciality and natural food items. Treats from the Indian Bay Bakery. Open daily, year-round. $

- The Highwheeler Café, Chebucto St, Baddeck; 295-3006. The perfect place to stock up for a picnic — deli sandwiches, cookies, cakes, fruit and pasta salads. Open daily 7:30 am–6 pm, longer hours in summer (closed Sun in off-season). $

- Inverary Inn and Resort, Shore Rd, Baddeck; 295-3500; www.inveraryresort.com. Flora's dining room offers a full-scale menu, with Scottish touches like smoked salmon and bannock. Lakeside Café on the waterfront is more casual, and features seafood appetizers and entrées. Open daily Apr–Dec for breakfast, lunch and dinner; café lunch and dinner only. $$$

- ★Keltic Lodge, Middle Head Peninsula, Ingonish Beach; 800 565-0444; www.signatureresorts.com. Fine formal dining in the Purple Thistle dining room. Five-course evening meal, menu changes daily. Open daily for breakfast and dinner (to 9 pm), mid-May–mid-Oct. $$$

- Markland Coastal Resort,

Dingwall; 383-2246;
www.marklandresort.com. Fresh
lamb and local seafood, with a
beautiful view of Aspy Bay from
the oceanside deck. Enjoy a walk
on the beach before dinner. Open
mid-June–mid-Oct, 7:30–10:30
am, 6–9 pm. $$$
- The Mull Café, 11630 Cabot
Trail, Mabou; 945-2244. Casual
and quick, hearty deli
sandwiches with take-out
available. Open daily 11 am–9
pm; shorter hours off-season. $
- Normaway Inn, Egypt Rd,
Margaree Valley; 800 565-9463;
www.normaway.com.
Beautifully situated in the
Margaree Valley. Four-course
country gourmet meals with
attentive but unobtrusive service.
Open for breakfast and dinner
mid-June–mid-Oct. $$$
- Red Shoe Pub, 11533 Hwy 19,
Mabou; 945-2996;
www.redshoepub.com. Owned by
the Rankin family. Entertainment
every evening. Open June–mid-
Oct, full menu served 11:30
am–9:30 pm. Late night menu
served 10 pm–1:30 am.
- Rita's Tea Room, Big Pond; 828-
2667. Baked goods and Rita's
Tea Room Blend Tea. Rita
MacNeil's awards and
photographs are on display.
Open daily 9 am–7 pm,
June–mid-Oct. $
- The Water's Edge, 22 Water St,
Baddeck; 295-3600. An
interesting menu of dishes that
are a little out of the ordinary,
and excellent desserts. A nice
setting in the middle of town.
Open May–Oct, noon–9 pm. $$

FLEUR-DE-LIS AND MARCONI TRAILS AND METRO CAPE BRETON

★Gowrie House, 840 Shore Rd,
Sydney Mines; 800 372-1115;
www.gowriehouse.com. Antique-
filled country inn, beautiful
grounds and gardens. Fine meals
are prepared from the freshest
Nova Scotia ingredients. One of
the province's best dining
experiences. Open daily, one
sitting at 7:30 pm, Apr–Dec.

Reservations essential. Dinner
for guests only rest of the year.
Bring your own wine. $$$
- Vollmer's Island Paradise,
Janvrin Island; 226-1507. Make
reservations a day ahead for fish
or meat. No smoking. Open daily
7 pm by appointment only. $$

ATTRACTIONS

The *Nova Scotia Doers' and
Dreamers' Guide* (see Travel
Essentials) provides exhaustive
listings of the province's
attractions. Guided walking tours
or brochures for self-guided tours
are available for many Nova Scotia
communities (make inquiries at the
closest visitor information centre).
Here we provide a selective listing
of many of the points of interest.
The area code for all of Nova
Scotia is 902. See Museums p. 14
and Places p. 74.

HALIFAX
- Alexander Keith's Nova Scotia
Brewery, 1496 Lower Water St,
Halifax; 877 612-1820;
www.keiths.ca. Costumed guides
lead historic tours of the oldest
working brewery in North
America.
- Anna Leonowens Gallery, 1891
Granville St, Halifax; 494-8223;
www.nscad.ns.ca (Nova Scotia
College of Art and Design
University)
★Art Gallery of Nova Scotia, 1723
Hollis St, Halifax; 424-7542;
www.agns.gov.ns.ca
- Bedford Institute of
Oceanography, located near the
Dartmouth end of MacKay
Bridge; 426-2373;
www.bio.gc.ca
- Black Cultural Centre for Nova
Scotia, 1149 Main St, Route 7 at
Cherrybrook Rd, Dartmouth; 800
465-0767; www.bccns.com
- *Bluenose II*, at the wharf by the
Maritime Museum of the
Atlantic when in Halifax; 866
579-4909;
www.schoonerbluenose2.ca
- Brewery Market, Hollis and
Lower Water St, Halifax;
farmers' market on Saturdays.

- Cathedral Church of All Saints, 1320 Tower Rd, Halifax; 423-6002; www.cathedralchurchof allsaints.com
- Cole Harbour Heritage Farm Museum, 471 Poplar Dr, Cole Harbour (outside Dartmouth) 434-0222
- Dartmouth Heritage Museum, 26 Newcastle St, Dartmouth; 464-2300; www.dartmouthheritage museum.ns.ca
- Discovery Centre, 1593 Barrington St, Halifax; 492-4422; www.discoverycentre.ns.ca
- Government House, 1451 Barrington St, Halifax. Lieutenant-governor's residence since early 1800s
- Grand Parade, between Barrington St and Argyle St, Halifax
- ★Halifax Citadel National Historic Site of Canada, overlooking downtown Halifax (you can't miss it); 426-5080; www.pc.gc.ca/lhn-nhs/ns/halifax
- ★Halifax Public Gardens, Spring Garden Rd at South Park St, Halifax
- Halifax Regional Library, 5381 Spring Garden Rd, Halifax; 490-5700; www.halifaxpubliclibraries.ca
- Hemlock Ravine Park, Kent Ave, off Bedford Highway
- Historic Properties, on the Halifax waterfront; 429-0530
- ★HMCS Sackville: Canada's Naval Memorial, at the wharf of the Maritime Museum, Halifax; 429-2132; www.hmcssackville-cnmt.ns.ca
- Little Dutch (Deutch) Church, Brunswick St at Gerrish, Halifax; 423-1059
- Maritime Command Museum, Admiralty House, 2725 Gottingen St, Halifax; 427-0550 ext 8250
- ★Maritime Museum of the Atlantic, 1675 Lower Water St, Halifax; 424-7490; www.maritime.museum.gov.ns.ca
- Museum of Natural History, 1747 Summer St, Halifax; 424-7353; www.nature.museum.gov.ns.ca
- Nova Scotia Centre for Craft and Design, 1061 Marginal Rd, Halifax; 492-2522; www.craft-design.ns.ca
- Old Burying Ground and Welsford-Parker Monument, Barrington St (across from Government House), Halifax; 429-2240
- Old Town Clock, at the base of the Citadel. Halifax's most famous landmark
- ★Pier 21 National Historic Site of Canada, 1055 Marginal Rd, Halifax; 425-7770; www.pier21.com
- Prince of Wales Tower National Historic Site of Canada, Point Pleasant Park (Tower Rd entrance), Halifax; 426-5080; www.pc.gc.ca/lhn-nhs/ns/prince
- ★Province House, 1726 Hollis St, Halifax; 424-4661; www.gov.ns.ca/legislature
- Quaker House, 57–59 Ochterloney St, Dartmouth; 464-2253; www.dartmouthheritage museum.ns.ca
- ★St. George's Round Church, 2222 Brunswick St, Halifax; 423-1059
- St. Paul's Anglican Church, at the Grand Parade, Halifax; 429-2240; www.stpaulshalifax.org
- Shearwater Aviation Museum, at CFB Shearwater; 720-1113; www.shearwateraviation museum.ns.ca
- Sir Sanford Fleming Park (the Dingle), Dingle Rd, off Purcell's Cove Rd on Northwest Arm, Halifax
- York Redoubt National Historic Site of Canada, Purcell's Cove Rd, Halifax; 426-5080; www.pc.gc.ca/lhn-nhs/ns/york

LIGHTHOUSE ROUTE

Peggys Cove and Hubbards
- The Shore Club; 857-9555; www.lobstersupper.com
- ★Village of Peggys Cove and lighthouse
- William E. deGarthe Memorial Monument, Peggys Cove

Chester to Mahone Bay
- Amos Pewter, interpretive workshop, 589 Main St, Mahone Bay; 800 565-3369; www.amospewter.com
- Lordly House Museum and Park,

133 Central St, Chester; 275-3842
- Mahone Bay Settlers' Museum, 578 Main St, Mahone Bay; 624-6263; www.settlersmuseum.ns.ca
- Ross Farm Living Museum of Agriculture, New Ross (on Rte 12, exit 9 from Hwy 103 at Chester Basin; 689-2210; www.rossfarm.museum.gov.ns.ca
- The Three Churches, Edgewater Rd (Hwy 3), Mahone Bay

Bridgewater and Lunenburg
★*Bluenose II*, at the Fisheries Museum wharf; 866 579-4909; www.schoonerbluenose2.ca
- Captain Angus J. Walters House Museum, 37 Tannery Rd, Lunenburg; 634-2010; www.explorelunenburg.ca
- DesBrisay Museum, 130 Jubilee Rd, Bridgewater; 543-4033; www.town.bridgewater.ns.ca/museum.htm
★Fisheries Museum of the Atlantic, Montague St (on the waterfront), Lunenburg; 866 579-4909; www.fisheries.museum.gov.ns.ca
- Fort Point Museum, Fort Point Rd, off Rte 331, LaHave; 688-1632; www.fortpointmuseum.com. Site of Fort Ste. Marie de Grâce, the first capital of New France (1632-1636).
- Lunenburg Academy, Kaulbach St, Lunenburg; it can be seen from any road into Lunenburg
- Knaut-Rhuland House Museum, 125 Pelham St, Lunenburg; 634-3498; www.lunenburgheritagesociety.ca
★St. John's Church, Cumberland St, Lunenburg; 634-4994; www.stjohnslunenburg.com
- Wile Carding Mill, 242 Victoria Rd, Bridgewater; 543-8233; www.cardingmill.museum.gov.ns.ca

Liverpool and Shelburne
- Archelaus Smith Museum, Route 330, Centreville, Cape Sable Island (across the causeway); 745-3361
- Argyle Township Courthouse & Gaol, 8168 Hwy 3, Tusket; 648-2493; www.argylecourthouse.com
- The Dory Shop Museum, Dock St, Shelburne; 875-3219;

www.doryshop.museum.gov.ns.ca
- Fort Point Lighthouse Park, Main St, Liverpool; 800 655-5741
- Hank Snow Country Music Centre, 148 Bristol Ave, Liverpool; 354-4675; www.hanksnow.com
- Perkins House Museum, 105 Main St, Liverpool; 354-4058; www.perkins.museum.gov.ns.ca
- Queens County Museum, 109 Main St, Liverpool; 354-4058; www.queensmuseum.netfirms.com
- Rossignol Cultural Centre, 205 Church St, Liverpool; 354-3067; www.rossignolculturalcentre.com
- Ross-Thomson House and Store Museum, 9 Charlotte Lane, Shelburne; 875-3141; www.rossthompson.museum.gov.ns.ca
- Shelburne County Museum, 20 Dock St, Shelburne; 875-3219; www.historicshelburne.com
- Sherman Hines Museum of Photography & Galleries, 219 Main St, Liverpool; 354-2667; www.shermanhinesphotographymuseum.com

Barrington
- Barrington Woolen Mill Museum, 2368 Hwy 3, Barrington; 637-2185; www.woolenmill.museum.gov.ns.ca
- The Old Meeting House, 2048 Hwy 3, Barrington; 637-2185; www.meetinghouse.museum.gov.ns.ca
- Seal Island Light Museum, Hwy 3, Barrington; 637-2185; maxwelbm@gov.ns.ca

Pubnico and Yarmouth
- Firefighters Museum of Nova Scotia, 451 Main St, Yarmouth; 742-5525; www.firefighters.museum.gov.ns.ca
- Killam Brothers Shipping Office, 90 Water St, at the foot of Central St on the waterfront; 742-5539
- Village Historique Acadien (Historical Acadian Village), Old Church Rd, West Pubnico; 762-2530; museum.gov.ns.ca/av
- Yarmouth County Museum and Archives, 22 Collins St, Yarmouth; 742-5539; yarmouthcountymuseum.ednet.ns.ca
- Yarmouth Light, Route 304,

Cape Fourchu Scenic Drive; 742-4522

EVANGELINE TRAIL

Mount Uniacke, Windsor, Wolfville

- Fort Edward National Historic Site, near Exit 6 on Hwy 101, Windsor; 798-4706
- Grand Pré National Historic Site, 866 542-3631; www.grand-pre.com
- ★Haliburton House, 414 Clifton Ave, Windsor; 798-2915; www.haliburton.museum.gov.ns.ca
- Howard Dill Enterprises, 400 College Rd, Windsor; 798-2728; www.howarddill.com
- K C Irving Environmental Science Centre and Harriet Irving Botanical Gardens, Wolfville; 585-5242; www.acadiau.ca/KCIrving_Centre
- ★Prescott House, 1633 Starrs Pt Rd (off Hwy 358) Starrs Point (near Wolfville); 542-3984; www.prescott.museum.gov.ns.ca
- Randall House Historical Museum, 259 Main St, Wolfville; 542-9775
- Robie Tufts Nature Centre, Front St, Wolfville
- ★Shand House Museum, 389 Avon St, Windsor; 798-8213; www.shand.museum.gov.ns.ca
- ★Uniacke Estate Museum Park, 758 Main Rd (Hwy 1), Mount Uniacke; 866-2560; www.uniacke.museum.gov.ns.ca
- Windsor Hockey Heritage Centre, 128 Gerrish St, Windsor; 798-1800; www.birthplaceofhockey.com

Kentville to Middleton

- Annapolis Valley Macdonald Museum, 21 School St, Middleton; 825-6116; www.macdonaldmuseum.ca
- Kentville Agricultural Centre and Blair House Museum, Route 1, Kentville; 679-5333
- Kings County Museum, in the old Kings County courthouse, 37 Cornwallis St, Kentville; 678-6237; www.okcm.ca
- Oaklawn Farm Zoo, Hwy 101, exit 16, Aylesford; 847-9790; www.oaklawnfarmzoo.ca

Digby and Annapolis Royal

- Admiral Digby Museum, 95 Montague Row, Digby; 245-6322; www3.ns.sympatico.ca/admuseum
- ★Annapolis Royal Historic Gardens, 441 Saint George St, Annapolis Royal; 532-7018; www.historicgardens.com
- Annapolis Tidal Generating Station, at the Annapolis River Causeway; 532-5454
- ARTs PLACE, 396 Saint George St, Annapolis Royal; 532-7069; www.arcac.ca
- deGannes-Cosby House, 477 Saint George St, Annapolis Royal.
- ★Fort Anne National Historic Site, St George St, Annapolis Royal; 532-2321; www.pc.gc.ca/fortanne
- North Hills Museum, 5065 Granville Rd, Granville Ferry; 532-7754; www.northhills.museum.gov.ns.ca
- O'Dell House Museum, 136 Lower Saint George St, Annapolis Royal; 532-7754; www.annapolisheritagesociety.com
- ★Port Royal National Historic Site of Canada (the Habitation), Route 1 to Granville Ferry, 12 kilometres southwest at Port Royal; 532-2898; www.pc.gc.ca/portroyal
- Sinclair Inn Museum, 232 St George St, Annapolis Royal; 532-7754; www.annapolisheritagesociety.com
- Upper Clements Park, 2931 Hwy 1.6 kilometres west of Annapolis Royal; 888 248-4567; www.upperclementspark.com
- Upper Clements Wildlife Park, Hwy 1.6 kilometres west of Annapolis Royal; 532-5924; www3.ns.sympatico.ca/ucwlp

Acadian Shore

- Université Sainte-Anne, Church Point; 769-2114; www.ustanne.ca
- L'Église Saint-Bernard (St Bernard Church), Route 1, St. Bernard; 837-5687; www.baiesaintemarie.com
- L'Église Sainte-Marie (St Mary's Church), and St. Mary's Museum, Church Point; 837-5408; www.geocities.com/st_marys_church2001/st.html

GLOOSCAP TRAIL

Amherst and Springhill
- Anne Murray Centre, 36 Main St, Springhill; 597-8614; www.annemurray.com
- Cumberland County Museum, 150 Church St, Amherst; 667-2561; www.cumberlandcounty museum.com
- Springhill Miners' Museum, 145 Black River Rd, Springhill; 597-3449; www.town.springhill.ns.ca/miner s_museum.htm

Joggins to Parrsboro
- Age of Sail Centre, Port Greville; 348-2030; www.ageofsailmuseum.ca
- ★Fundy Geological Museum, 162 Two Islands Rd, Parrsboro; 866 856-3466; www.fundygeo.museum.gov.ns.ca
- Joggins Fossil Centre, Main St, Joggins; 251-2727
- Ottawa House Museum by-the-Sea, 1155 Whitehall Rd, near Parrsboro; www.parrsboro.com/ottawa house.htm
- Parrsboro Rock and Mineral Shop and Museum, 349 Whitehall Rd, Parrsboro; 254-2981

Truro, Maitland, Shubenacadie
- Glooscap Heritage Centre, 65 Treaty Trail, (Exit 13A off Hwy 102) just outside Truro; 843-3496; www.glooscapheritagecentre.com
- Lawrence House Museum, 8660 Hwy 215, Maitland; 261-2628; www.lawrence.museum.gov.ns.ca
- Shubenacadie Provincial Wildlife Park, near exit 11 on Hwy 102, Shubenacadie; 758-2040 or 424-5937; www.wildlifepark.gov.ns.ca
- Victoria Park, Park Rd. and Brunswick St, Truro; 893-6078

SUNRISE TRAIL

Pictou and Stellarton
- Hector Exhibit & Research Centre, 86 Old Haliburton Rd, Pictou; 485-4563; www.rootsweb.com/~nspcghs
- ★Hector Heritage Quay, 33 Caladh Ave, Pictou; 877 574-2868; www.townofpictou.com
- Mc Culloch House Museum, 100 Old Haliburton Rd, Pictou. www.museum.gov.ns.ca/mch
- Northumberland Fisheries Museum, 71 Front St, Pictou; 485-4972; www.northumberlandfisheries museum.com
- Nova Scotia Museum of Industry, Hwy 104 at exit 24, Stellarton; 755-5425; www.industry.museum.gov.ns.ca

Tatamagouche to Amherst
- Balmoral Grist Mill Museum, 660 Matheson Brook Rd, off Route 311, Balmoral Mills; 657-3016; www.gristmill.museum.gov.ns.ca
- ★Jost Vineyards, off Route 6, between Tatamagouche and Pugwash at Malagash; 800 565-4567; www.jostwine.com
- Northumberland Arts Council Fraser Cultural Centre, Main St, Tatamagouche; 657-3285, 657-3667 (off-season)
- Sutherland Steam Mill Museum, off Route 326, Denmark; 657-3016; www.steammill.museum.gov.ns.ca

MARINE DRIVE
- Canso Islands National Historic Site, Union St, 1 km off the coast of Canso; 295-2069; www.pc.gc.ca/lhn-nhs/ns/canso
- Canso Museum, Whitman House, Canso; 366-2170 or 366-2525; canconn@atcon.com
- Fisherman's Life Museum, 58 Navy Pool Loop, Jeddore, off Route 7 at Oyster Pond; 889-2053; www.fishermanslife.museum. gov.ns.ca
- Memory Lane Heritage Village, Route 7, Lake Charlotte; 877 287-0697; www.heritagevillage.ca
- Moose River Gold Mines Museum, Moose River Rd, Route 224; Moose River Gold Mines; 384-2006; www.mvta.net
- Musquodoboit Railway Museum, Main St (Route 7), Musquodoboit Harbour;

889-2689;
www.halifaxinfo.com/museums-galleries.php
- Nova Scotia Lighthouse Interpretive Centre, Route 211, Port Bickerton; 364-2000
- ★Sherbrooke Village, off Route 7, near the modern village of Sherbrooke; 888 743-7845; www.sherbrookevillage.museum.gov.ns.ca

CABOT TRAIL AND CEILIDH TRAIL

Cabot Trail
- Acadian Museum, 15067 Main St (at Co-operative Artisinale de Cheticamp Ltée), Cheticamp; 224-2170; www.co-opartisanale.com
- ★Alexander Graham Bell National Historic Site, Chebucto St (Hwy 205), Baddeck; 295-2069; www.pc.gc.ca/lhn-nhs/ns/grahambell
- ★Cape Breton Highlands National Park, 888 773-8888; www.pc.gc.ca/pn-np/ns/cbreton
- Centre de la Mi-Carême, 12615 Cabot Trail, St. Joseph du Moine; 224-1016 or 224-2665; www.collections.ic.gc.ca/micareme
- Les Trois Pignons Museum of the Hooked Rug and Home Life, 15584 Main St, Cheticamp; 224-2642 or 224-2612; www.lestroispignons.com
- The Great Hall of the Clans at the Gaelic College of Celtic Arts and Crafts, South Gut St. Anns; 295-3441 or 295-2912; www.gaeliccollege.edu
- Giant MacAskill Museum, Route 312, Englishtown; 929-2925
- Highland Village Museum, 4119 Route 223, Iona; 725-2272; www.highlandvillage.museum.gov.ns.ca
- L'Église Saint-Pierre (Church of St. Peter), Cheticamp; 224-2062
- Lone Shieling, at the base of North Mountain, Cape Breton Highlands National Park
- MacAskill House Museum, St. Peter's; fortress.uccb.ns.ca/historic/askill.html. Works of great marine photographer Wallace MacAskill.
- Margaree Salmon Museum,

60 East Big Intervale Rd, North East Margaree; 248-2848
- Orangedale Station Museum, 1428 Main St, Orangedale; 756-3384. Rolling stock and rail history of the area.
- Wagmatcook Culture and Heritage Centre, Wagmatcook; 295-2999; www.wagmatcook.com
- Whale Interpretive Centre, Pleasant Bay; 224-1411

Ceilidh Trail
- An Drochaid (The Bridge) Museum, 11513 Rte 19, Mabou; 945-2790
- Cape Breton's Celtic Music Interpretive Centre, Judique; 787-2708; www.celticmusicsite.com
- Glenora Distillery, Single Malt Whisky Economuseum; 800 839-0491; www.glenoradistillery.com
- Inverness Miners' Museum, in the old CNR station, Inverness; 258-3822

FLEUR-DE-LIS AND MARCONI TRAILS AND METRO CAPE BRETON
- Cape Breton Centre for Heritage and Science, 225 George St, Sydney. 539-1572
- Cape Breton Miners' Museum, 42 Birkley St, Quarry Point, Glace Bay; 849-4522; www.minersmuseum.com
- Cossit House Museum, 75 Charlotte St, Sydney; 539-7973 or 539-1572; www.cossit.museum.gov.ns.ca
- ★Fortress of Louisbourg National Historic Site of Canada, Louisbourg; 733-2280, 733-3546; www.pc.gc.ca/louisbourg
- Jost Heritage House, 54 Charlotte St, Sydney; 539-0366
- LeNoir Forge Museum, Lower St, Arichat; 226-9364
- Marconi National Historic Site of Canada, Timmerman St, Glace Bay; 295-2069; www.pc.gc.ca/lhn-nhs/marconi
- St Patrick's Church Museum, 87 Esplanade, Sydney; 562-8237
- Sydney and Louisburg Railway Museum, Louisbourg; 733-2157; fortress.uccb.ns.ca/historic/s_l.html
- Two Rivers Wildlife Park, Grand

Mira North Rd, Marion Bridge
(off Rte 327); 727-2483;
www.tworiverspark.ca

FESTIVALS AND EVENTS

What follows is a listing by area of
some of the best and most popular
festivals and events in the
province. For a complete listing,
consult the *Nova Scotia Festivals
and Events Guide*, available at
visitor information centres or at
www.novascotia.com. The
scheduling of many of these events
is subject to change; the Check In
Reservation and Information
Service will provide updated
information (800 565-0000). See
Fairs, Festival and Events p. 40.

PROVINCE-WIDE

May/June
- Musique Royale. Early and
  traditional music in historic
  venues all summer.
  www.musiqueroyale.com
- Studio Rally Weekend. Craft
  studios across the province open
  to the public. www.studiorally.ca

HALIFAX

Year-round
- Halifax Farmers' Market at the
  Brewery Market (Halifax).
  Saturday morning farmers'
  market where local crafts, baked
  goods and produce are available
- St Cecilia Concert Series.
  Classical music at Lillian Piercey
  Concert Hall and other venues.
  www.stcecilia.ca

May/June
- Scotia Festival of Music.
  Internationally renowned festival
  of chamber music.
  www.scotiafestival.ns.ca

June
- Greek Festival. Three-day feast
  put on by the Halifax Greek
  community. www.greekfest.org
- Halifax Celtic Feis. Celebration
  of Scottish and Irish heritage.
  www.halifaxcelticfeis.com
- Halifax Highland Games and

Scottish Festival. The Garrison
Grounds, Halifax.
www.halifaxhighlandgames.com
- Nova Scotia Multicultural
  Festival, Dartmouth. Food,
  music and dancing offered by
  Nova Scotia's different ethnic
  communities. www.multifest.ca

July
- Africville Reunion. The spirit of
  the Black community of
  Africville is revived at a picnic,
  church service and dance.
- Atlantic Jazz Festival. Outdoor
  concerts and late-night sessions
  in city bars. www.jazzeast.com
- Maritime Fiddle Festival,
  Dartmouth. Top-notch
  competitors from Canada and the
  United States.
  www3.ns.sympatico.ca/
  marfiddlefest
- Nova Scotia Designer Crafts
  Council Summer Festival. A
  juried market draws many of the
  province's best craftspeople.
  www.nsdcc.ns.ca
- Royal Nova Scotia International
  Tattoo. A musical extravaganza
  with a military flavour.
  www.nstattoo.ca

August
- Halifax International Busker
  Festival. Street performers,
  including jugglers and clowns,
  provide 10 days of fun along the
  waterfront. www.buskers.ca

September
- Atlantic Film Festival.
  Independent films and parties
  celebrating the industry.
  www.atlanticfilm.com
- Atlantic Fringe Festival.
  Alternative plays performed
  around the city.
  www.atlanticfringe.com
- DRUM. A musical production of
  drums and dance of four cultures
  on the waterfront to mid-
  October. www.drumshow.ca
- Maritime Fall Fair. Brings the
  country to the city; animals,
  food, entertainment.
  www.maritimefallfair.com
- Nova Scotia International
  Airshow. Atlantic Canada's
  largest demonstration of aerial

acrobatics. www.nsairshow.ca
- Word on the Street. Book sales, displays, author readings and entertainment. www.thewordonthestreet.ca

LIGHTHOUSE ROUTE

May
- Liverpool International Theatre Festival (every second year). www.astortheatre.ns.ca

June/July
- Music at the Three Churches, Mahone Bay. Classical music every second Friday all summer. www.threechurches.com
- Festival Acadien de Wedgeport, Argyle.
- Privateer Days, Liverpool. Festival recalling the town's tumultuous early years.

July
- Lunenburg Craft Festival. Quality crafts from the province's top artisans.
- Shelburne Founders' Days. Commemorates the arrival of thousands of United Empire Loyalists in the 1780s.
- South Shore Exhibition, Bridgewater. Century-old agricultural exhibition featuring ox-pulls among the many events.
- Whirligig and Weathervane Festival. Shelburne. Prizes for contestants. Observers help judge and may buy the wonderful, whimsical creations.
- Yarmouth Seafest

August
- Chester Race Week. Atlantic Canada's largest regatta. The Front and Back harbours are crowded with sleek yachts.
- Hank Snow Tribute. Bridgewater Exhibition Grounds.
- Lunenburg Fishermen's Picnic and Reunion. A festival for the fisheries that features unusual and entertaining competitions like net mending, scallop shucking and dory racing.
- Lunenburg Folk Harbour Festival. The Lunenburg waterfront provides an idyllic setting for a series of

performances by folk musicians. www.folkharbour.com
- Mahone Bay Classic Boat Festival. Boatbuilding competitions and demonstrations, and events recalling the town's shipbuilding tradition. www.woodenboatfestival.org
- Nova Scotia Folk Art Festival. Celebrates the work of Nova Scotia's best folk artists. www.nsfolkartfestival.com

September
- Lights Along the Shore Lighthouse Festival, at various sites along the South Shore. www.ssta.com

October
- Great Scarecrow Festival and Antique Fair, Mahone Bay. Dozens of vendors in three venues; music, food, activities for kids, and scarecrows everywhere. www.mahonebay.com

November/December
- Father Christmas Festival, Mahone Bay. Larger than life Father Christmas figures, candle-lit streets, horse-drawn taxi, Victorian carolers. www.mahonebay.com

EVANGELINE TRAIL

May
- Annapolis Valley Apple Blossom Festival, Windsor to Digby. Community-based celebrations herald the arrival of another growing season. www.appleblossom.com
- Musique de la Baie, Venues throughout Clare. Acadian kitchen parties all summer. www.baiesaintmarie.com

June
- Musique Saint-Bernard, Saint Bernard. Fine music in St. Bernard Church Sunday afternoons in summer. www.baiesaintmarie.com
- Fox Mountain Bluegrass Festival, Berwick. www.foxmountaincampingpark.com

- Rhododendron Sunday, Kentville Agricultural Centre

July
- Festival Acadien de Clare. Colourful Acadian celebration that runs the length of the Acadian Shore. www.festivalacadiendeclare.ca
- Heart of the Valley Days, Middleton. Parade, concert and fireworks. www.town.middleton.ns.ca
- Journée Acadienne de Grand Pré. Grand Pré. Acadian music, heritage, culture. www.grand-pre.com

August
- Annapolis Valley Exhibition, Lawrencetown. Showcase of Valley agriculture, with top-name entertainment.
- Digby Scallop Days. A feast of Digby scallops, scallop-shucking competition. www.townofdigby.ns.ca
- Natal Days Craft and Antique Show, Annapolis Royal. Fast-growing community of craftspeople displays its wares.

September/October
- Annapolis Royal Arts Festival. Best-selling Canadian authors are among the participants at this annual gathering.
- Deep Roots Music Festival. Wolfville. A celebration of the music of the peoples who have settled Nova Scotia. www.deeprootsmusic.ca
- Hants County Exhibition, Windsor. North America's oldest agricultural fair. www.hantscounty.com
- Pumpkin Festival, Hants County Exhibition Grounds, Windsor. Growers of giant pumpkins vie for World's Biggest Pumpkin title. www.worldsbiggestpumpkins.com
- Pumpkin Regatta, Windsor. Giant gourds take to the water for riotous races. www.worldsbiggestpumpkins.com

GLOOSCAP TRAIL

May
- Truro International Tulip Festival. www.downtowntruro.ca

August
- Nova Scotia's Gem and Mineral Show, Parrsboro. An agate and amethyst hunt along Parrsboro-area beaches. museum.gov.ns.ca/fgm/mineralgem/show.html
- Nova Scotia Provincial Exhibition, Truro. Parade, equestrian events, animals, food, entertainment. www.nspe.ca
- Wild Blueberry Harvest Festival, throughout central Nova Scotia. Teas, suppers, pancake breakfasts — all starring blueberries. www.wildblueberryfest.com

SUNRISE TRAIL

July
- Antigonish Highland Games. Highland competitions from dancing to caber tossing make this Nova Scotia's best Scottish festival. www.antigonishhighlandgames.com
- Festival of the Tartans, New Glasgow. Includes piping, dancing, drumming and Scottish heavy events.
- Gathering of the Clans and Fishermen's Regatta, Pugwash. A Scottish festival capped off by a lobster dinner. www.pugwashvillage.com/gathering.html
- Kites and Kayaks Festival, Pictou Lodge, Pictou. Family fun on the water and in the sky
- New Glasgow Riverfront Music Jubilee, New Glasgow. www.jubilee.ns.ca
- Pictou Lobster Carnival. Fishermen's competitions and Northumberland Strait lobsters are the highlights at this community festival. www.townofpictou.com

August
- Hector Festival, Pictou. Celebrates the coming of the Scots to Nova Scotia aboard the *Hector*.
- Pictou County Dragon Boat Festival, New Glasgow.
- Race on the River, New Glasgow.

September
- Oktoberfest, Tatamagouche.

Post-war immigration to the North Shore gave rise to this traditional German celebration. www.nsoktoberfest.ca

MARINE DRIVE

July
- Stan Rogers Folk Festival, Canso. A celebration of the music of one of Canada's most celebrated folk musicians. www.stanfest.com

August
- Clam Harbour Beach Sand Castle and Sculpture Contest. The fine, white sand along one of Nova Scotia's best beaches is an ideal building material.

CAPE BRETON ISLAND

June to September
- Ceilidhs at the Creamery. Port Hawkesbury. Tuesdays all summer. www.ceilidh.ca
- Mabou Ceilidhs. See for yourself why this village of 400 is home to several of Nova Scotia's best musicians. Tuesdays. There are also Wednesday-night ceilidhs throughout July and August in Judique. www.invernesscounty.com

July
- Big Pond Festival. Cape Breton music highlighting Big Pond's most famous resident, Rita MacNeil.
- Broad Cove Scottish Concert, near Inverness. A highlight of the summer ceilidh season. www.broadcoveconcert.ca
- Judique-on-the-Floor Days. More of Cape Breton's best music. www.invernesscounty.com

July/August
- Festival de l'Escaouette, Cheticamp. An Acadian celebration featuring a special mass in Cheticamp's exquisite church. www.festivallescaouette.com
- Inverness Gathering. Inverness. Ceilidhs, dinners, song and dance.
- Granville Green Concerts. Port Hawkesbury. Free concerts every Sunday. www.granvillegreen.com
- Louisbourg Crab Festival. Louisbourg. Early August.

August
- Baddeck Regatta. Highlight of Baddeck's summer sailing season since 1904.
- Feast of St. Louis. An 18th-century feast at the Fortress of Louisbourg.
- Gaelic Mod, South Gut St. Anns. Music and other Gaelic arts at the home of the Gaelic College. www.gaeliccollege.edu

September/October
- Hike the Highlands Festival, on the Cabot Trail. 18 guided hikes; entertainment, BBQs and more. www.hikethehighlandsfestival.com
- Celtic Colours. An island-wide celebration of Celtic music featuring Cape Breton and international performers. www.celtic-colours.com

THEATRE

Halifax is home to Neptune Theatre, Nova Scotia's only professional live repertory theatre group. Also, a surprising number of communities throughout the province, including Halifax, are summertime venues for live theatre. Many productions are distinctly Nova Scotian, revealing much about the province and its people.

The area code for all of Nova Scotia is 902. See Theatre p.26.

- 2b Theatre Company, 5670 Macara Street, Halifax; 453-6267
- Astor Theatre, Gorham St, Liverpool; 354-5250; www.litf.ca. Featuring the Liverpool International Theatre Festival (bi-annually) in May.
- Atlantic Theatre Festival, Wolfville; www.atf.ns.ca
- Bicentennial Theatre, 12390 Route 224, Middle Musquodoboit; 384-2819; www3.ns.sympatico.ca/ bicentennial.theatre
- Bus Stop Theatre, 2203 Gottingen St, Halifax
- Centrestage Theatre, 363-R Main St, Kentville; 678-8040; www.centrestagetheatre.ca
- The Chester Playhouse, Pleasant St, Chester; 275-3933, 800 363-7529; www.chesterplayhouse.ns.ca. Site of the Chester Theatre

Festival April to December.
- DalTheatre, 6135 University Ave, Halifax; 800 874-1669; www.theatre.dal.ca
- Dartmouth Players Theatre, 5 Crichton Ave, Dartmouth; 465-7529; www.dartmouthplayers.ns.ca
- deCoste Entertainment Centre, Water St, Pictou; 800 353-5338; www.decostecentre.ca
- Eastern Front Theatre, Alderney Landing, Dartmouth; 463-7529; www.easternfront.ns.ca
- Exodus Theatre, Halifax; www.exodustheatre.ns.ca
- Festival Antigonish, Bauer Theatre, St. Francis Xavier University, Antigonish; 800 563-7529; www.festivalantigonish.com (July-August).
- Grafton Street Dinner Theatre, 1741 Grafton St, Halifax; 425-1961; www.graftonstdinnertheatre.com
- Halifax Feast Dinner Theatre, Maritime Centre, Barrington St, Halifax; 420-1840; www.feastdinnertheatre.com
- Irondale Ensemble, 2182 Gottingen St, Halifax; 429-1370; www.irondale.ca. Critical and thoughtful alternative theatre.
- King's Theatre, Lower St. George St, Annapolis Royal; 800 818-8587; www.kingstheatre.ca. Site of the Annapolis Royal Summer Theatre Festival in July and August.
- Louisbourg Playhouse, 11 Aberdeen St, Louisbourg; 888 733-2787 (June-Oct); www.louisbourgplayhouse.com
- Mermaid Theatre, 132 Gerrish St, Windsor; 798-5841; www.mermaidtheatre.ns.ca. Touring puppet theatre for children.
- Mulgrave Road Theatre, 68 Main St, Guysborough; 533-2092; www.mulgraveroad.ca
- Neptune Theatre, 1593 Argyle St, Halifax; 429-7070; 800 565-7345; www.neptunetheatre.com
- The Rebecca Cohn, Dalhousie Arts Centre, University Ave, Halifax; 494-3820; www.dal.ca/artscentre. A variety of live performances including the Symphony Nova Scotia concert series.
- Savoy Theatre, 19 Union St, Glace Bay; 842-1577; www.savoytheatre.com. Highlights include the Cape Breton Summertime Revue, a lively blend of Celtic music and satire.
- Shakespeare by the Sea, Halifax. Open air theatre in Point Pleasant Park; 422-0295; www.shakespearebythesea.ca
- ★Ship's Company Theatre, 38 Main St, Parrsboro; 800 565-7469; www.shipscompany.com. New theatre incorporating MV *Kipawo*, a restored car ferry (July-Sept).
- Theatre Arts Guild, The Pond Playhouse, 6 Parkhill Rd, Halifax; 477-2663; www.tagtheatre.com
- Th'YARC, 76 Parade St, Yarmouth; 800 561-1103; www.thyarc.ca. Yarmouth Summer Stage is held in July and August.
- Two Planks and a Passion Theatre Company. Touring company. www.twoplanks.ca
- Zuppa Circus. www.zuppacircus.com

SHOPPING
See Arts and Crafts p. 20

CRAFT SHOPS AND STUDIOS
- Arts North, just west of Cape North on the Cabot Trail. Specializing in Cape Breton pottery and jewellery, the gallery also features silk, weaving, prints, quilts and basketry by resident artisans. Open daily from mid-June–mid-Oct.
- ArtWare, Diligent River. 254-2972; www.artware.ns.ca. Krista Wells makes masks, prints, collage jewellery from found materials, paint clay and handmade paper. Open by chance or appointment.
- Black Duck, 8 Pelham St, Lunenburg. A long-standing craft co-operative with adjoining art gallery and a fine selection of books on Nova Scotia and the Maritimes. Open year-round.
- Co-operative Artisanale de Cheticamp Ltée, 15067 Cabot Trail, Cheticamp. This is the place for hooked rugs in all shapes and sizes (as well as mats, coasters and wall-

hangings). Watch how the hooking is done during one of the frequent daily demonstrations here or at any one of the numerous craft shops in Cheticamp. Open daily 8 am–9 pm, June 15–Sept 15, variable hours in off-season.

- deWeever's Wovens, 3486 Hwy 1, Aylesford. Contemporary styling in quality handwoven clothing.
- Flight of Fancy, Main St, Bear River. Selling the works of over 200 craftspeople, this is a beautifully appointed shop in the picturesque village of Bear River — worth a trip just for the drive. Open May–Oct, Mon–Sat 9–7.
- Flora's, Point Cross (near Cheticamp) on the Cabot Trail. Large craft shop with a wide selection of hooked rugs. Open daily during tourist season.
- Glooscap Trading Post, Hwy 102, Exit 13, Truro. Traditional Mi'kmaq crafts, featuring woven baskets and twig furniture. The wonderful smell of sweet grass will make you want to browse just a little longer. Open 9 am–5:30 pm, year-round.
- Grey Seal Weaving, 3886 Rte 247, Point Michaud. 587-2777/2494. Damask silk scarves, shawls and framed pieces woven by E. Del Zoppo on a draw loom. Open by chance or appointment.
- Inverness County Centre for the Arts, Route 19, Inverness; www.invernessarts.ca. Gallery and gallery shop. Open year-round Mon – Fri 10 am–5 pm; summer weekends 1–5.
- Jennifer's of Nova Scotia, 5635 Spring Garden Rd, Halifax. Easy to find on Halifax's main downtown shopping street, Jennifer's features primarily Nova Scotian crafts, especially pottery, pewter and knitted items. Open 9 am–6 pm Mon, Tues, Sat; Wed, Thurs and Fri to 9 pm; Sun 11 am–5 pm.
- Leather Works, at Indian Brook (between Baddeck and Ingonish) on the Cabot Trail. Historic reproductions and a variety of contemporary leather goods by John Roberts. Open daily May–Oct.

- Lizzy Bugs, 6913 Tupper Grove, Halifax. 423-2102. Larger than life metal insects by Elizabeth Goluch. Open by chance or appointment.
- Out of Hand, 135 Montague St, Lunenburg. Arts & crafts gallery, unusual gifts. Open May–Dec 9 am–6 pm, July–Aug 9 am–9 pm.
- Raspberry Bay Stone, 5759 Hwy 2, Bass River. 647-2287; www.raspberrybaystone.com. Hand-carved natural stone. Open most days, call for hours.
- Suttles and Seawinds, 466 Main St, Mahone Bay. Fashion and home accessories by local designer Vicki Lynn Bardon. Also vibrant quilts and patchwork accessories. Open year-round.
- Tudor Tile, 1003 Little Harbour Rd, Sable River. 656-3298. Handmade custom-designed ceramic tile. Open by chance or appointment.

FINE JEWELLERY AND CRYSTAL

- Fire Works Gallery, 1569 Barrington St, Halifax. An eclectic mix of silver and gold jewellery, some made by the shop's resident jewellers, and art glass, pottery by well-known local artists. Open daily except Sunday.
- Nova Scotian Crystal, 5080 George St, at Lower Water St, Halifax. Canada's only mouth-blown and hand-cut crystal in the centuries-old tradition of Waterford. Stemware, vases, bowls, giftware. Open daily except Sunday.

PEWTER

- Amos Pewter, 589 Main St, Mahone Bay. Interpretive workshop and studio. Contemporary designs including picture frames, goblets and jewellery. Open Mon–Sat 9 am–5:30 pm, Sun afternoons.
- Seagull Pewter, Route 6, 9926 Durham St, Pugwash. Full line of pewter products. Canada's largest giftware manufacturer, now international in scope. Open daily. Also on Spring Garden Rd, Halifax.

POTTERY

- Birdsall-Worthington Pottery Ltd, 590 Main St, Mahone Bay. Slip-decorated earthenware pottery, including commemorative plates and handmade earrings. Open Mon–Sat 10 am–5 pm, Sun 1 pm–5 pm, July–Sept; limited hours in off-season.
- Cape Breton Clay, East Big Intervale Rd, Margaree Valley. 235-2467; www.capebretonclay.com. Pottery features maritime motifs of trout, lobster, mussels. Open daily June–Oct.
- Nova Scotia Folk Pottery, Front Harbour, Chester; 275-3272. Colourful platters, bowls, vases and serving dishes by Jim Smith. Open daily 10 am–6 pm, Sun noon–6 pm, June–Sept; off-season by appointment.
- Nova Terra Cotta Pottery, 10 Dufferin St, Lunenburg. 634-8902; www.joanbruneau.com. Open daily in summer, 9:30 am–5:30 pm; shorter fall hours.
- Shape Shift Pottery, at St. Anns on the Cabot Trail. Deanie Cox makes raku and functional dinnerware. Open daily 9 am–5 pm, June–Sept.

FINE ART AND FOLK ART

- Argyle Fine Art, 1869 Upper Water St, Halifax. 425-9456; www.argylefa.com. Wide variety of contemporary art by established and emerging Canadian artists. Open year-round, Mon–Sat.
- Folk Art by Reed Timmons, Pleasant Bay on the Cabot Trail. Specializing in hand-carved whales, gulls, roosters and fishermen. Open daily June–Oct.
- Fundy Adventures Studio, 1417 Whitehall Rd, Parrsboro. Randy Corcoran creates folk art and sculpture from wood, bone and stone.
- Gallery Shop, Art Gallery of Nova Scotia, 1741 Hollis St at Cheapside, Halifax. Good selection of works by a wide variety of Nova Scotia artists and craftspeople. Open daily except Monday. Evening hours on Thursday.
- Houston North Gallery, 110 Montague St, Lunenburg; 634-8869. Large selection of Inuit carvings and prints, Nova Scotia folk art, silk screens and intaglio. Open year-round.
- Iron Art and Photographs, 48084 Cabot Trail, Tarbot. 929-2821; www.ironart.ca. Fine art photography by Carol Kennedy and metal sculptures and iron work by Gordon Kennedy. Open June–Oct, 10 am–6 pm.
- Le Motif, 15423 Cabot Trail, Cheticamp. Specializing in rag rugs, carvings, twig baskets and the folk art of proprietor Diane Bourgeois. Open daily, June–mid-Oct.
- Lyghtesome Gallery, 166 Main St, Antigonish. 863-5804; www.lyghtesome.ns.ca. Local and Maritime artists. Open Mon–Sat, 9 am–5 pm.
- Page and Strange Gallery, Granville Square, Halifax. 422-8995; www.pageandstrange.com. Established artists with a special connection to Nova Scotia. Open Mon–Fri 10 am–6 pm, Sat –5.
- Secord Gallery, 6301 Quinpool Rd, Halifax. 423-6644; www.secordgallery.com. Nova Scotian artists. Open Mon–Thurs, 9:30 am–5:30 pm, Fri–8, Sat 10–5.
- Skipping Stone Craft and Art Gallery, Guysborough; 533-2078. Works by Nova Scotian artists and artisans. Open mid-May–Oct.
- Studio 21, 1223 Lower Water St, Halifax. 423-1852; www.studio21.ca. Original contemporary art by top Canadian artists. Open Tues–Fri 11 am–6pm, Sat 10–5; Sun noon–5.
- Sunset Art Gallery, Cheticamp. Bright, whimsical wood carvings (lots of people and birds) by William Roach. Open daily May 24–Oct 15 or by appointment.
- Water's Edge Gallery, Water St, Baddeck; 295-1209. A collection

of artworks with a primarily maritime theme and featuring new and established artists of Atlantic Canada.

- Zwicker's Gallery, 5415 Doyle St, Halifax. 423-7662; www.zwickersgallery.ca. Eastern Canada's oldest gallery. Works of over 80 Maritime and Canadian artists. Open Mon–Fri, 9 am–5 pm; Sat from 10 am.

GIFT SHOPS

- Blomidon Inn's House of Gifts, Wolfville. Kitchen wares, glass, pottery, knitted garments. Open May–Christmas.
- Blue Heron Gift Shop, Chebucto St, Baddeck. Large selection of Nova Scotian books and CDs. Open daily year-round, 9 am–9 pm in summer.
- Frieze and Roy General Store, 8787 Hwy 215, Maitland. Oldest continuously operating general store in Canada (since 1839). Gifts and Canadian crafts.
- Kidston Landing, Chebucto St, Baddeck. Extensive selection of Nova Scotia crafts, Scottish woolens, men's and women's clothing, including wool and cotton sweaters. Open daily 9 am–9 pm.
- Sea Shanty Antiques and Crafts, Beach Point at the Englishtown Ferry. Interesting collectibles, including vintage china and glassware, and a good selection of new and antique quilts. Open daily mid-May–mid-Oct.
- Seawinds Chandlery, on the Government Wharf, Baddeck. Fine handmade sweaters, gift items and marine supplies. Open daily during tourist season, 9 am–9 pm.
- Sou'wester Gift Shop, Peggys Cove. Large selection of Nova Scotia crafts including hand-knitted sweaters. Open year-round.
- Sunrise Mercantile, Tatamagouche. 657-1094; www.sunmerc.com. An eclectic yarn and fibre arts studio, gift shop and gourmet food store. Open daily May–Oct, 10 am–sunset; shorter winter hours.

- The Teazer, Edgewater Rd (Route 3), Mahone Bay. Upscale local crafts and imported gift items, kitchen ware. Open daily (Sunday in afternoon only), Apr–Christmas.
- Warp and Woof, Water St, Chester. Local art and crafts; fine gift items. Open daily, May–Oct.

SPECIALTY SHOPS

- The Book Room, 1546 Barrington St, Halifax. Enjoy browsing in the city's oldest bookstore. Large selection of regional books. Open Mon–Sat.
- Box of Delights, Main St, Wolfville. Good general bookstore with the valley's best selection of local titles. Open year-round.
- Days Gone By Collectibles, 3192 Port LaTour Rd, Shelburne County; 768-2870. Large selection of antique and collectible folk art, hooked rugs, quilts, decoys, books, glass and more. Open May–Oct; closed Mon.
- For The Birds, 647 Main St, Mahone Bay. Feeders, books, binoculars and all bird-related things. Open May–Dec Mon–Sat; Feb–Apr Tues–Sat.
- Grohmann Knives, 116 Water St, Pictou. Fine knives for every use made on-site. Plant tours Mon–Fri 9 am–3 pm. Open Mon–Fri 9 am–5 pm, weekends seasonal.
- Halifax Folklore Centre, 1528 Brunswick St, Halifax. Large selection of traditional musical instruments and Nova Scotian recordings. Open Mon–Wed noon–5:30 pm, Thurs–Fri noon–9 pm, Sat 10 am–5 pm.
- Lismore Sheep Farm Wool Shop, 1389 Louisville Rd, River John. Wool, sheepskin and knitted products. Working sheep farm. Open daily May–Christmas.
- MacIsaac Kiltmakers, 4 MacAskill Dr, St Peter's; 866 343-4000; www.mackilts.com. Handmade kilts; kilt accessories.
- Magasin Campus (Campus Bookstore), Université Sainte-Anne, Pointe de l'Église. Books

dealing with the history and culture of the Acadians. Open Mon–Sat 9 am–5 pm.

- Negemow Basket Shop, Whycocomagh. Quality Mi'kmaq baskets sold by the Googoo family for more than 30 years.
- Outdoor Store, Chebucto St, Baddeck. Quality outdoor clothing, equipment and gifts. Open Apr–Christmas daily 9 am–8 pm; Sun 11 am–7pm.
- Port of Wines, 5431 Doyle St, Halifax. Wide selection and knowledgeable staff. Open Mon–Sat.
- Puddle Dock Emporium, 504 Main St, Mahone Bay. Asian antique furniture, collectibles and crafts. Open daily Apr–Christmas.
- Sew Inclined, Wreck Cove on the Cabot Trail. Specializing in designer vests, hats and pants. Custom orders and sewing services available. Open daily June–Oct.

TREATS

- Clearwater Lobster Shops, 757 Bedford Hwy, Bedford; Halifax International Airport; and other locations in metro Halifax. Live lobster packed for travel. Open daily.
- Domaine de Grand Pré Winery, Grand Pré. Stroll the grounds, taste the wine, enjoy Swiss cuisine at on-site restaurant.
- Italian Gourmet, 5431 Doyle St, Halifax. A few tables for lunch and lots of Italian goodies to take away. Open daily 9am–7pm (Sat –5).
- J. Willie Krauch and Sons Smoked Fish, Tangier. Danish-smoked Atlantic salmon, mackerel and eel; orders filled worldwide. Open daily from 8 am.
- Jost Vineyards, Route 6, Malagash. Family-run winery on 10 hectares. Retail store, daily tours at 3 pm in summer. Open daily to 6 pm (closed Sunday mornings); shorter hours in off-season.
- LaHave Bakery, Route 331, LaHave. Whole grain and herb breads, and sweets. From Lunenburg, a short drive and cable ferry ride across the LaHave River; also at 3 Edgewater Rd in Mahone Bay.
- Lunenburg County Winery,

Newburne; 644-2415. U-pick blueberries. Wine tastings and sales. Open year-round 9am–6 pm, 9 pm in summer.
- Sainte Famille Wines, corner Dyke Rd and Dudley Park Lane, Falmouth. Vineyard at site of early Acadian settlement. Daily tours 11 am and 2 pm. Wine, gift baskets and crafts at gift shop. Open daily to 6 pm (Sun noon–5 pm).
- St. Mary's River Smokehouse, Sherbrooke. www.thebestsmokedsalmon.com.
- Spring Garden Place Market, Spring Garden Rd, Halifax. Specialty foods available from a variety of shops. Open daily.
- Sugar Moon Farm, Earltown, off Rte 331; 657-3348. Maple syrup, maple sugar and other maple treats. Open weekends year-round; daily in summer.
- The Tangled Garden, Route 1, Grand Pré. Herb jellies and vinegars; also finely crafted dried-flower wreaths and other arrangements. Open daily 10 am–6 pm.

WINERIES

- Blomidon Estate Winery, 10318 Hwy 21, Canning; 877 582-7565; www.blomidonwine.com. Open May–Oct 10 am–6pm; Apr and Nov 11 am–5 pm.
- Domaine de Grand Pré Winery, Grand Pré; 542 7177; www.grandprewines.ns.ca. Stroll the grounds, taste the wine, enjoy Swiss cuisine at on-site restaurant. Open 10am – 6pm (Sundays 11am – 6pm); off-season open Wed – Sun, 11am – 5pm.
- Jost Vineyards, Route 6, Malagash; 800 565-4567; www.jostwines.com. Family-run winery on 10 hectares. Retail store, daily tours at 3 pm in summer. Open daily to 6 pm (closed Sunday mornings); shorter hours in off-season.
- Lunenburg County Winery, Newburne; 644-2415; www.canada-wine.com. U-pick blueberries. Wine tastings and sales. Open year-round 9 am–6 pm, 9 pm in summer.
- Sainte Famille Wines, corner Dyke Rd and Dudley Park Lane, Falmouth; 800 565-0993; www.st-famille.com. Vineyard at

site of early Acadian settlement. Daily tours 11 am and 2 pm. Wine, gift baskets and crafts at gift shop. Open daily to 6 pm (Sun noon–5 pm).

OUTDOOR RECREATION

PARKS AND NATURAL ATTRACTIONS

Included among the province's outstanding natural attractions are two national parks, Kejimkujik and Cape Breton Highlands. Nova Scotia also has 126 provincial parks. These range from sites of natural or historical significance to pleasant spots for a picnic or swim. Some have campgrounds. For more information on provincial parks, consult the detailed listings in the *Nova Scotia Doers' and Dreamers' Guide* (see Travel Essentials) or write to the Nova Scotia Department of Natural Resources, RR1 Belmont, NS, B0M 1C0. The area code for all of Nova Scotia is 902.

Halifax
★Point Pleasant Park, in the South end of Halifax. Although thousands of trees were destroyed by Hurricane Juan in 2003, the park continues to afford peaceful walks and views of Halifax Harbour and the Northwest Arm.
- Seaview Park, near Halifax ramp to A Murray McKay Bridge. Site of former community of Africville.
- Shubie Park, off Waverley Rd, Dartmouth. Two locks of the Shubenacadie Canal can be viewed from here.
- Sir Sandford Fleming Park (The Dingle), off Purcells Cove Rd, overlooking the Northwest Arm in Halifax. Beautiful view of the Arm along walking trails. Dedicated in 1912, the Dingle Tower was built to commemorate 150 years of representative government for Nova Scotia.

Peggys Cove
- See the waves, the rocks and the lighthouse at Nova Scotia's most famous fishing village.

Lunenburg
- Blue Rocks, east of Lunenburg on Lunenburg Bay. This tiny, rockbound fishing village is a favourite haunt of local and visiting artists.
- Ovens Natural Park, Route 332 southeast of Lunenburg, near Riverport. Coastal caves and cliffside hiking trails highlight this privately owned park.

Liverpool and Shelburne
★Kejimkujik Seaside Adjunct National Park, off Route 3 between Port Joli and Port Mouton. This beautiful stretch of isolated coastline is accessible by hiking trails. This is a nesting area for the endangered piping plover and sections of the beach are closed mid-Apr–mid-Aug.

Annapolis Valley
- Blomidon Provincial Park, Blomidon. Good hiking, scenic views of Minas Basin and rockhounding.
- The Look-off, Route 358 north of Wolfville, on Cape Blomidon. Panoramic view of the Minas Basin and six river valleys.

Maitland Bridge
★Kejimkujik National Park, off Route 8 between Annapolis Royal and Liverpool. Situated in the interior of southwestern Nova Scotia, this 381-square-kilometre wilderness area is a favourite of campers and canoeists. For more information contact Kejimkujik National Park, PO Box 236, Maitland Bridge, NS, B0T 1B0; 682-2772; www.pc.gc.ca/pn-np/ns/kejimkujik

Glooscap Trail
- Cape Chignecto Provincial Park, near Advocate Harbour. Forty-eight kilometres of coastal wilderness trails; Nova Scotia's premier hiking destination.
- Cape d'Or Lighthouse Look-off, off Route 209, Advocate Harbour. Breathtaking view of the Bay of Fundy and Minas Channel.
- Five Islands Provincial Park, Route 2 east of Parrsboro, at Five Islands. Camp, hike or picnic in this beautiful park overlooking

five islands in the Minas Basin.
- Joggins Fossil Cliffs, Joggins. Sandstone cliffs with 300-million-year-old fossil material. The cliffs themselves are off-limits but erosion ensures a steady supply of fossils on the beach. Tours available (see listing under Attractions).
- South Maitland Village Park, Maitland. Good place to watch the Tidal Bore.
- Victoria Park, Brunswick St and Park Rd, Truro. Recreational facilities, hiking trails and two waterfalls make this 1000-acre park ideal for family outings.

Marine Drive
- Taylor Head Provincial Park, Route 7 east of Spry Bay. Hiking trails, wildlife habitat and coastal views along Taylor Head Peninsula.
- Tor Bay Provincial Park, Tor Bay (south of Larry's River). Contemplate the vastness of the Atlantic while picnicking on this rocky point.

Cape Breton and the Cabot Trail
★Cape Breton Highlands National Park, northern Cape Breton. Nova Scotia's most spectacular scenery. The 950-square-kilometre park affords abundant opportunities for camping and hiking. For more information contact Cape Breton Highlands National Park, Ingonish Beach, NS, B0C 1L0; 285-2691; www.pc.gc.ca/pn-np/ns/cbreton
- Cabot's Landing Provincial Park, Cape North. Reputed to be the site where John Cabot landed in 1497. Picnic and enjoy the pleasant views of Aspy Bay.
- Marble Mountain, on the shores of the Bras d'Or, overlooking the village of the same name. After a steep hike, beautiful views of Cape Breton's inland sea. Swimming at the crushed marble beach.
- Uisage Bahn Falls Park, near Baddeck Bridge. A network of hiking trails leads through hardwood forest to a dramatic gorge and waterfalls.

GOLF
There are more than 60 golf courses in Nova Scotia that welcome green-fee players. Golf Nova Scotia members are committed to making tee times available to visitors. For a complete list of member courses contact www.golfnovascotia.com or for reservations call 800 565-0001. For more information on golf courses in Nova Scotia, visit the Nova Scotia Golf Association website at www.nsga.ns.ca. See Golf p. 45.
- Abercrombie Golf & Country Club (18-hole), New Glasgow; 755-4653; www.abercrombiegolf.com
- Amherst Golf & Country Club (18-hole), Amherst; 667-8730; www.amherstgolfclub.com
- Antigonish Golf Club (18-hole), Antigonish; 863-2228; www.antigonishgolfclub.ns.ca
- Avon Valley Golf and Country Club (18 hole), Falmouth; 798-2673; www.avonvalleygolf.com
- Bell Bay Golf Club (18-hole), Baddeck; 800 565-3077; www.bellbaygolfclub.com
- Bluenose Golf Club (9-hole), Lunenburg; 634-4260; www.bluenosegolfclub.com
- Chester Golf Club (18-hole), Chester; 275-4543; www.chestergolfclub.ca
- Clare Golf and Country Club (18 hole), Comeauville; 769-2124; www.claregolf.ca
- Dundee Resort and Golf Club (18-hole), Dundee (on the south shore of the Bras d'Or); 345-0420; www.dundeeresort.com
- Fox Hollow Golf Club (18 hole), Stewiacke; 639-2535
- Glen Arbour Golf Course (18-hole), Hammonds Plains (near Halifax); 877 835-4653; www.glenarbour.com
- Glen Lovat Golf Club (18-hole), New Glasgow; 877 774-4536; www.glenlovat.ca
- Grandview Golf & Country Club (18-hole), Dartmouth; 435-3767; www.grandviewgolfandcountryclub.com
- Granite Springs Golf Club (18-hole), Prospect Road (near Halifax); 852-4653; www.granitespringsgolf.com

- Greenfield Golf (9 hole), Greenfield; 893-2827
- Highlands Links (18-hole), Ingonish Beach (at Keltic Lodge); 800 441-1118; www.highlandslinksgolf.com
- Ken-Wo Golf & Country Club (18-hole), New Minas; 681-5388; www.ken-wo.com
- LePortage Golf Club (18-hole), Cheticamp; 224-3338; www.leportagegolfclub.com
- Linacy Greens Golf Club (18-hole), New Glasgow; 866 990-5200; www.linacygreens.com
- Liverpool Golf & Country Club (9-hole), White Point Beach; 800 565-5068; www.whitepoint.com
- Mountain Golf and Country Club (18 hole), Truro; 893-2841; www.mountaingolf.ca
- Northumberland Links (18-hole), 1776 Gulf Shore Rd, Pugwash; 243-2808; www.northumberlandlinks.com
- Oakfield Golf & Country Club (18-hole), Grand Lake (near Halifax International Airport); 861-2658; www.oakfieldgolf.com
- Osprey Ridge (18-hole), Bridgewater; 543-6666; www.ospreyridge.ns.ca
- Paragon Golf & Country Club (18-hole), Kingston; 877 414-2554
- Pictou Golf Club (9-hole), Pictou; 485-4435
- Digby Pines Resort Golf Course (18-hole), Digby; 800 667-4637; www.signatureresorts.com
- River Oaks Golf Club (18-hole), Meaghers Grant (Route 357 through the Musquodoboit River valley); 384-2033; www.riveroaksgolfclub.ca
- Sunrise Beach Golf Club (9-hole), Tatamagouche; 657-2666; www.sunrisebeachgolf.com
- Riverrun Golf Club (9-hole), Truro; 893-8215
- The Links at Montague (9-hole), Dartmouth; 433-3330; www.thelinksatmontague.com
- Truro Golf Club (18 hole), Truro; 893-4650; www.trurogolfclub.com

BOAT TOURS (SIGHTSEEING, WHALE- AND BIRD-WATCHING, FISHING)

- Amoeba Sailing Tours, Baddeck; 295-7780/1426; www.amoebasailingtours.com. Daily 1 1/2 hr sailings on schooner *Amoeba*. June–Oct.
- Bird Island Tours Ltd, Big Bras d'Or; 800 661-6680; www.birdisland.net. Narrated tour to Bird Islands; see puffins, seabirds, eagles and seals from covered boat. Mid-May–mid-Sept.
- Brier Island Whale and Seabird Cruises, Westport; 800 656-3660; www.brierislandwhalewatch.com. Cruises two to five times daily, three to five hour cruises on the Fundy. Greatest variety of whales in Nova Scotia waters. Rainchecks are given on the rare occasions when no sightings are made.
- Capt. Cox's Whale and Bird Watch, Bay St. Lawrence; 888 346-5556. Seabirds and whales in the waters off Cape Breton's northernmost tip; marine biologist guide. Daily tours.
- Capt. Mark's Whale and Seal Cruise, Pleasant Bay; 888 754-5112; www.whaleandsealcruise.com. Five trips daily (three off-season). Hear and see whales, cruise past sea caves, waterfalls and pioneer settlements.
- Elsie Yacht Charters, Inverary Resort, Shore Rd, Baddeck; 800 565-5660. Daily sails on the 18-metre yacht built for Alexander Graham Bell in 1917. June–Sept.
- Four Winds Charters, Cable Wharf, Unit 4, Halifax and St. Margarets Bay; 877 274-8421; www.fourwindscharters.com. Whale-watching, history tours, ferry to Georges and McNabs islands.
- Hummer Ocean Tours, Lunenburg and Mahone Bay; 866 468-3073; www.hummeroceantours.com.
- Peggys Cove Water Tours, Route 333, Peggys Cove; 866 468-3073; www.hummeroceantours.com. One hour 45 min sightseeing and bird-watching tours in 12-person zodiac.

- Murphy's on the Water: *Mar II* Tall Ship Sailing Tours, *Harbour Queen I*, *Haligonian III*, *Theodore Tugboat*. Cable Wharf, 1751 Lower Water St, Halifax; 420-1015; www.murphysonthewater.com.
- Seaquarium Whale Watching Tours, North Ingonish; 285-2103; www.ingonish.com/seaquarium. See whales, marine life, bald eagles and seabirds with experienced captain and tour guide. Three cruises daily, June–Sept.
- Seaside Whale & Nature Cruises, Cheticamp; 800 959-4253; www.loveboatwhalecruises.com. Three tours daily. Accommodation and cruise packages available through Laurie's Motor Inn (see Lodging).
- Sea Visions Whale Watch, Ingonish Ferry; 285-2628. Three trips daily. See whales and seabirds from an 18-metre schooner.
- Tall Ship *Silva*, Halifax; 429-9463; www.tallshipsilva.com. Daily tours around Halifax Harbour.
- Whale Cruisers (Cheticamp) Ltd, Cheticamp; 800 813-3376; www.whalecruises.com. Frequent sightings of pilot, minke and finback whales. Landward view of the coastline of Cape Breton Highlands National Park. Three cruises daily.

Hiking

Hikers will find plenty to choose from in Nova Scotia — spectacular ocean views, desolate highland plateaus, thick boreal forest and more. There are trails suitable for family outings and trails to challenge the most serious hikers. See Hiking p. 53.

Useful information for hikers is available from a number of sources. The *Nova Scotia Atlas* includes 90 pages of topographic maps that cover the whole of Nova Scotia at a scale of 1:150,000. Available from bookstores and online at www.gov.ns.ca/snsmr/maps. *Hiking Trails of Nova Scotia*, a publication of the Canadian Hostelling Association, is also available in bookstores. These publications can also be purchased at outfitters throughout the province.

For information on hiking trails in Nova Scotia's two national parks, Kejimkujik and Cape Breton Highlands, write to Parks Canada, Atlantic Region, Historic Properties, Upper Water St, Halifax, NS, B3J 1S9; 426-3436. *Walking in the Highlands* is a guide to the 28 marked and serviced trails in the Cape Breton Highlands park.

Tidal Bore Rafting

The tidal bore on the Shubenacadie River provides a unique rafting experience. Check ahead to find out when the bore is at its peak.

- Shubenacadie River Adventure Tours, South Maitland; 888 878-8687; www.shubie.com. Open June–Sept. Reservations recommended.
- Shubenacadie River Runners, 8681 Route 215, Maitland; 800 856-5061; www.tidalborerafting.com. Open June–Sept. Reservations recommended.
- Tidal Bore Rafting Park, 12215 Route 215, Urbania; 800 565-7238; www.tidalboreraftingpark.com. Open May–Oct.

Birding

Nova Scotia is an important stopover on the Atlantic flyway for many species of migratory birds. Late summer sees thousands congregate on Fundy shores. Whale-watching tours (see listings above) also provide an excellent opportunity to observe seabirds, guillemots, kittiwakes, gannets, cormorants and more. Atlantic puffins and bald eagles are special attractions. See Birding p. 69.

Canoeing and Sea Kayaking

Opportunities for freshwater paddling and sea kayaking in Nova Scotia are practically unlimited. Much of the interior of the province is a wilderness area studded with lakes and creased by rivers and streams. There are also long stretches of sheltered coastline on both the Atlantic and the Fundy shores. The *Nova Scotia Doers' and Dreamers' Guide* lists a number of outfitters, as well as suppliers of equipment, maps and useful information. See Sea Kayaking p. 65.

BICYCLING

An extensive series of secondary roads has helped to make cycling one of the fastest growing sports in Nova Scotia. Serious cyclists can challenge the world-famous Cabot Trail while others may choose a gentler route like the Sunrise Trail along the shores of the Northumberland Strait. *Bicycle Tours in Nova Scotia,* which describes 20 of the province's best routes, can be purchased from the Touring Chairman, Bicycle Nova Scotia, PO Box 3010 South, Halifax, NS, B3J 3G6. See Cycling p. 50.

The Nova Scotia Bicycle Book, with extensive route information, is available from Atlantic Canada Cycling, PO Box 1555, Station C, Halifax, NS, B3J 2Y3; 423-2453; www.atlanticcanadacycling.com.

CAMPING

Nova Scotia's two national parks, Kejimkujik and Cape Breton Highlands, and many of the province's 120 provincial parks have campground facilities (see Parks and Natural Attractions for addresses and information). There are also close to 130 privately owned campgrounds in Nova Scotia. Extensive listings and information on camping facilities are provided in the *Nova Scotia Doers' and Dreamers' Guide* (see Travel Essentials).

FISHING

Deep-Sea Fishing
Options for saltwater fishing range from relaxing outings, often in combination with some cultural or historical commentary, where sedentary groundfish are the catch, to serious searches for large gamefish — bluefin tuna, shark and bluefish. Murphy's on the Water (www.murphysonthewater.com) is one of several charter companies that operate out of Halifax

Harbour. For complete listings consult the *Nova Scotia Doers' and Dreamers' Guide* (see Travel Essentials).

Freshwater Fishing
Many species are caught in Nova Scotia lakes and rivers, but the province owes its lofty reputation among anglers to the speckled trout and the Atlantic salmon. The Margaree River in western Cape Breton and St Mary's River on the Eastern Shore have attracted anglers from around the world. These rivers and several others in the province are posted for fly-fishing only. Information on scheduled rivers, licenses, seasons and bag limits is available from outfitters and tackle shops or from all district offices of the Department of Natural Resources (Halifax; 424-5419). For information on the salmon fishery, write to the federal Department of Fisheries and Oceans, PO Box 550, Halifax, NS, B3J 2S7; 426-5952.

SAILING

Nova Scotia is a popular destination for sailors. The island-studded bays and sheltered harbours of the South Shore and the unique sailing experience afforded by Cape Breton's inland sea, the Bras d'Or, have created yachting havens like Chester and Baddeck. Yacht clubs at these communities and several others, including Halifax, host colourful regattas during the summer months. See Sailing p. 61.

Operators of pleasure craft are required to report to Canada Customs by calling 888 226-7277 on arrival in the first Canadian port of call. Customs information concerning pleasure craft, and a list of Customs offices providing marine services, are available from Revenue Canada, Customs Border Services, PO Box 520, Halifax, NS, B3J 2R7; 426-2911, 800 461-9999; fax 426-6522.

USEFUL ADDRESSES

It is possible to make detailed plans for your Nova Scotia

vacation before leaving home by contacting Nova Scotia's Check In Reservation and Information Service. Travel counsellors will provide invaluable advice, reservation services and a wealth of written material to make travel planning easier. In North America, call 800 565-0000 or email info@checkinnovascotia.com.

Once in Nova Scotia, the same services are available at provincial and community visitor information centres. These are indicated by a "?" on the Nova Scotia Scenic Travelways Map, and can be found at key locations throughout the province, including the New Brunswick-Nova Scotia border and the Halifax International Airport.

Visitors from the United States who need to contact home in case of an emergency may do so through the Consulate General of the United States of America, 1969 Upper Water St, Halifax, NS, B3J 3R7; 429-2480.

SPECIAL TRAVEL SERVICES

Visitors with Special Needs
The *Nova Scotia Doers' and Dreamers' Guide* indicates, with the international symbols, which lodgings and attractions are wheelchair-accessible and non-smoking. To find out what additional services may be available, visitors are urged to make specific inquiries. Where possible, it is advisable to book in advance. For assistance, contact the Nova Scotia Check In Reservation and Information Service at 800 565-0000 (North America), www.checkinnovascotia.com or Nova Scotia League for Equal Opportunities at 455-6942; nsleo@eastlink.ca. The Abilities Foundation website (www.enablelink.org) and their magazine, *Abilities* (available online), offer some travel information.

Students
Student discounts are available for a variety of travel services. In order to qualify, students are advised to buy an International Student Identity Card. In Canada, cards may be purchased at Travel Cuts, a travel agency for students found on many Canadian university campuses. Halifax branches are located at St. Mary's University (494-7027) and Dalhousie University (494-2054) and at 1589 Barrington St (482-8000). Students from the US can call 800 592-2887 for information or the location of the nearest Travel Cuts branch.

To find out about hostelling in the province, contact Hostelling International — Nova Scotia, 1253 Barrington St, Halifax, NS, B3J 1Y3; 422-3863; www.hihostels.ca.

Seniors
There are discounts for seniors on many travel services including transportation and accommodation. Make inquiries before making reservations and have your senior citizen identification card at the ready.

Many of the private tour operators in the province offer coach tours at reduced rates for seniors (several companies are listed in the Getting Around section).

GENEALOGICAL SOURCES

- Nova Scotia Archives and Records Management, 6016 University Ave, Halifax, B3H 1W4; 424-6060; www.gov.ns.ca/nsarm. Hours are 8:30 am-4:30 pm, Mon–Fri;(open until 9 pm Wed); 9 am–5 pm, Sat. Closed Sun, holidays and Sat on holiday weekends.
- Genealogical Association of Nova Scotia, PO Box 641, Station Central, Halifax, B3J 2T3; 454-0322; www.chebucto.ns.ca/Recreation/GANS
- Acadia University, Vaughan Library, 50 Acadia St, PO Box 4, Wolfville, NS, B0P 1X0; www.library.acadiau.ca
- Admiral Digby Museum, PO Box 1644, Digby, NS, B0V 1A0; www.klis.com/digby/museum
- Annapolis Valley Macdonald Museum, 21 School St.,

Middleton, NS, B0S 1P0;
www.macdonaldmuseum.ca
- Argyle Township Courthouse and Archives, PO Box 101, Tusket, NS, B0W 3M0; www.argylecourthouse.com
- Cape Breton Genealogy and Historical Association, 120 Braemar Dr, Sydney, NS, B1R 1V9
- Centre d'Etudes Acadiennes, Université de Moncton, Moncton, NB, E1A 3E9; www.umoncton.ca/etudeacadiennes/centre/cea
- Colchester Historical Society, 29 Young Street, Truro, NS, B2N 5C5; www.colchesterarchives@ns.aliantzinc.ca
- Deputy Registrar-General, Box 157, Halifax, NS, B3J 2M9; www.gov.ns.ca/snsmr/vstat
- Kings County Museum, 37 Cornwallis Street, Kentville, NS, B4N 2E2; genealogy@okcm.ca
- Memory Lane Heritage Village, Box 1937, Lake Charlotte, NS, B0J 1Y0; www.heritagevillage.ca
- Pictou County Genealogy and Heritage Society, PO Box 1210, Pictou, NS, B0K 1H0; pcghs@gov.ns.ca
- Shelburne County Genealogical Society, 168 Water St, Shelburne, NS, B0T 1W0; gencentre@ns.sympatico.ca
- South Shore Genealogical Society, 68 Bluenose Dr, Lunenburg, NS, B0J 2C0; www.rootsweb.com/~nslssgs
- West Hants Historical Society, 281 King St, Windsor, NS, B0N 2T0; www.glinx.com/~whhs/links
- Yarmouth County Historical Society, 22 Collins Street, Yarmouth, NS, B5A 3CB; yarmouthcountymuseum.ednet.ns.ca

CONTRIBUTORS

ADRIANE ABBOTT is the founder of the Nova Scotia Studio Rally.
COLLEEN ABDULLAH is a writer, visual communication designer and marketing consultant. She lives in Mahone Bay on Nova Scotia's beautiful South Shore, where she chats with visitors from all over the world in her antiques shop.
ELEANOR ANDERSON has been actively involved for many years in golf marketing in Nova Scotia.
LINETTE CHIASSON recently returned to her native Halifax after studying theatre and English in Ottawa, where she appeared in a variety of roles.
SCOTT CUNNINGHAM, a biologist, is author of *Sea Kayaking in Nova Scotia*. He lives in Tangier, where he operates Coastal Adventures.
DALE DUNLOP is a native Nova Scotian who has explored every highway and byway in the province and is co-author, with his wife Alison Scott, of *Exploring Nova Scotia*. Dale is a litigation lawyer by profession.
ELAINE ELLIOTT is the author, with her sister Virginia Lee, of the *Flavours* series of cookbooks and guidebooks, the most recent being *Fall Flavours*. She has an unparalleled knowledge of Nova Scotian restaurants and cuisine.
MICHAEL ERNST started Sail Mahone Bay in 1994. He has enjoyed sailing for 40 years, and for 20 years was a sailing instructor in Britain under the Royal Yachting Association.
AL KINGSBURY is a journalist and author who lives in the Annapolis Valley.
ALLAN LYNCH is a freelance writer based in Nova Scotia's Annapolis Valley who focuses on travel, business and the business of travel.
ROBERT MCCALLA is a geographer and author of *The Maritime Provinces Atlas*.
TERRY PUNCH is Past President of the Royal Nova Scotia Historical Society and has written numerous books and pamphlets on genealogical research in Nova Scotia.
JOAN WALDRON is an avid birder, and since her retirement from the Nova Scotia Museum she has been spotting birds around the world.
PEGGY WALT is a publicist with her ear to the vibes of the music world in Nova Scotia from her Halifax-based business, Cultural Affairs Consulting and Promotion.

INDEX

208

PHOTO CREDITS

Photo Credits

Legend: Top=T; Centre=C; Bottom=B
Photographs by Keith Vaughan, except as noted below:
Stewart Applegath: p.23T; Parker Bagnell: p.73C, p.167; Bay Ferries
Limited: p.113C; Julian Beveridge: p.18, p.21T, p.23B, p.35, p.36T&B,
p.37C, p.38B, p.86T; Firefighters' Museum/Percy Cottreau: p.15; Cape
Breton Highlands Project: p.53B, p.64B, p.67T, p.68, p.153C, p.156C; Ted
Coldwell: p. 36C, p.37T; Brookes Diamond p. 32T; Golf Nova Scotia: p.45,
p.47, p.48T, p.49B; Fortress of Louisbourg/Joel Berard: p.17, p.166T;
Fortress of Louisbourg/Chris Reardon: p.166B; Freewheeling Adventures:
p.50, p.51T, p.52B; Elizabeth Goluch: p.24B; Grafton Street Dinner
Theatre: p.26; Steven Isleifson: p.104B; Jocelyne Lloyd: p.120B;
Lunenburg Folk Harbour Festival: p.32B; Robert MacGregor: p.88C;
Wendy MacGregor: p.59; Mermaid Theatre: p.28B; Nova Scotia Tourism,
Culture and Heritage: p.2C, p.3B, p.55B, p.73B, p.84B, p.109T, p.121C,
p.127B, p.145T&B, p.158B; Parks Canada: p.109C; Port Bickerton and
Area Planning Association: p.144B; Kristina Rapson: p.31; Royal Nova
Scotia International Tattoo: p.40; Ron Scott/scottwalking.com: p.53T, p.54T,
p.55; Shakespeare by the Sea: p.27B; Sherbrooke Village/Walley Hayes and
Roger Lloyd): p.13, p.141T; Ship's Company Theatre: p.29; Murdock
Smith: p.33B; La Société Saint-Pierre: p152T; Richard Stern: p.70T, p.71C;
Tempest Restaurant, Wolfville: p.37B, p.39T

Maps by Peggy McCalla: pp.4-5, p.76, p.77, p.95, p.115, p.131, p.135,
p.141, p.147, p. 162.

Formac Publishing Company Limited
5502 Atlantic Street
Halifax, Nova Scotia B3H 1G4
www.formac.ca

Distributed in the United States by:
Casemate
1016 Warrior Rd. Suite C
Drexel Hill, PA 19026

Distributed in the United Kingdom by:
Portfolio Books Limited
Unit 5, Perivale Industrial Park
Horsenden Lane South
Greenford, UK, UB6 7Rl

Printed and bound in China